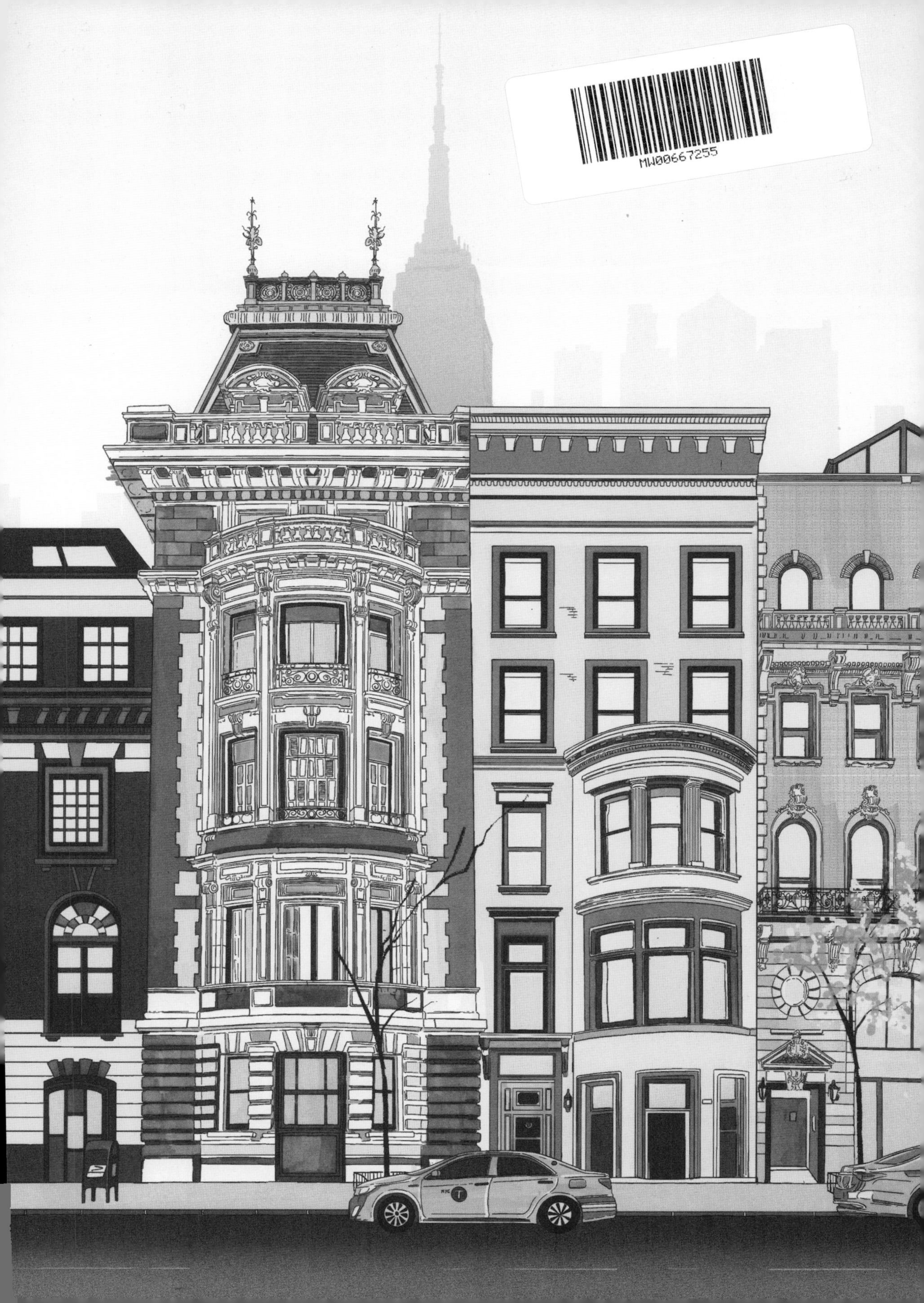
NYC

THIS BEAUTIFUL, RIDICULOUS CITY

A Graphic Memoir

by kay sohini

TEN SPEED GRAPHIC

An imprint of TEN SPEED PRESS

California | New York

To the two greatest loves of my life: Shah Rukh Khan and New York—for all the magic in my world.

And to a third: my husband, Shil Sen—for all the laughs and for keeping me grounded amid the chaos in my head.

This book wouldn't have existed without all the time you made for me to basically draw twelve or more hours a day for six months straight.

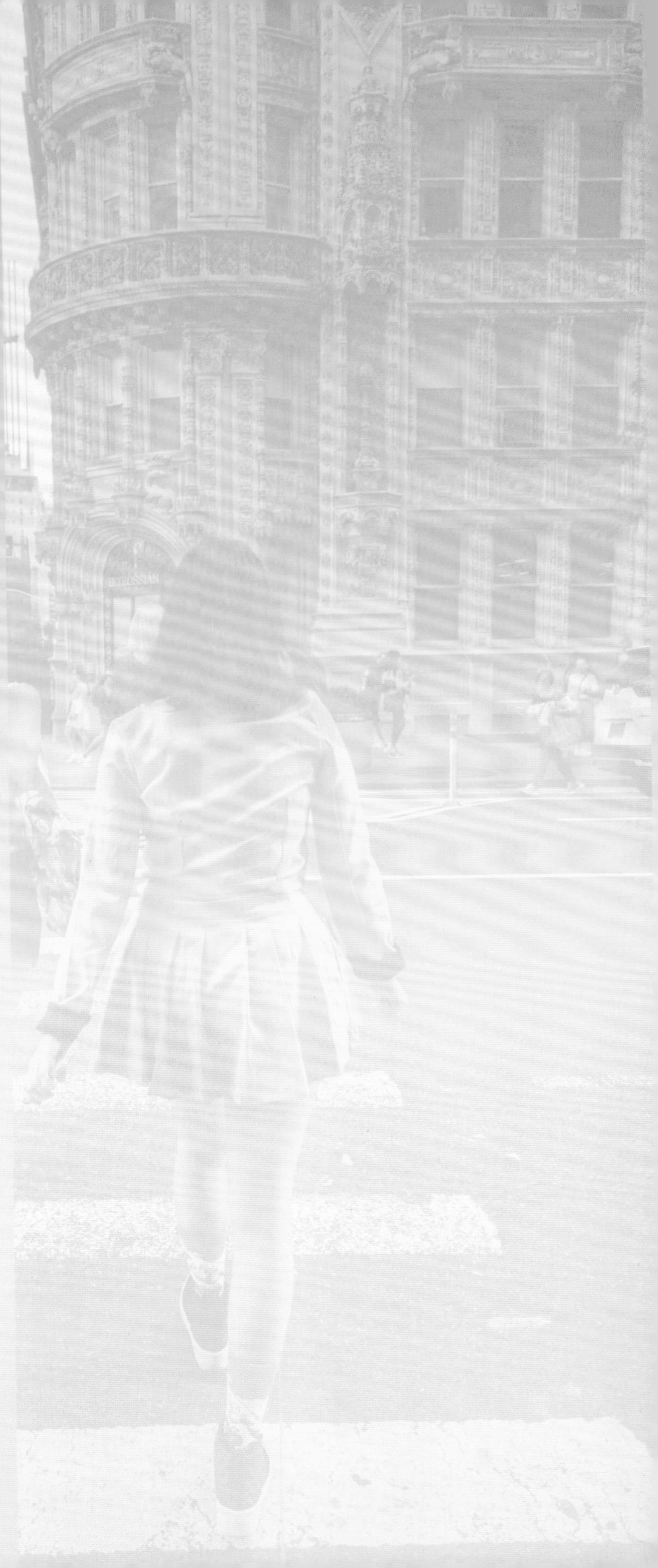

"In the country there are a few chances of sudden rejuvenation—a shift in weather, perhaps, or something arriving in the mail. But in New York the chances are endless. I think that although many persons are here from some excess of spirit (which caused them to break away from their small town) some, too, are here from a deficiency of spirit, who find in New York a protection, or an easy substitution."

E. B. White, *Here Is New York*

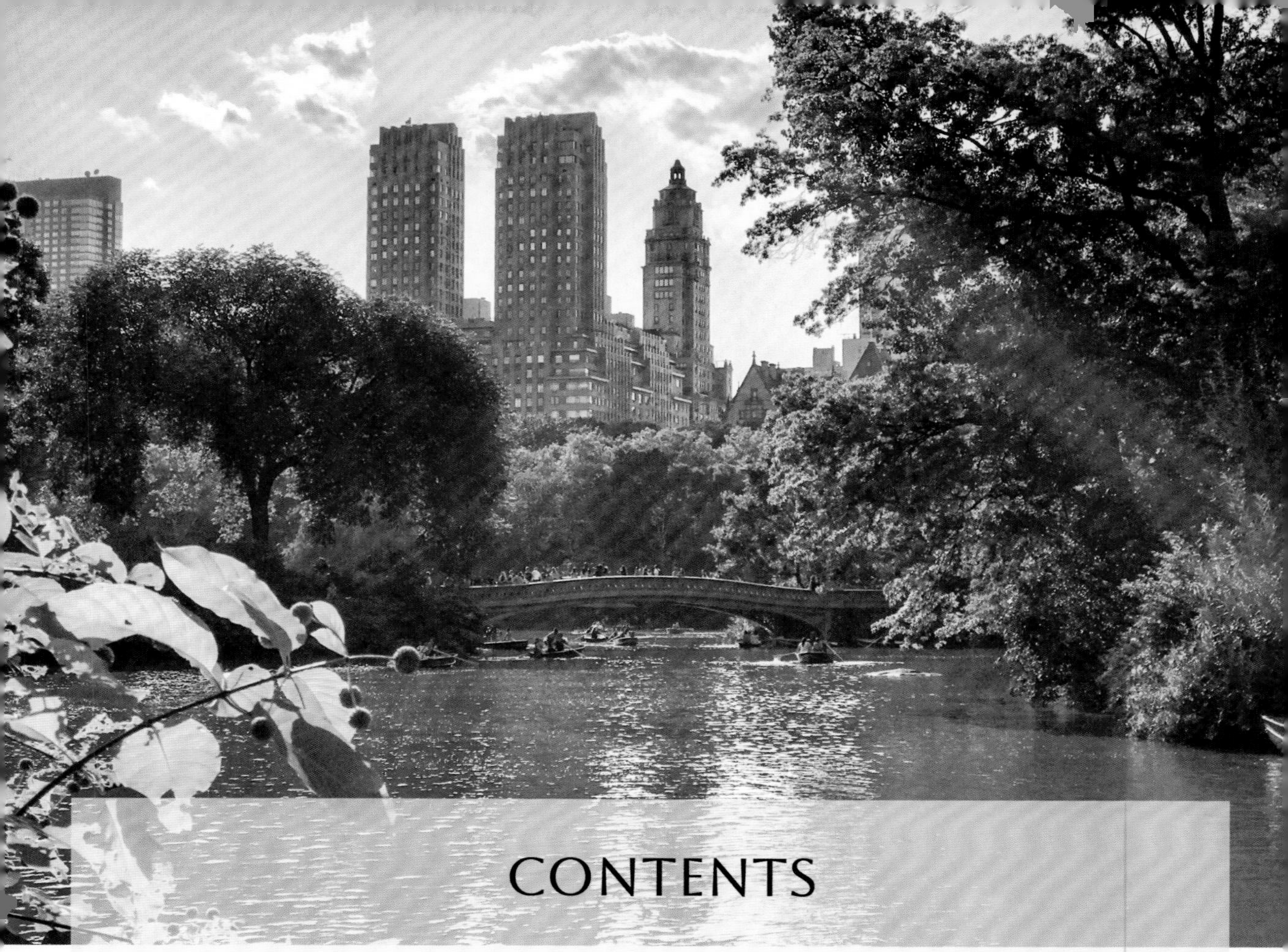

CONTENTS

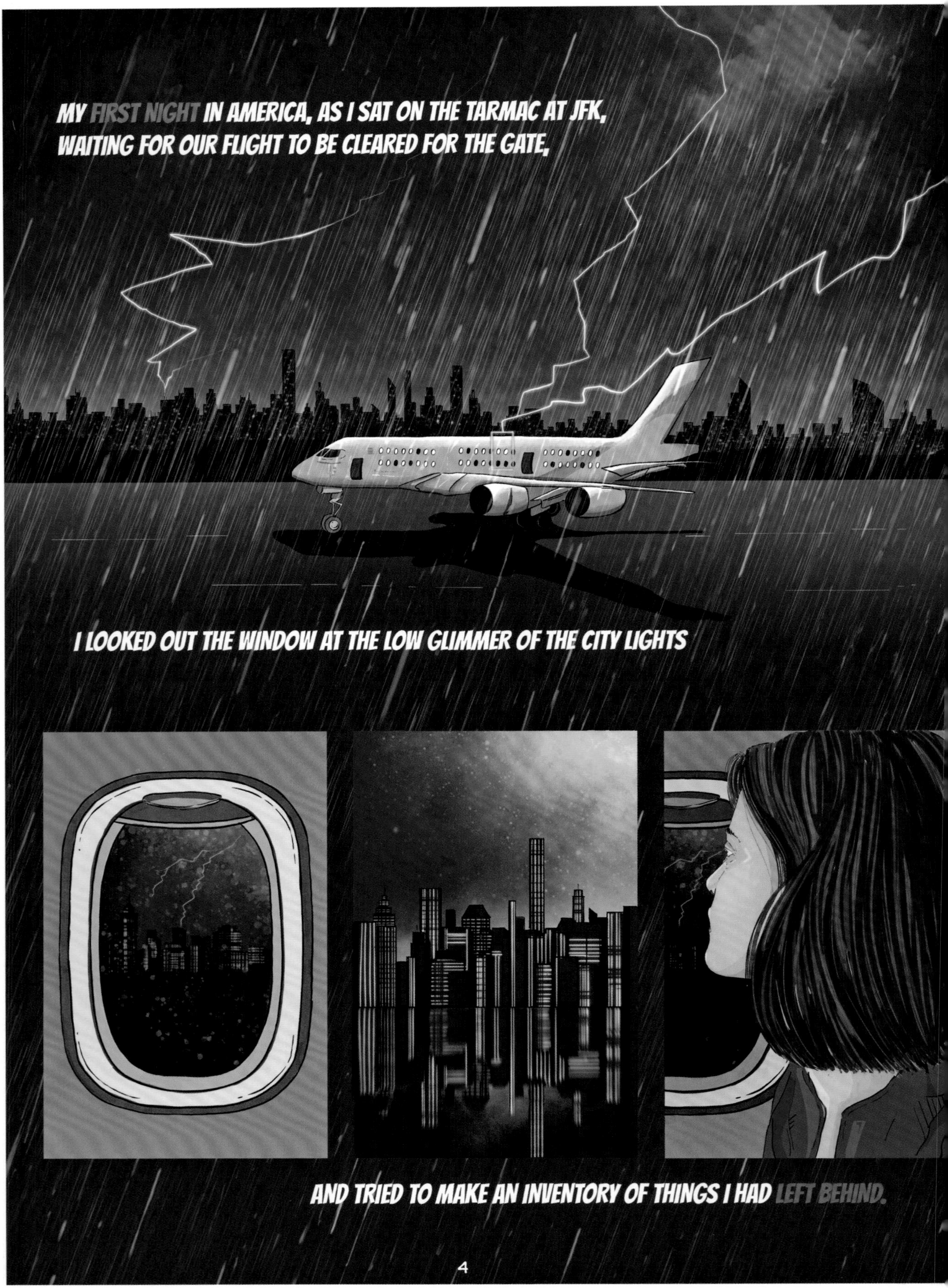
MY FIRST NIGHT IN AMERICA, AS I SAT ON THE TARMAC AT JFK, WAITING FOR OUR FLIGHT TO BE CLEARED FOR THE GATE,
I LOOKED OUT THE WINDOW AT THE LOW GLIMMER OF THE CITY LIGHTS
AND TRIED TO MAKE AN INVENTORY OF THINGS I HAD LEFT BEHIND.

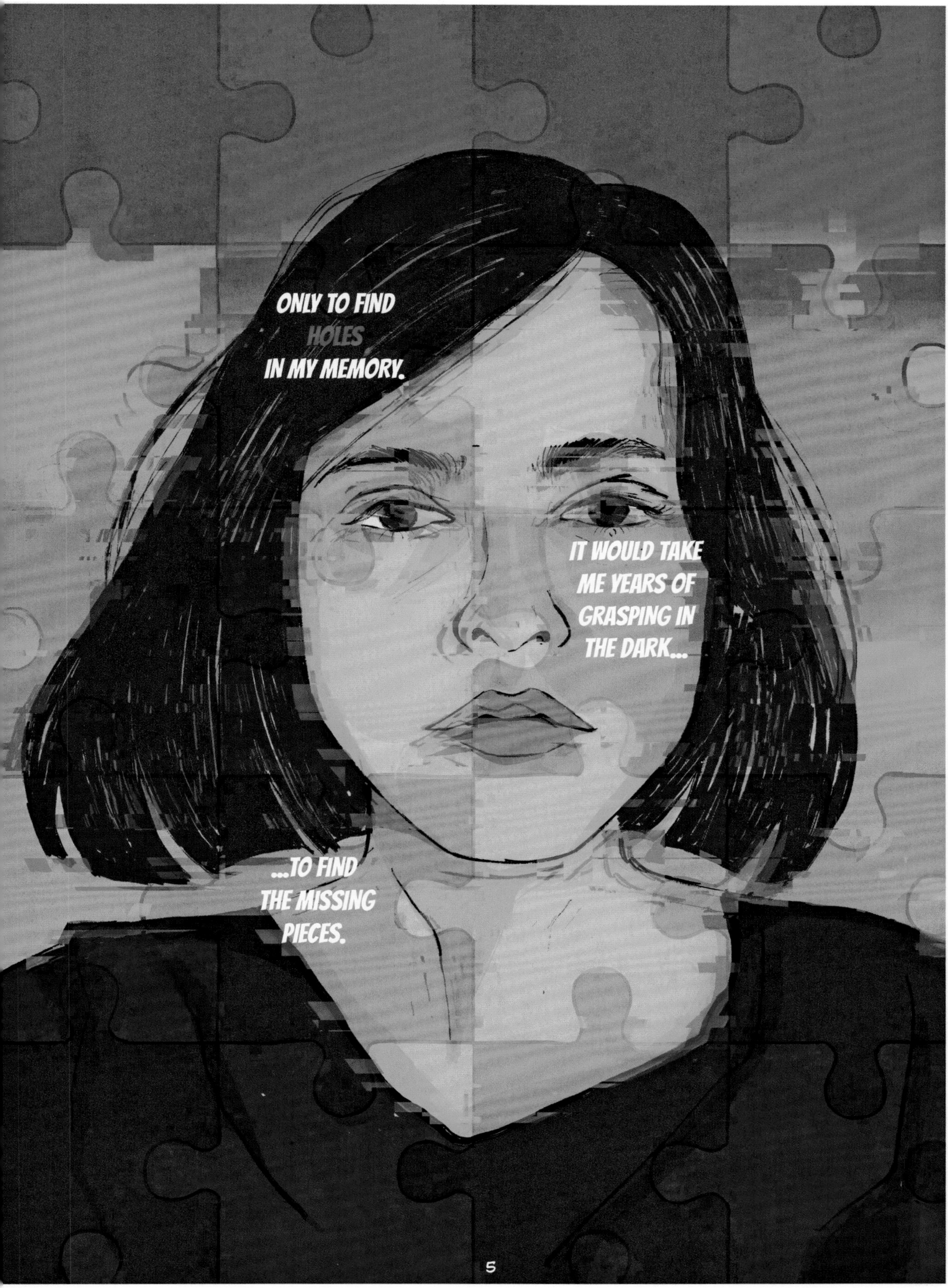
ONLY TO FIND HOLES IN MY MEMORY.
IT WOULD TAKE ME YEARS OF GRASPING IN THE DARK...
...TO FIND THE MISSING PIECES.

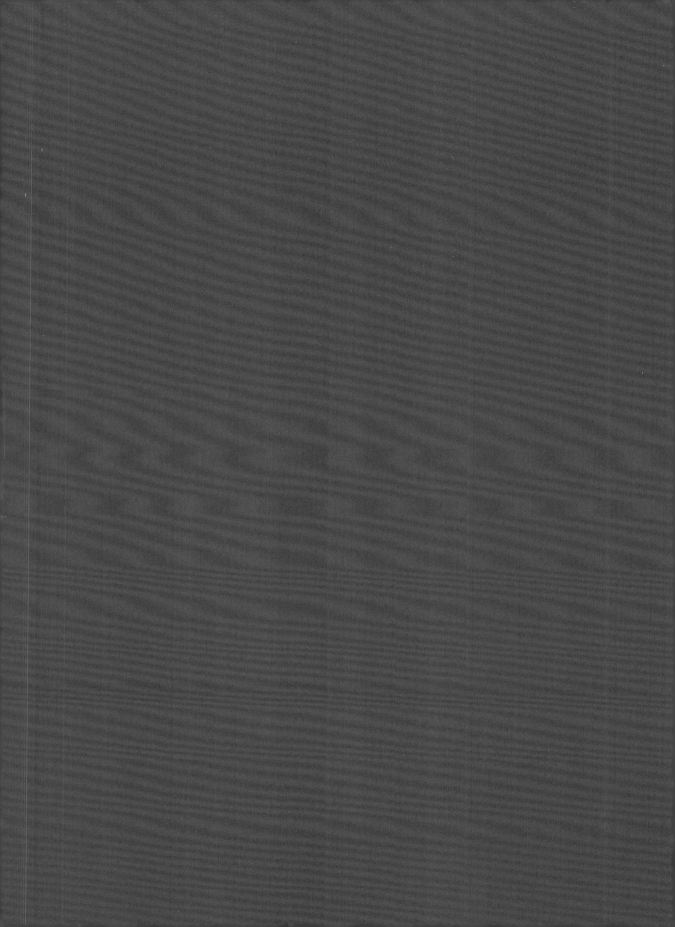

NEW YORK BEFORE NEW YORK

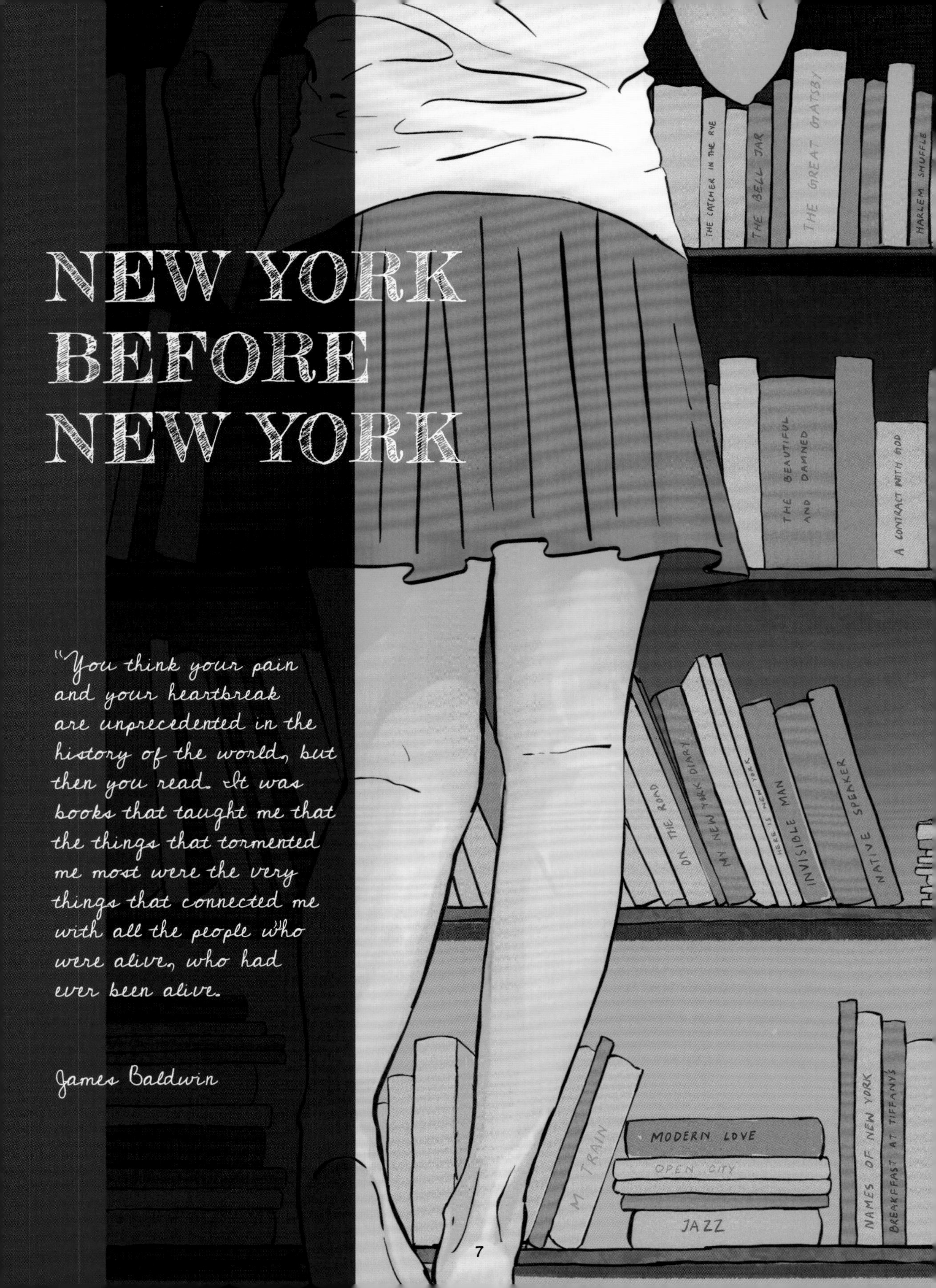
THE CATCHER IN THE RYE
THE BELL JAR
THE GREAT GATSBY
HARLEM SHUFFLE
THE BEAUTIFUL AND DAMNED
A CONTRACT WITH GOD
ON THE ROAD
MY NEW YORK DIARY
HERE IS NEW YORK
INVISIBLE MAN
NATIVE SPEAKER
M TRAIN
MODERN LOVE
OPEN CITY
JAZZ
NAMES OF NEW YORK
BREAKFAST AT TIFFANY'S

"You think your pain and your heartbreak are unprecedented in the history of the world, but then you read. It was books that taught me that the things that tormented me most were the very things that connected me with all the people who were alive, who had ever been alive.

James Baldwin

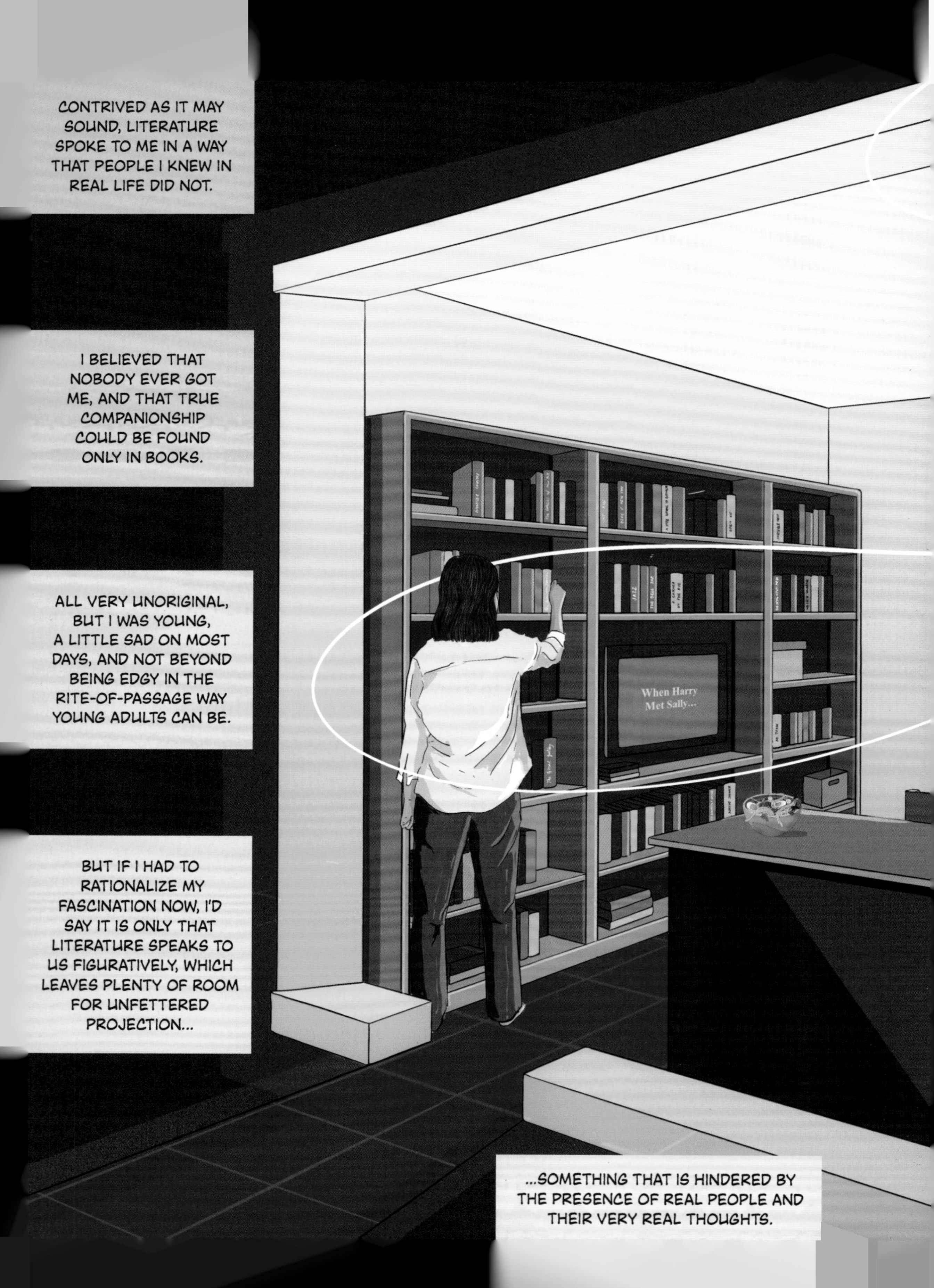
CONTRIVED AS IT MAY SOUND, LITERATURE SPOKE TO ME IN A WAY THAT PEOPLE I KNEW IN REAL LIFE DID NOT.
I BELIEVED THAT NOBODY EVER GOT ME, AND THAT TRUE COMPANIONSHIP COULD BE FOUND ONLY IN BOOKS.
ALL VERY UNORIGINAL, BUT I WAS YOUNG, A LITTLE SAD ON MOST DAYS, AND NOT BEYOND BEING EDGY IN THE RITE-OF-PASSAGE WAY YOUNG ADULTS CAN BE.
BUT IF I HAD TO RATIONALIZE MY FASCINATION NOW, I'D SAY IT IS ONLY THAT LITERATURE SPEAKS TO US FIGURATIVELY, WHICH LEAVES PLENTY OF ROOM FOR UNFETTERED PROJECTION...
When Harry Met Sally...
...SOMETHING THAT IS HINDERED BY THE PRESENCE OF REAL PEOPLE AND THEIR VERY REAL THOUGHTS.

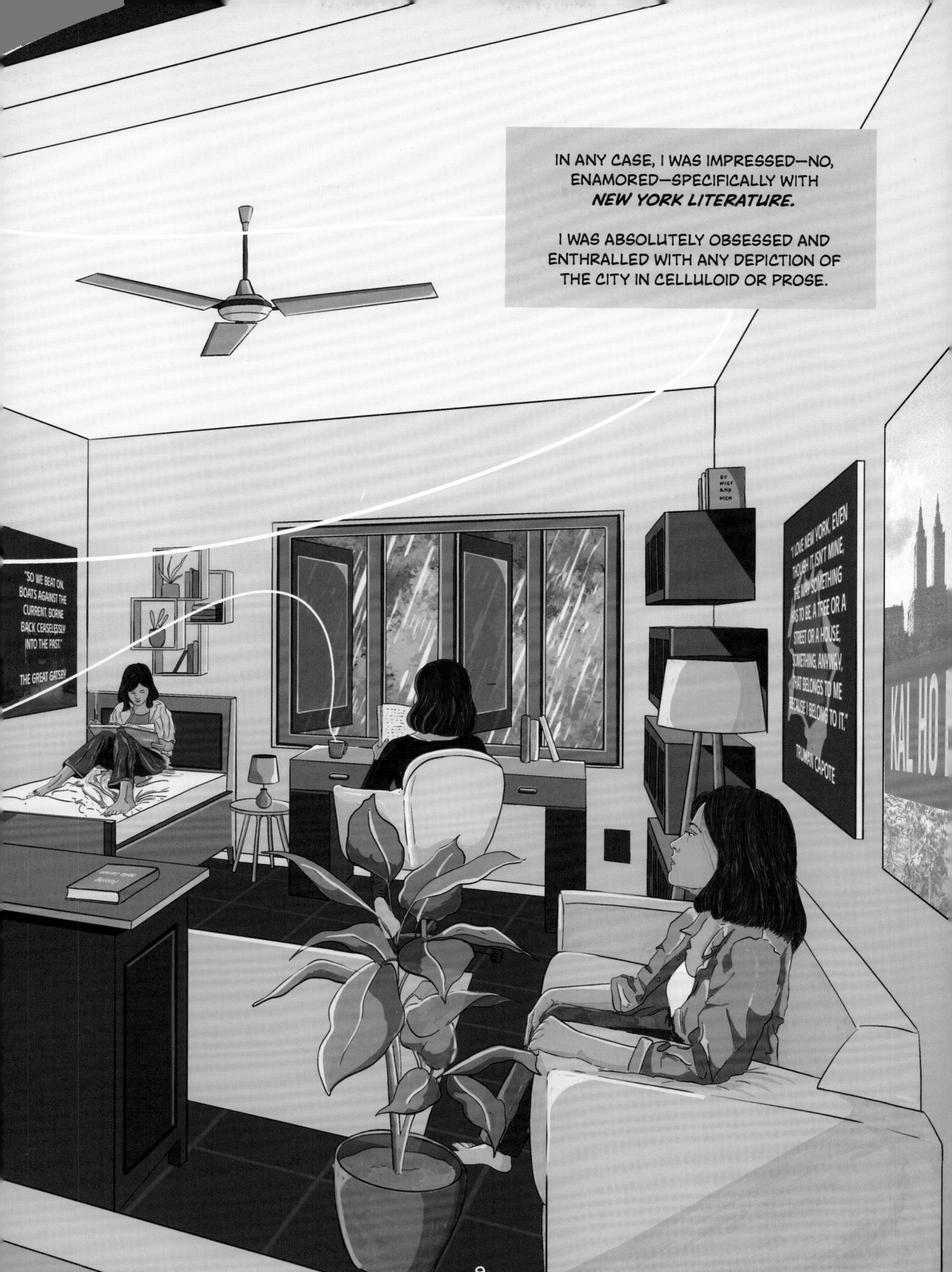
IN ANY CASE, I WAS IMPRESSED—NO, ENAMORED—SPECIFICALLY WITH ***NEW YORK LITERATURE.***
I WAS ABSOLUTELY OBSESSED AND ENTHRALLED WITH ANY DEPICTION OF THE CITY IN CELLULOID OR PROSE.
"SO WE BEAT ON, BOATS AGAINST THE CURRENT, BORNE BACK CEASELESSLY INTO THE PAST."
THE GREAT GATSBY
OF MICE AND MEN
"I LOVE NEW YORK, EVEN THOUGH IT ISN'T MINE, THE WAY SOMETHING HAS TO BE, A TREE OR A STREET OR A HOUSE, SOMETHING, ANYWAY, THAT BELONGS TO ME BECAUSE I BELONG TO IT."
TRUMAN CAPOTE
KAL HO

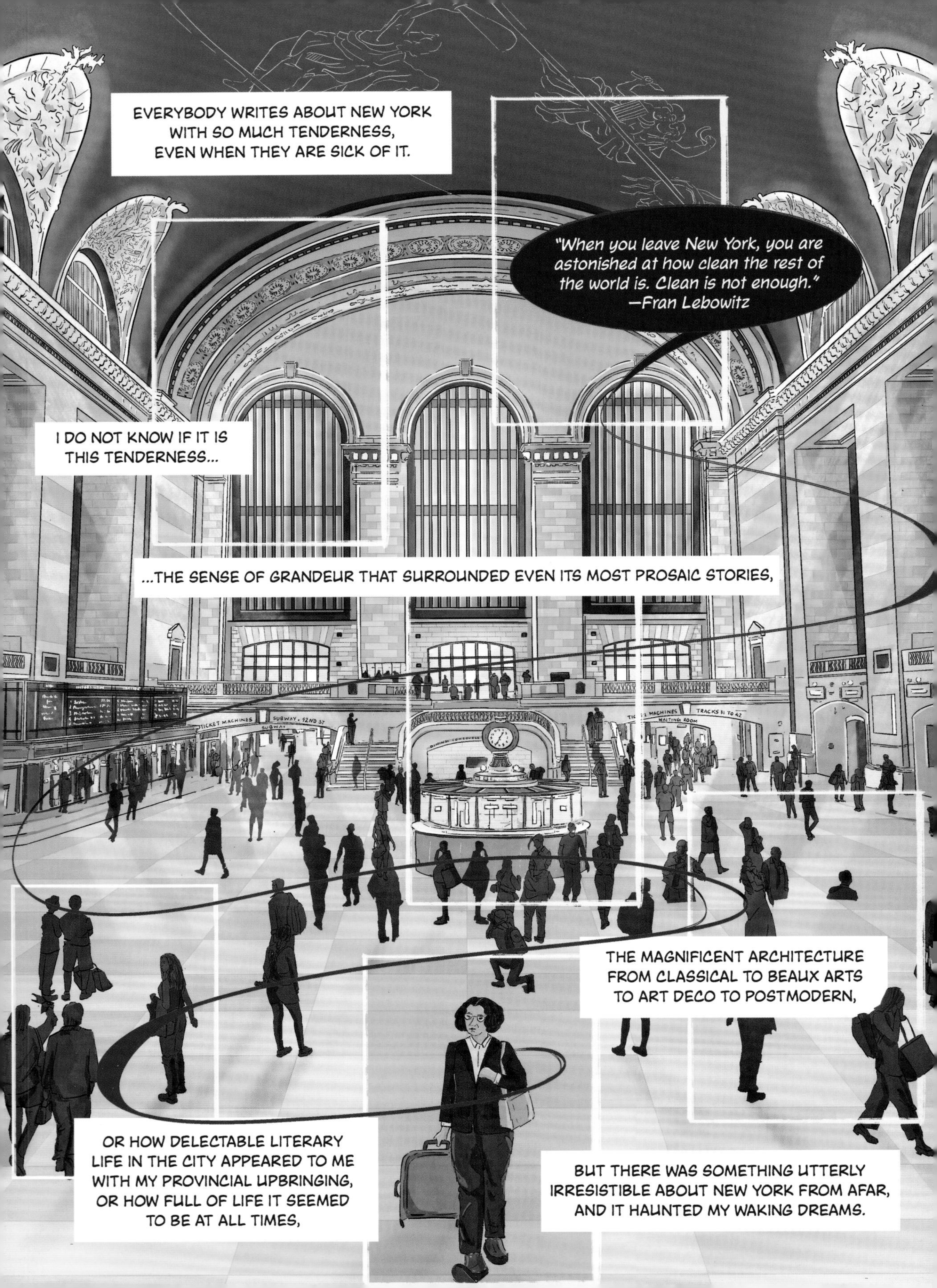
EVERYBODY WRITES ABOUT NEW YORK WITH SO MUCH TENDERNESS, EVEN WHEN THEY ARE SICK OF IT.
"When you leave New York, you are astonished at how clean the rest of the world is. Clean is not enough." —Fran Lebowitz
I DO NOT KNOW IF IT IS THIS TENDERNESS...
...THE SENSE OF GRANDEUR THAT SURROUNDED EVEN ITS MOST PROSAIC STORIES,
TICKET MACHINES
SUBWAY · 42ND ST
SUBWAY
TICKET MACHINES
TRACKS 31 TO 42
WAITING ROOM
THE MAGNIFICENT ARCHITECTURE FROM CLASSICAL TO BEAUX ARTS TO ART DECO TO POSTMODERN,
OR HOW DELECTABLE LITERARY LIFE IN THE CITY APPEARED TO ME WITH MY PROVINCIAL UPBRINGING, OR HOW FULL OF LIFE IT SEEMED TO BE AT ALL TIMES,
BUT THERE WAS SOMETHING UTTERLY IRRESISTIBLE ABOUT NEW YORK FROM AFAR, AND IT HAUNTED MY WAKING DREAMS.

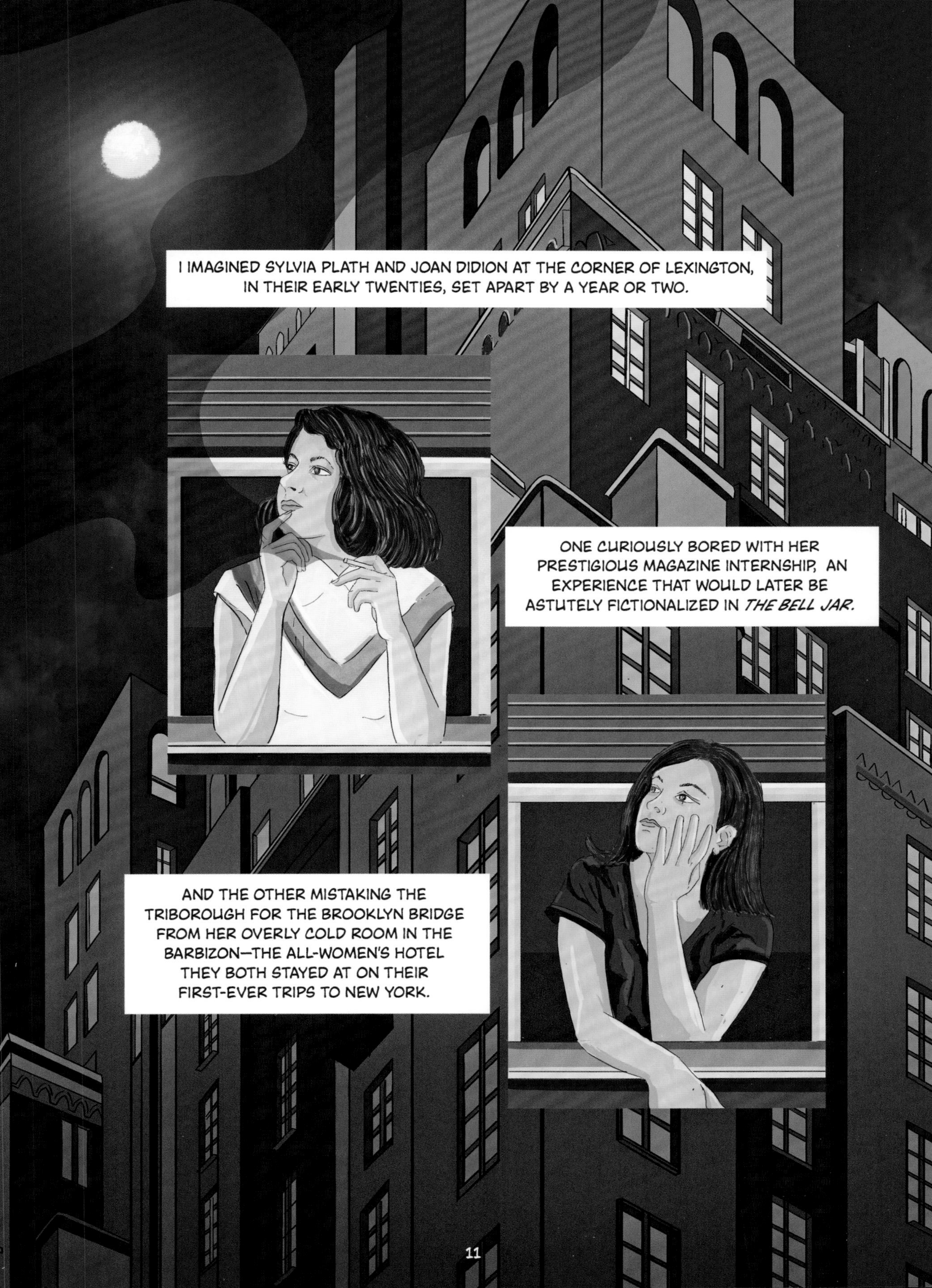
I IMAGINED SYLVIA PLATH AND JOAN DIDION AT THE CORNER OF LEXINGTON, IN THEIR EARLY TWENTIES, SET APART BY A YEAR OR TWO.
ONE CURIOUSLY BORED WITH HER PRESTIGIOUS MAGAZINE INTERNSHIP, AN EXPERIENCE THAT WOULD LATER BE ASTUTELY FICTIONALIZED IN *THE BELL JAR.*
AND THE OTHER MISTAKING THE TRIBOROUGH FOR THE BROOKLYN BRIDGE FROM HER OVERLY COLD ROOM IN THE BARBIZON—THE ALL-WOMEN'S HOTEL THEY BOTH STAYED AT ON THEIR FIRST-EVER TRIPS TO NEW YORK.

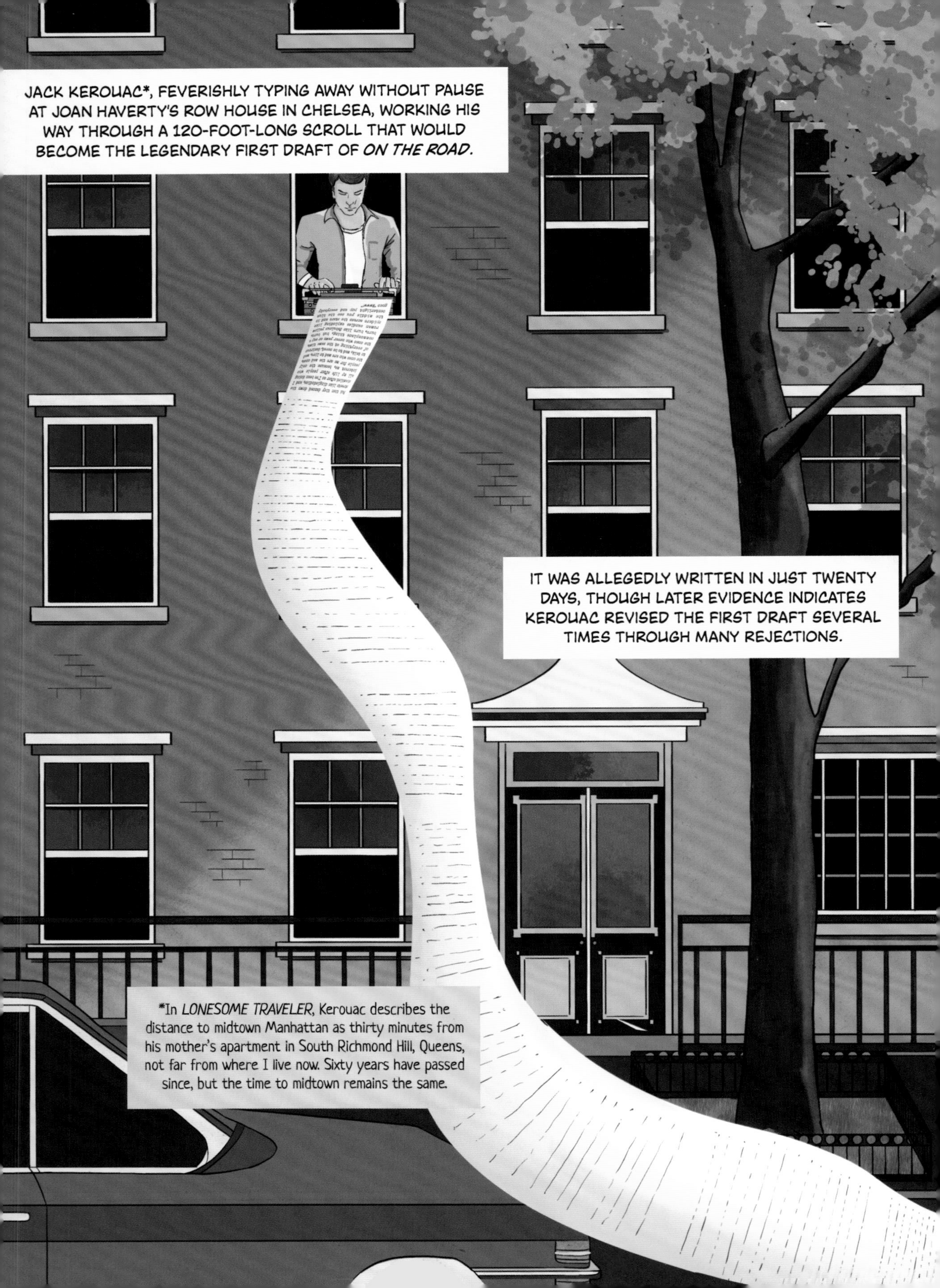

JACK KEROUAC*, FEVERISHLY TYPING AWAY WITHOUT PAUSE AT JOAN HAVERTY'S ROW HOUSE IN CHELSEA, WORKING HIS WAY THROUGH A 120-FOOT-LONG SCROLL THAT WOULD BECOME THE LEGENDARY FIRST DRAFT OF *ON THE ROAD*.
IT WAS ALLEGEDLY WRITTEN IN JUST TWENTY DAYS, THOUGH LATER EVIDENCE INDICATES KEROUAC REVISED THE FIRST DRAFT SEVERAL TIMES THROUGH MANY REJECTIONS.
*In *LONESOME TRAVELER*, Kerouac describes the distance to midtown Manhattan as thirty minutes from his mother's apartment in South Richmond Hill, Queens, not far from where I live now. Sixty years have passed since, but the time to midtown remains the same.

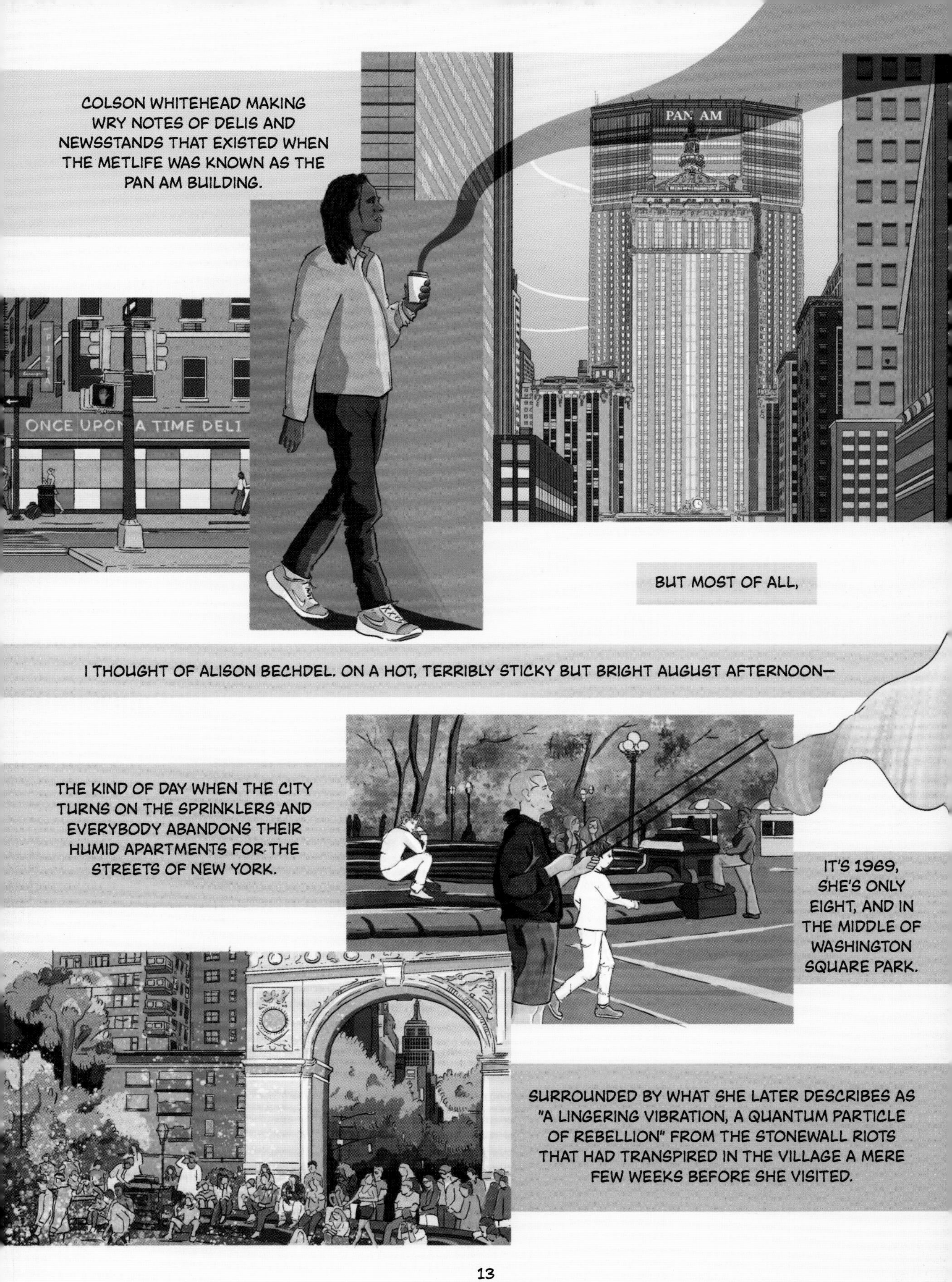
COLSON WHITEHEAD MAKING WRY NOTES OF DELIS AND NEWSSTANDS THAT EXISTED WHEN THE METLIFE WAS KNOWN AS THE PAN AM BUILDING.
PAN AM
PIZZA
ONCE UPON A TIME DELI
BUT MOST OF ALL,
I THOUGHT OF ALISON BECHDEL. ON A HOT, TERRIBLY STICKY BUT BRIGHT AUGUST AFTERNOON—
THE KIND OF DAY WHEN THE CITY TURNS ON THE SPRINKLERS AND EVERYBODY ABANDONS THEIR HUMID APARTMENTS FOR THE STREETS OF NEW YORK.
IT'S 1969, SHE'S ONLY EIGHT, AND IN THE MIDDLE OF WASHINGTON SQUARE PARK.
SURROUNDED BY WHAT SHE LATER DESCRIBES AS "A LINGERING VIBRATION, A QUANTUM PARTICLE OF REBELLION" FROM THE STONEWALL RIOTS THAT HAD TRANSPIRED IN THE VILLAGE A MERE FEW WEEKS BEFORE SHE VISITED.

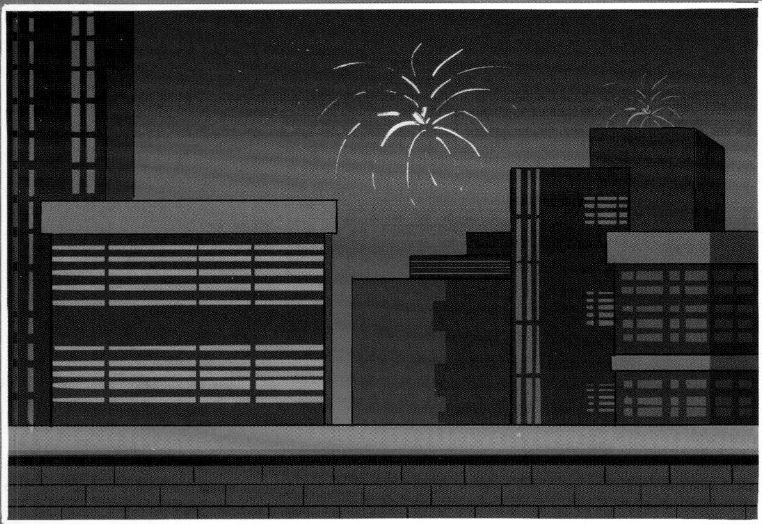

AT FIFTEEN, ON THE TERRACE OF A BLEECKER STREET APARTMENT THAT BELONGED TO HER MOTHER'S FRIEND, WITH AN UNEXCEPTIONAL VIEW OF THE FIREWORKS DURING THE BICENTENNIAL, FOR *"THE GREATEST PARTY EVER KNOWN"* WHEN IT SEEMED THAT THE ENTIRE WORLD HAD GATHERED IN NEW YORK FOR AMERICA'S 200TH BIRTHDAY, ENCOUNTERING QUEER CULTURE FOR THE FIRST TIME AT THE PIERS OVER-LOOKING THE HUDSON, AND REVELING IN HER OWN OPEN-MINDEDNESS.

IN THE EIGHTIES, RIGHT OUT OF COLLEGE, WORKING ODD OFFICE JOBS, MAKING HER WAY UP FROM BROOKLYN TO THE EAST VILLAGE, AT SOME POINT BEING REFUSED ENTRY INTO CHUMLEY'S—A HISTORIC PROHIBITION-ERA PUB THAT HER MOTHER HAD USED TO FREQUENT DURING HER TIME IN THE CITY AND WHICH ONCE HAD A TABLE THAT WAS CLAIMED AS FITZGERALD'S FAVORITE.

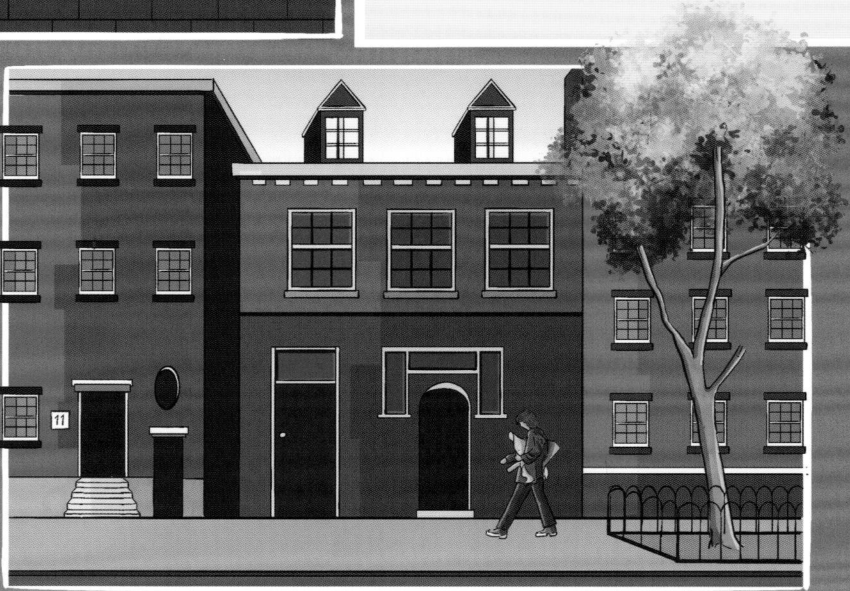
11

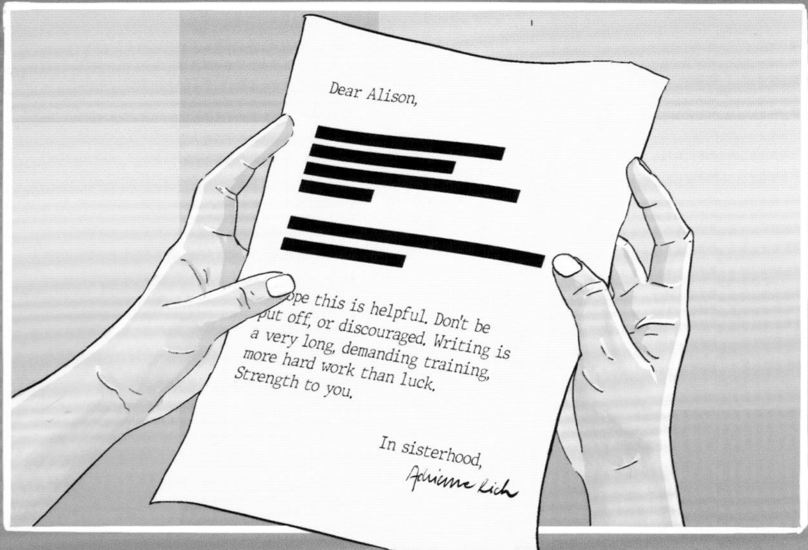
Dear Alison,
[redacted]
ope this is helpful. Don't be
put off, or discouraged. Writing is
a very long, demanding training,
more hard work than luck.
Strength to you.
In sisterhood,
Adrienne Rich

ATTEMPTING TO CHRONICLE HER RELATIONSHIP WITH HER MOTHER IN PROSE, HER SURPRISE AT RECEIVING A PERSONALIZED REJECTION LETTER FROM ADRIENNE RICH, AND THEN MOVING ON TO DRAWING LITTLE CARTOONS INSPIRED BY HER LIFE FOR THE FEMINIST NEWSPAPER SHE VOLUNTEERED AT, WHICH WOULD LATER CULMINATE IN *DYKES TO WATCH OUT FOR.*

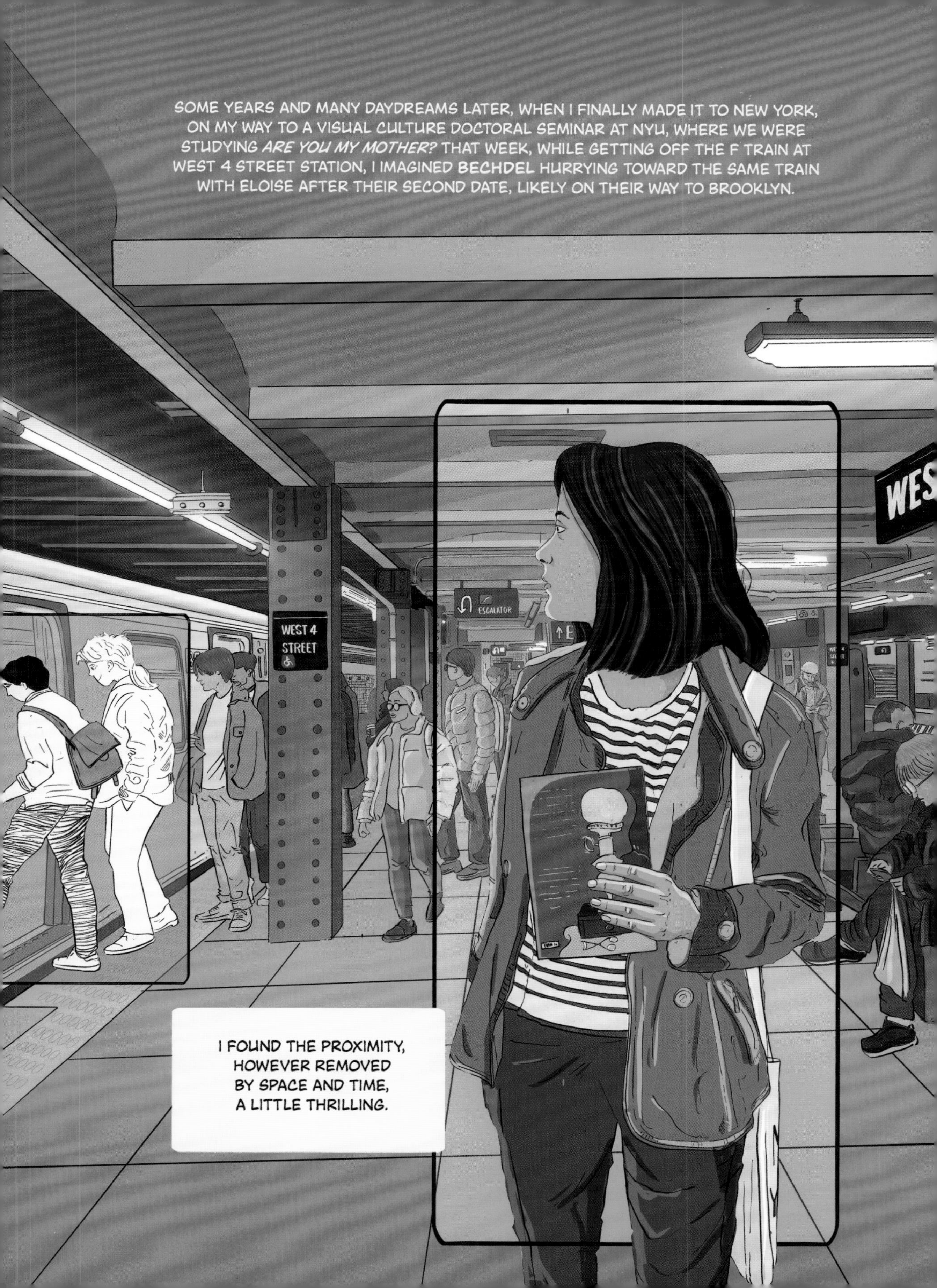
SOME YEARS AND MANY DAYDREAMS LATER, WHEN I FINALLY MADE IT TO NEW YORK, ON MY WAY TO A VISUAL CULTURE DOCTORAL SEMINAR AT NYU, WHERE WE WERE STUDYING *ARE YOU MY MOTHER?* THAT WEEK, WHILE GETTING OFF THE F TRAIN AT WEST 4 STREET STATION, I IMAGINED **BECHDEL** HURRYING TOWARD THE SAME TRAIN WITH ELOISE AFTER THEIR SECOND DATE, LIKELY ON THEIR WAY TO BROOKLYN.
WEST 4 STREET
ESCALATOR
WES
I FOUND THE PROXIMITY, HOWEVER REMOVED BY SPACE AND TIME, A LITTLE THRILLING.

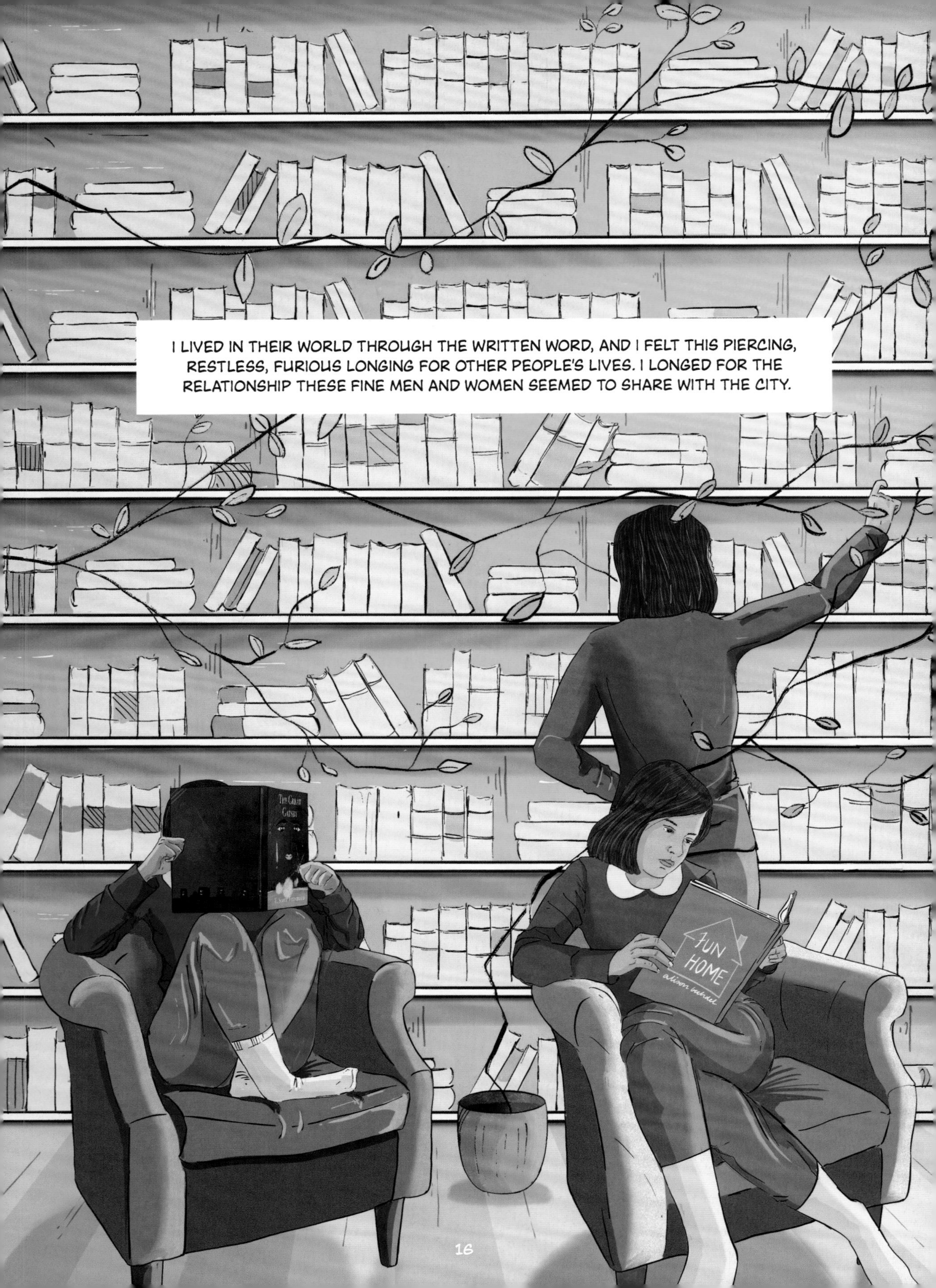
I LIVED IN THEIR WORLD THROUGH THE WRITTEN WORD, AND I FELT THIS PIERCING, RESTLESS, FURIOUS LONGING FOR OTHER PEOPLE'S LIVES. I LONGED FOR THE RELATIONSHIP THESE FINE MEN AND WOMEN SEEMED TO SHARE WITH THE CITY.
THE GREAT GATSBY
FUN HOME
alison bechdel

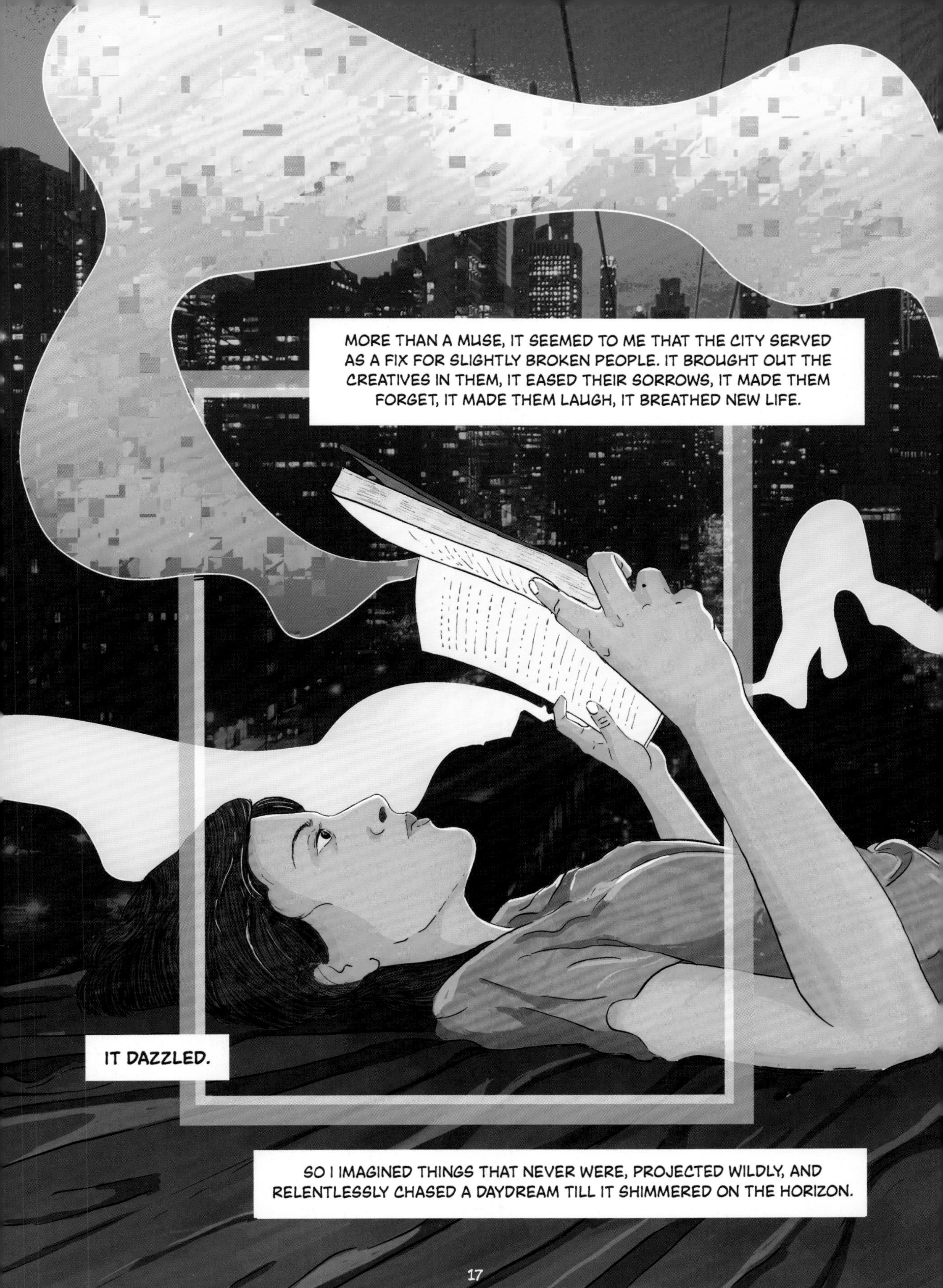
MORE THAN A MUSE, IT SEEMED TO ME THAT THE CITY SERVED AS A FIX FOR SLIGHTLY BROKEN PEOPLE. IT BROUGHT OUT THE CREATIVES IN THEM, IT EASED THEIR SORROWS, IT MADE THEM FORGET, IT MADE THEM LAUGH, IT BREATHED NEW LIFE.
IT DAZZLED.
SO I IMAGINED THINGS THAT NEVER WERE, PROJECTED WILDLY, AND RELENTLESSLY CHASED A DAYDREAM TILL IT SHIMMERED ON THE HORIZON.

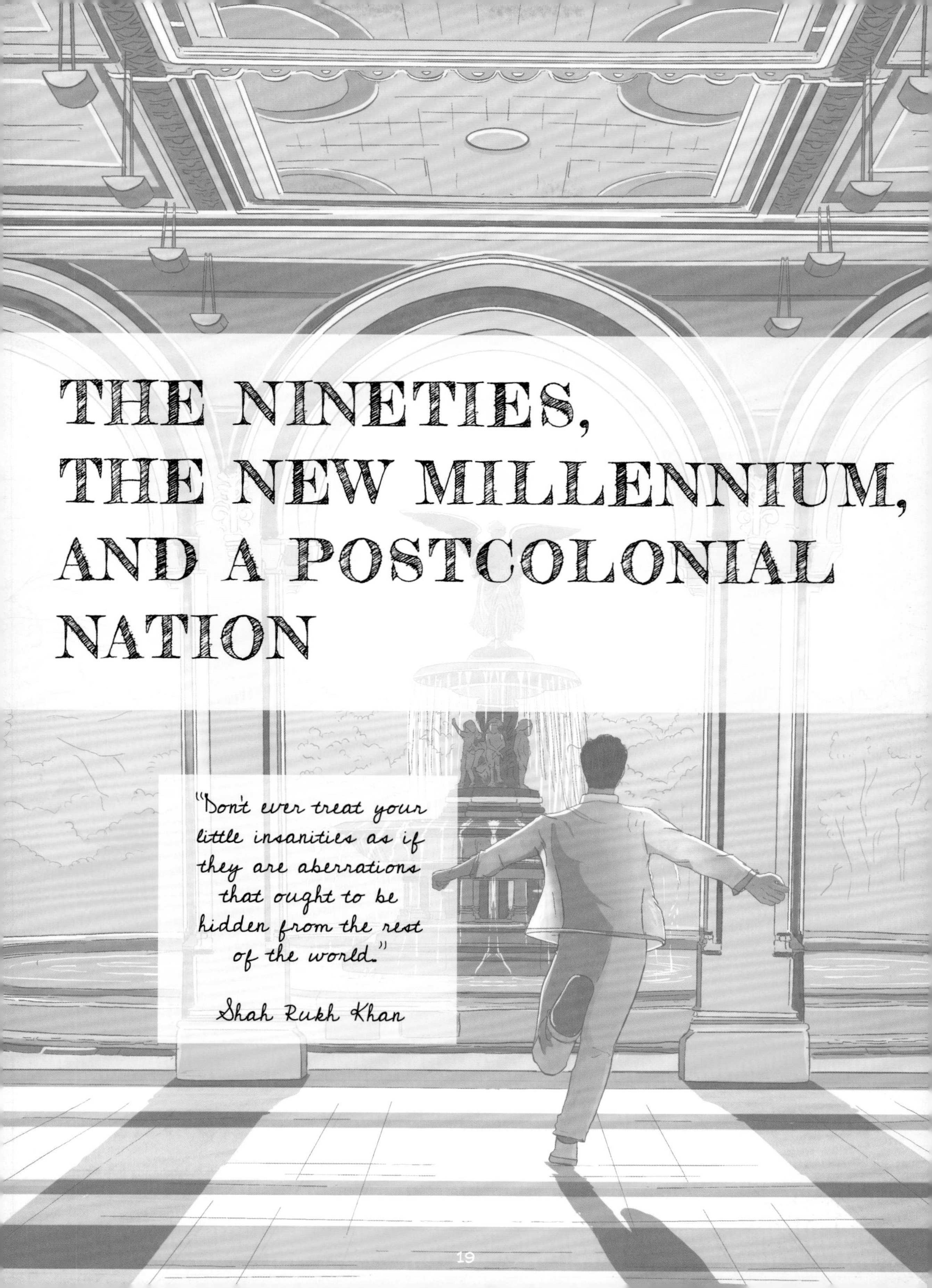

THE NINETIES, THE NEW MILLENNIUM, AND A POSTCOLONIAL NATION

"Don't ever treat your little insanities as if they are aberrations that ought to be hidden from the rest of the world."

Shah Rukh Khan

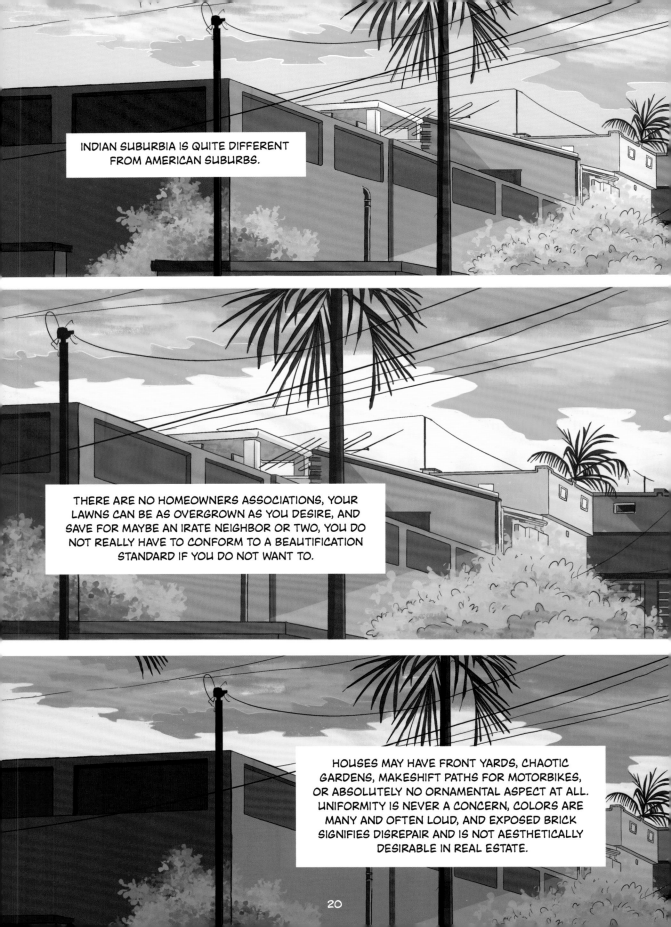

INDIAN SUBURBIA IS QUITE DIFFERENT FROM AMERICAN SUBURBS.

THERE ARE NO HOMEOWNERS ASSOCIATIONS, YOUR LAWNS CAN BE AS OVERGROWN AS YOU DESIRE, AND SAVE FOR MAYBE AN IRATE NEIGHBOR OR TWO, YOU DO NOT REALLY HAVE TO CONFORM TO A BEAUTIFICATION STANDARD IF YOU DO NOT WANT TO.

HOUSES MAY HAVE FRONT YARDS, CHAOTIC GARDENS, MAKESHIFT PATHS FOR MOTORBIKES, OR ABSOLUTELY NO ORNAMENTAL ASPECT AT ALL. UNIFORMITY IS NEVER A CONCERN, COLORS ARE MANY AND OFTEN LOUD, AND EXPOSED BRICK SIGNIFIES DISREPAIR AND IS NOT AESTHETICALLY DESIRABLE IN REAL ESTATE.

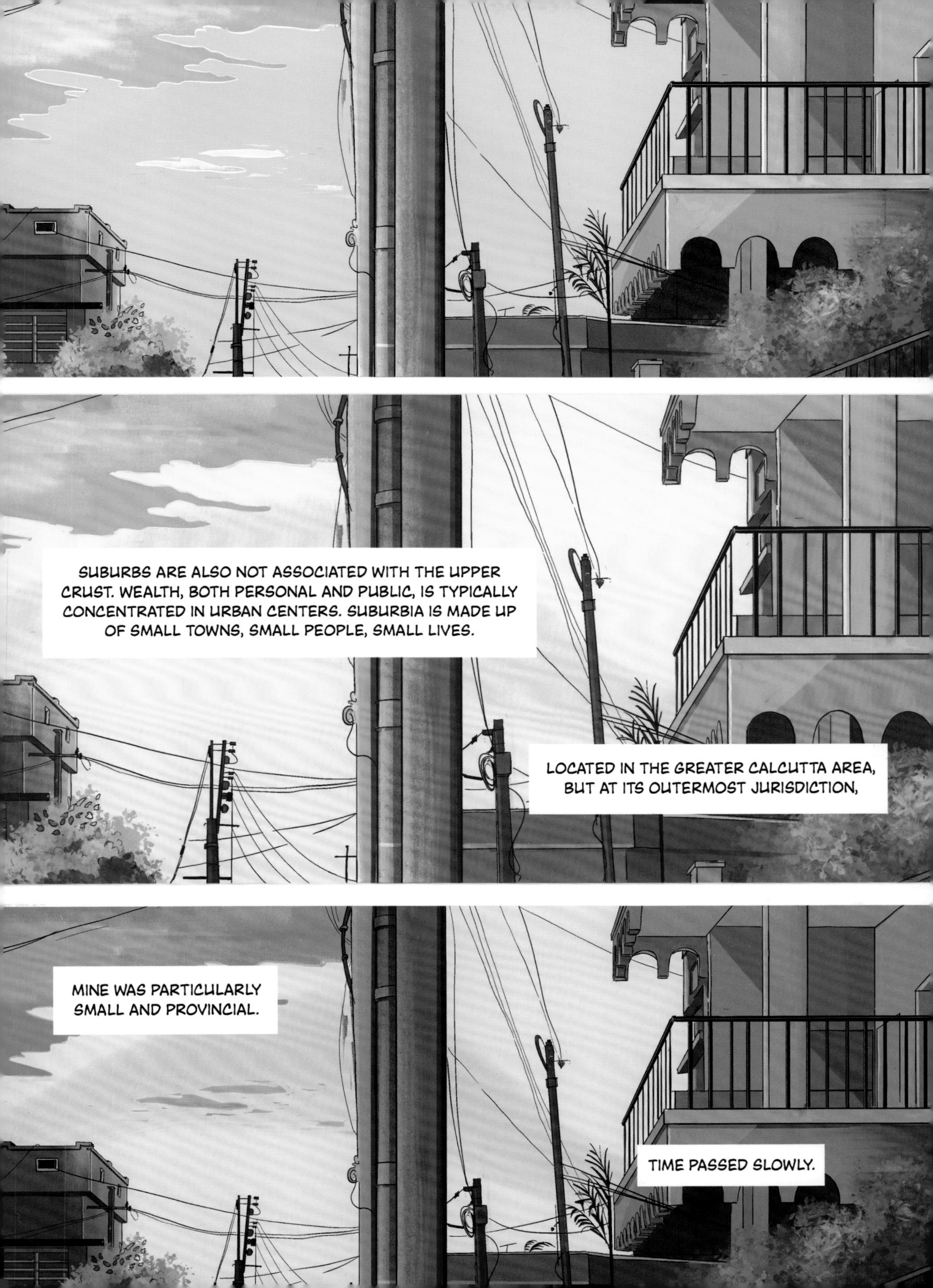
SUBURBS ARE ALSO NOT ASSOCIATED WITH THE UPPER CRUST. WEALTH, BOTH PERSONAL AND PUBLIC, IS TYPICALLY CONCENTRATED IN URBAN CENTERS. SUBURBIA IS MADE UP OF SMALL TOWNS, SMALL PEOPLE, SMALL LIVES.
LOCATED IN THE GREATER CALCUTTA AREA, BUT AT ITS OUTERMOST JURISDICTION,
MINE WAS PARTICULARLY SMALL AND PROVINCIAL.
TIME PASSED SLOWLY.

NEVERTHELESS, IN THE EARLY NINETIES, INDIA WAS AT THE DAWN OF **ECONOMIC LIBERALIZATION**, FOLLOWING THE PRESENTATION OF THE EPOCHAL BUDGET BY THEN FINANCE MINISTER MANMOHAN SINGH (WHO WENT ON TO BECOME THE PRIME MINISTER IN 2004).

"There is no time to lose. Neither the Government nor the economy can live beyond its means year after year."

ON JULY 24, 1991

"The room for maneuver, to live on borrowed money or time, does not exist any more."

"The basic challenge of our times is to ensure that wealth creation is not only tempered by equity and justice but is harnessed to the goal of removal of poverty and development for all."

IT CHANGED COMMERCE, TELECOMMUNICATION, AND ENTERTAINMENT. RESTRICTIONS ON IMPORTED GOODS WERE LIFTED, THE MARKET WAS OPENED TO INTERNATIONAL COMPANIES, AND EVEN IN THE OUTSKIRTS OF BIG CITIES, THINGS WERE CHANGING FAST.

Free Press Journal
Thursday, July 25, 1991   By Kunal Verma
Policy Opens Floodgates for Private Sector

The New York Times
Business Day
THURSDAY, JULY 25, 1991
India Retreats from Socialist Past

INDIAN EXPR
THURSDAY JULY 25, 1991
7,719-CR DEFICIT IN UNIO
Foreign investment libera

THE TIMES OF INDIA
BUDGET HITS RICH, GRAZES OTHERS
By Tapan Dasgupta
THURSDAY JULY 25, 1991

BY THE TIME I WAS GROWING UP, GLOBAL BRANDS HAD FLOODED THE INDIAN MARKET AT COMPETITIVE PRICES, SOME ADAPTING THEIR PRODUCTS TO CATER TO INDIAN PALATES.

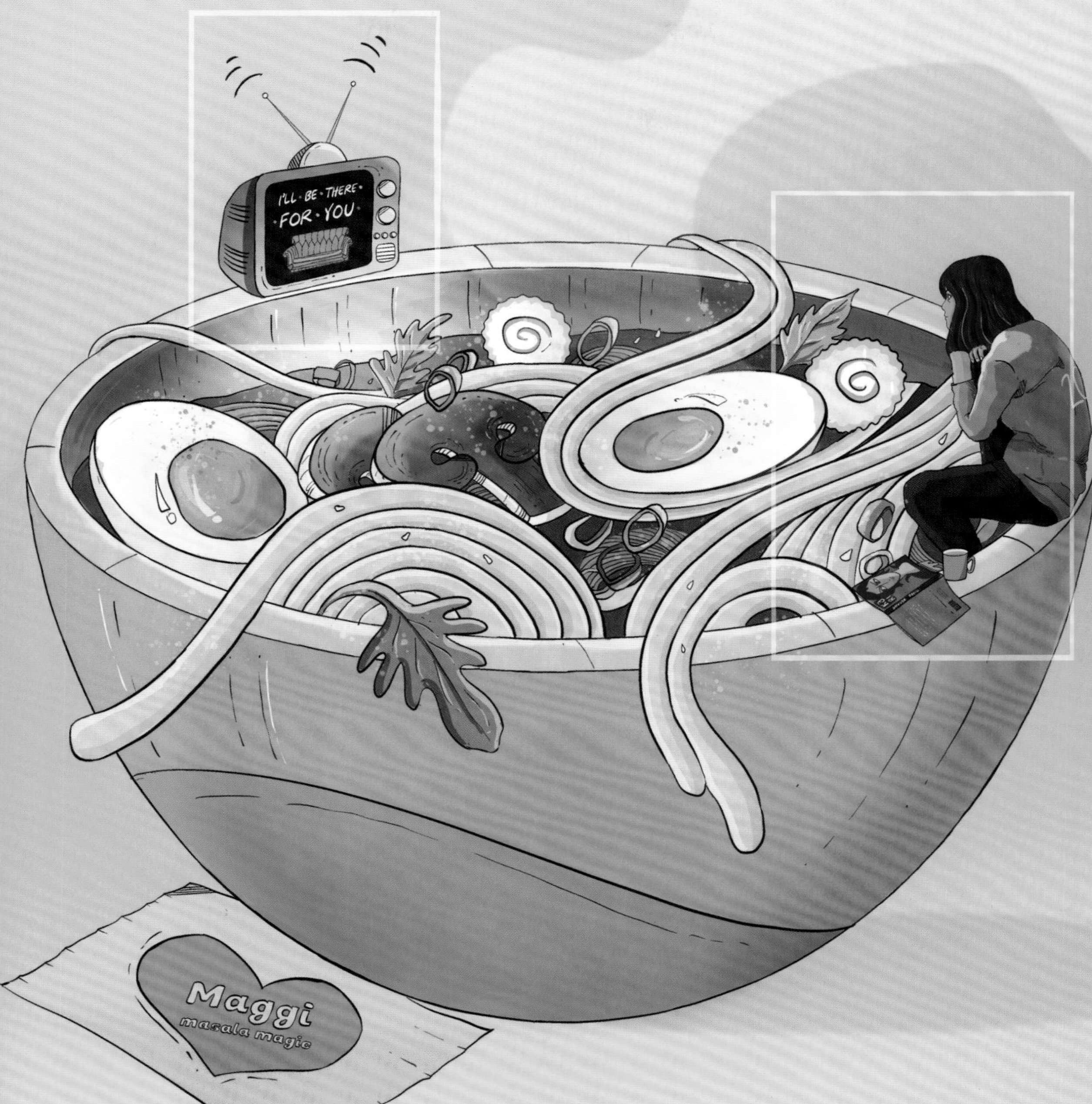
I'LL BE THERE FOR YOU
Maggi
masala magic

THE MOST PROMINENT EXAMPLE IS NESTLÉ MAGGI NOODLES, THE INSTANT RAMEN, WHICH BECAME PART-CURRY, PART-INDO-CHINESE FLAVORED IN THE SUBCONTINENT.

IN AN EFFORT TO CATCH UP WITH THE WORLD, INDIA ADOPTED RAPID INDUSTRIALIZATION, ALBEIT AT THE COST OF THE ENVIRONMENT. OVERNIGHT, FROM A "THIRD WORLD COUNTRY" WE BECAME A "DEVELOPING NATION." BETWEEN THE 1990S AND THE 2010S, THE ECONOMY GREW STEADILY, BUT DISPARITY AND RAMPANT POVERTY REMAINED EVEN AS THE GROSS DOMESTIC PRODUCT (GDP) AND THE INDIAN MIDDLE CLASS GREW. BY 2015, BETWEEN 300 MILLION AND 600 MILLION PEOPLE FELL INTO THE GROWING CATEGORY. WE LEARNED FROM THE WEST HOW TO TAKE PLEASURE IN UNABASHED MATERIALISM, AND GLOBAL BRANDS FOUND A LUCRATIVE MARKET IN OUR NUMBERS.

MALLS POPPED UP IN THE BIG CITIES, WITH DESIGNER STOREFRONTS, FOOD COURTS WITH AMERICAN FAST FOOD CHAINS (MARKETED AS A FANCIER COMMODITY THAN THEY WERE IN THE UNITED STATES), AND MULTIPLEXES WITH SURROUND SOUND. HOLLYWOOD MOVIES GOT REAL-TIME RELEASE DATES AND RAN ALONGSIDE HOMEGROWN ENTERTAINMENT.

ON THE STREETS, AMBASSADORS MANUFACTURED BY HINDUSTAN MOTORS WERE REPLACED BY SLEEK SEDANS FROM HYUNDAI AND FORD. LEVI'S, PEPE JEANS, REEBOK, NIKE, VAN HEUSEN, AND OTHERS OPENED STORES IN THE METROPOLISES, CHANGING THE WAY THE YOUTH AND THE MODERATELY AFFLUENT DRESSED.

PEPSI HIRED INDIA'S BIGGEST MOVIE STAR AND ITS MOST DECORATED CRICKETER TO BE ITS BRAND AMBASSADORS, AND THE SLOGAN "YEH DIL MAANGE MORE," THE CATCHY INDIAN EQUIVALENT OF JANET JACKSON'S "ASK FOR MORE" COMMERCIAL, BECAME UBIQUITOUS.

ADVERTISEMENTS, ONCE UTILITARIAN, BECAME INCREASINGLY COMPLEX PRODUCTIONS MEANT *TO SEDUCE, ENTERTAIN, AND CREATE A NEW CLASS OF CONSUMERS.*

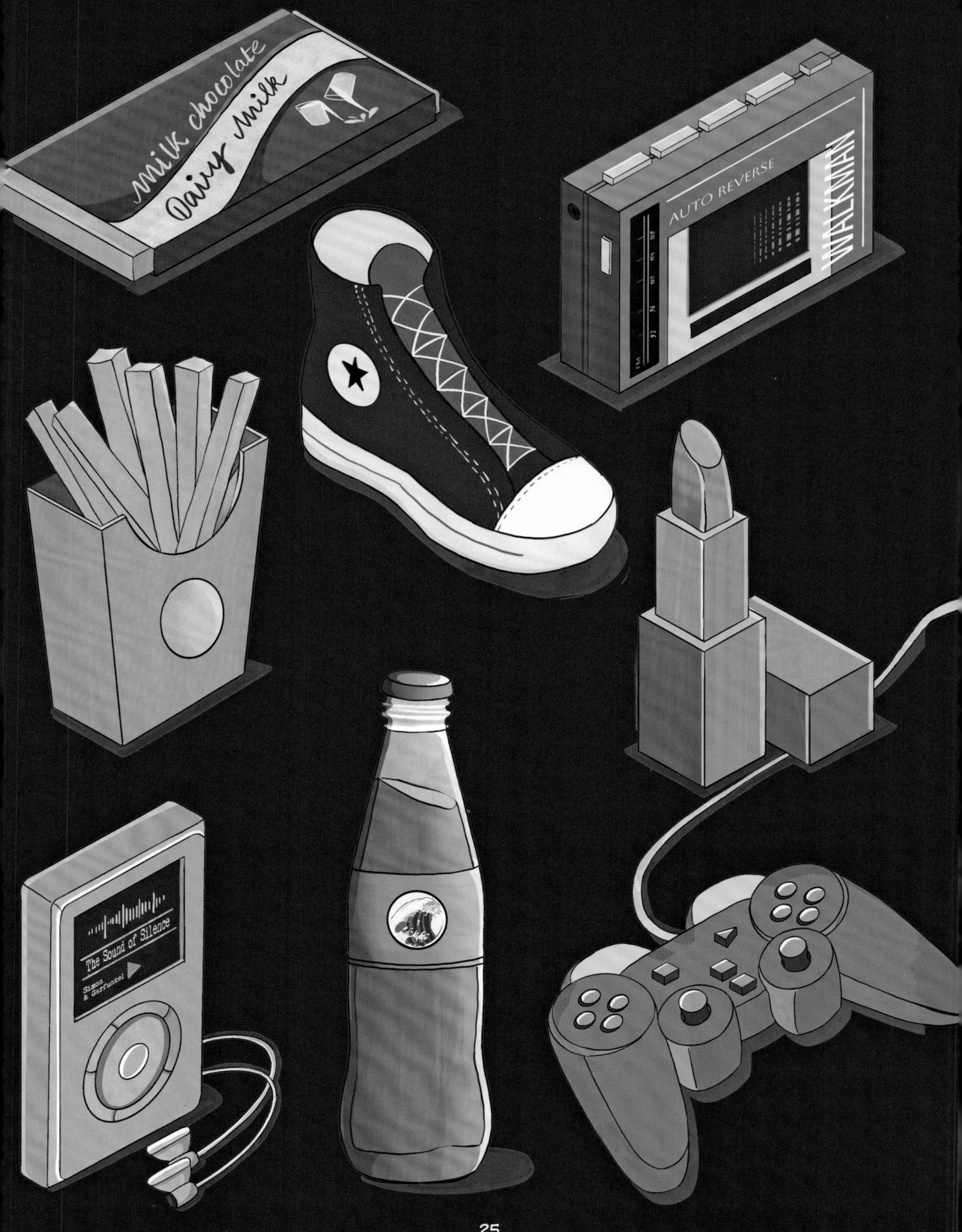
Milk chocolate
Dairy Milk
AUTO REVERSE
WALKMAN
FM
92 96 100 104 108
The Sound of Silence
Simon
& Garfunkel

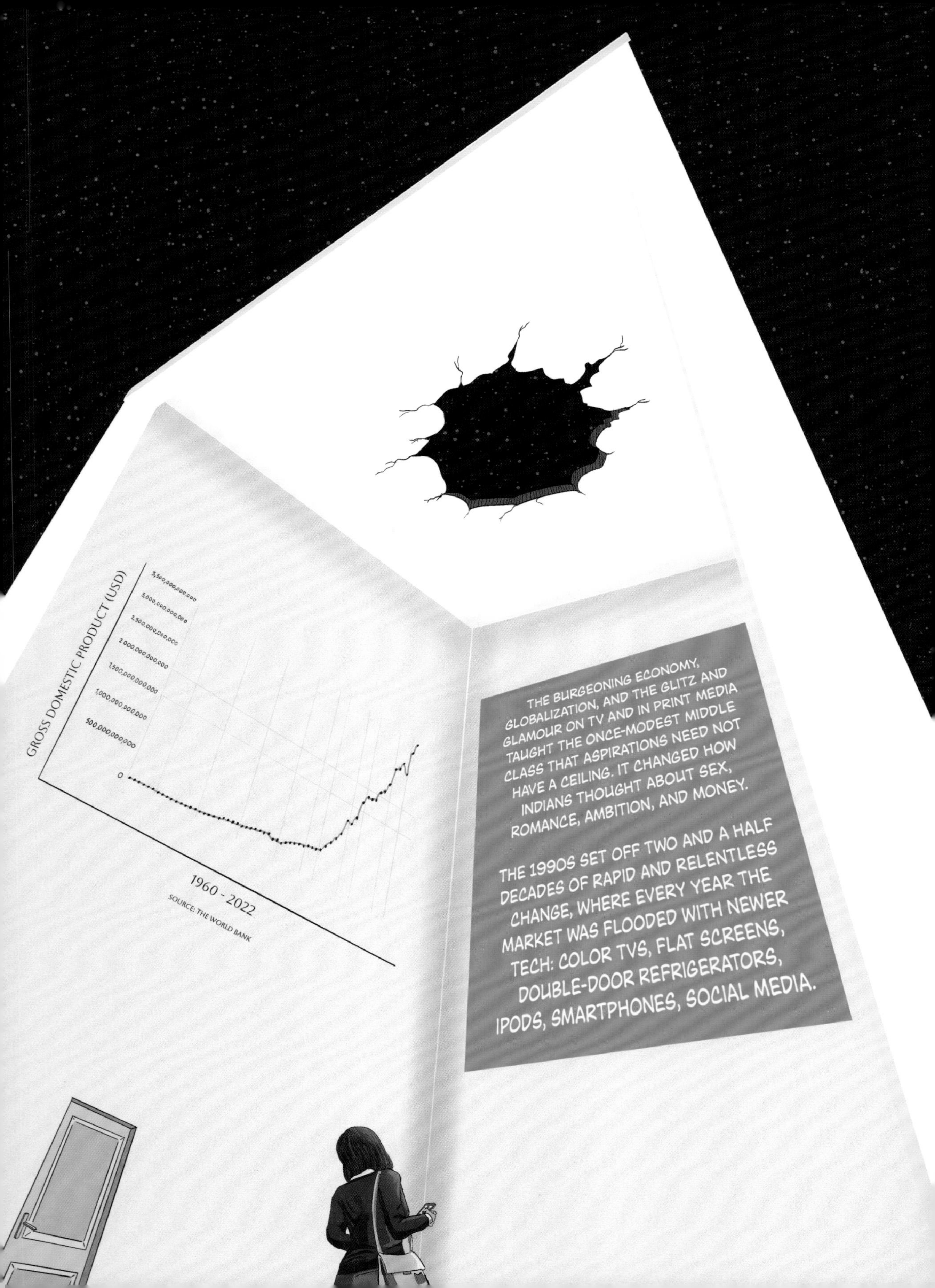
GROSS DOMESTIC PRODUCT (USD)
3,500,000,000,000
3,000,000,000,000
2,500,000,000,000
2,000,000,000,000
1,500,000,000,000
1,000,000,000,000
500,000,000,000
0
1960 - 2022
SOURCE: THE WORLD BANK
THE BURGEONING ECONOMY, GLOBALIZATION, AND THE GLITZ AND GLAMOUR ON TV AND IN PRINT MEDIA TAUGHT THE ONCE-MODEST MIDDLE CLASS THAT ASPIRATIONS NEED NOT HAVE A CEILING. IT CHANGED HOW INDIANS THOUGHT ABOUT SEX, ROMANCE, AMBITION, AND MONEY.
THE 1990S SET OFF TWO AND A HALF DECADES OF RAPID AND RELENTLESS CHANGE, WHERE EVERY YEAR THE MARKET WAS FLOODED WITH NEWER TECH: COLOR TVS, FLAT SCREENS, DOUBLE-DOOR REFRIGERATORS, IPODS, SMARTPHONES, SOCIAL MEDIA.

But it was not just the market that changed.

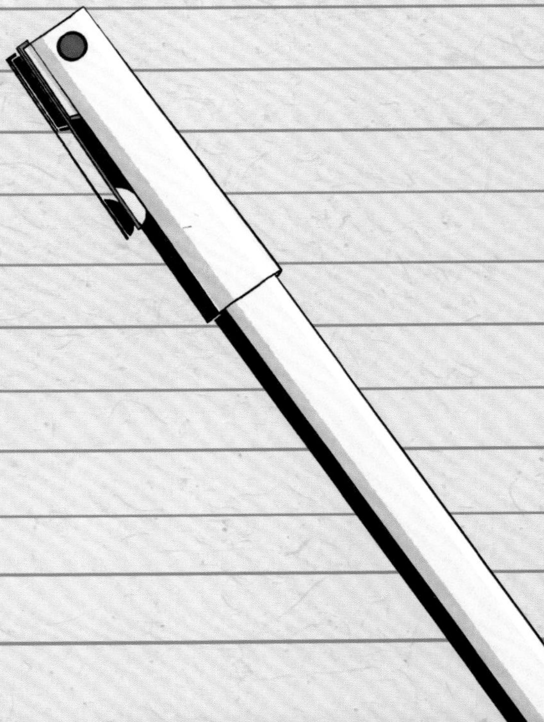

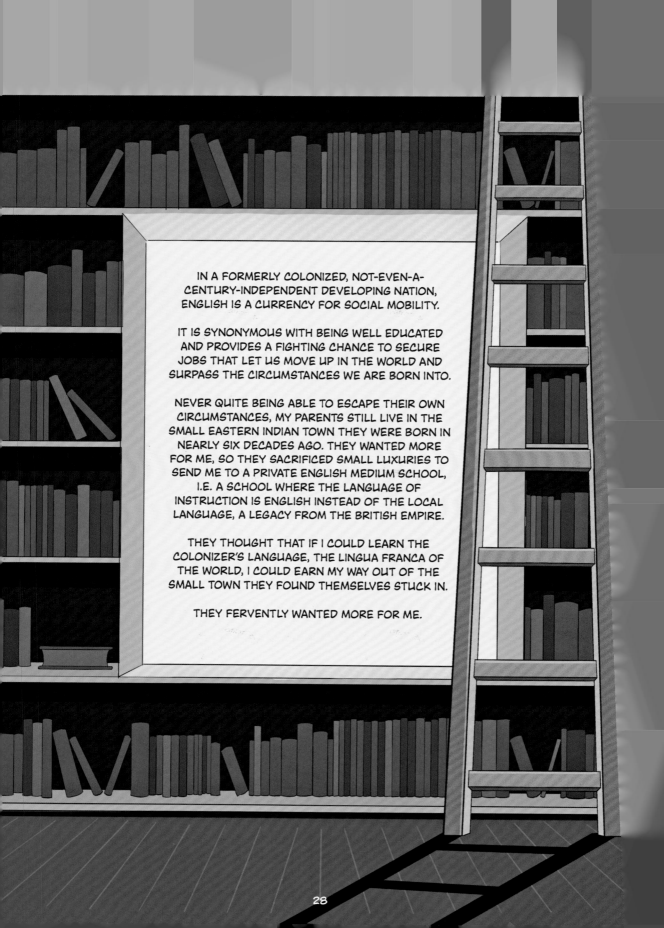

IN A FORMERLY COLONIZED, NOT-EVEN-A-CENTURY-INDEPENDENT DEVELOPING NATION, ENGLISH IS A CURRENCY FOR SOCIAL MOBILITY.

IT IS SYNONYMOUS WITH BEING WELL EDUCATED AND PROVIDES A FIGHTING CHANCE TO SECURE JOBS THAT LET US MOVE UP IN THE WORLD AND SURPASS THE CIRCUMSTANCES WE ARE BORN INTO.

NEVER QUITE BEING ABLE TO ESCAPE THEIR OWN CIRCUMSTANCES, MY PARENTS STILL LIVE IN THE SMALL EASTERN INDIAN TOWN THEY WERE BORN IN NEARLY SIX DECADES AGO. THEY WANTED MORE FOR ME, SO THEY SACRIFICED SMALL LUXURIES TO SEND ME TO A PRIVATE ENGLISH MEDIUM SCHOOL, I.E. A SCHOOL WHERE THE LANGUAGE OF INSTRUCTION IS ENGLISH INSTEAD OF THE LOCAL LANGUAGE, A LEGACY FROM THE BRITISH EMPIRE.

THEY THOUGHT THAT IF I COULD LEARN THE COLONIZER'S LANGUAGE, THE LINGUA FRANCA OF THE WORLD, I COULD EARN MY WAY OUT OF THE SMALL TOWN THEY FOUND THEMSELVES STUCK IN.

THEY FERVENTLY WANTED MORE FOR ME.

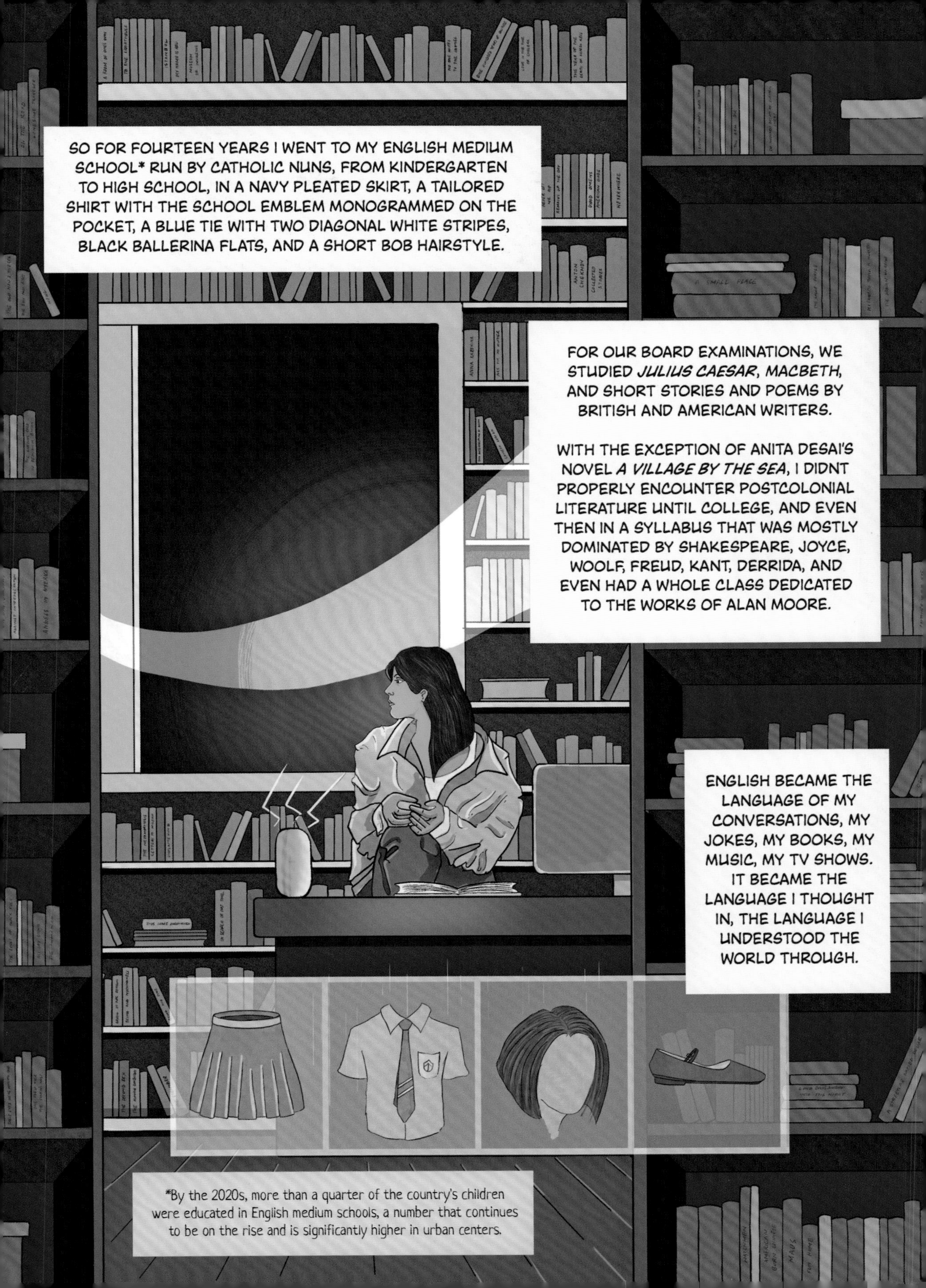
SO FOR FOURTEEN YEARS I WENT TO MY ENGLISH MEDIUM SCHOOL* RUN BY CATHOLIC NUNS, FROM KINDERGARTEN TO HIGH SCHOOL, IN A NAVY PLEATED SKIRT, A TAILORED SHIRT WITH THE SCHOOL EMBLEM MONOGRAMMED ON THE POCKET, A BLUE TIE WITH TWO DIAGONAL WHITE STRIPES, BLACK BALLERINA FLATS, AND A SHORT BOB HAIRSTYLE.
FOR OUR BOARD EXAMINATIONS, WE STUDIED *JULIUS CAESAR*, MACBETH, AND SHORT STORIES AND POEMS BY BRITISH AND AMERICAN WRITERS.
WITH THE EXCEPTION OF ANITA DESAI'S NOVEL *A VILLAGE BY THE SEA*, I DIDNT PROPERLY ENCOUNTER POSTCOLONIAL LITERATURE UNTIL COLLEGE, AND EVEN THEN IN A SYLLABUS THAT WAS MOSTLY DOMINATED BY SHAKESPEARE, JOYCE, WOOLF, FREUD, KANT, DERRIDA, AND EVEN HAD A WHOLE CLASS DEDICATED TO THE WORKS OF ALAN MOORE.
ENGLISH BECAME THE LANGUAGE OF MY CONVERSATIONS, MY JOKES, MY BOOKS, MY MUSIC, MY TV SHOWS. IT BECAME THE LANGUAGE I THOUGHT IN, THE LANGUAGE I UNDERSTOOD THE WORLD THROUGH.
*By the 2020s, more than a quarter of the country's children were educated in English medium schools, a number that continues to be on the rise and is significantly higher in urban centers.

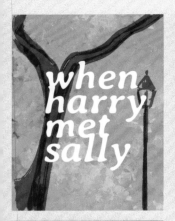

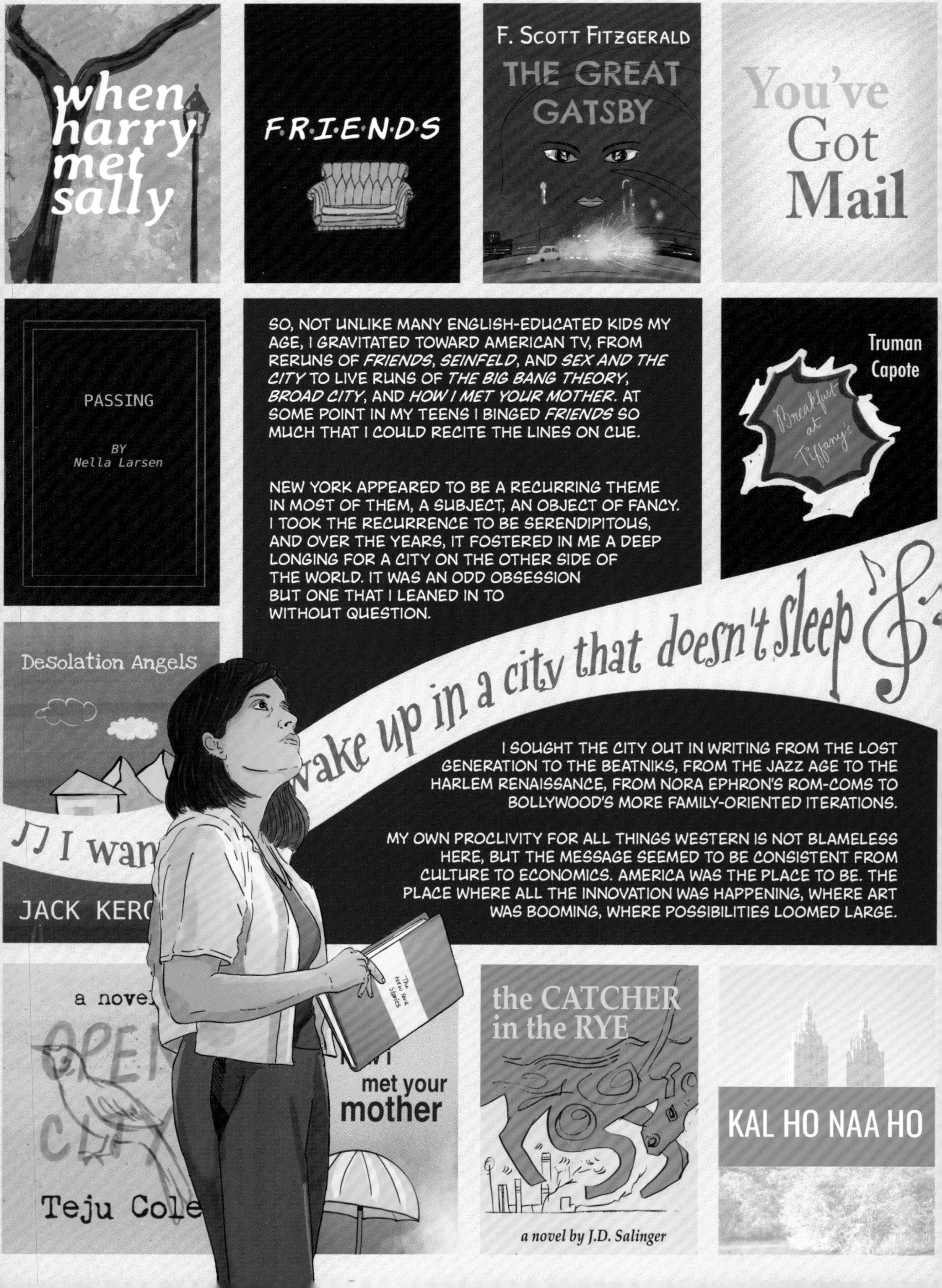

when harry met sally
F·R·I·E·N·D·S
F. SCOTT FITZGERALD
THE GREAT GATSBY
You've Got Mail
PASSING
BY
Nella Larsen
SO, NOT UNLIKE MANY ENGLISH-EDUCATED KIDS MY AGE, I GRAVITATED TOWARD AMERICAN TV, FROM RERUNS OF *FRIENDS*, *SEINFELD*, AND *SEX AND THE CITY* TO LIVE RUNS OF *THE BIG BANG THEORY*, *BROAD CITY*, AND *HOW I MET YOUR MOTHER*. AT SOME POINT IN MY TEENS I BINGED *FRIENDS* SO MUCH THAT I COULD RECITE THE LINES ON CUE.
NEW YORK APPEARED TO BE A RECURRING THEME IN MOST OF THEM, A SUBJECT, AN OBJECT OF FANCY. I TOOK THE RECURRENCE TO BE SERENDIPITOUS, AND OVER THE YEARS, IT FOSTERED IN ME A DEEP LONGING FOR A CITY ON THE OTHER SIDE OF THE WORLD. IT WAS AN ODD OBSESSION BUT ONE THAT I LEANED IN TO WITHOUT QUESTION.
Truman Capote
Breakfast at Tiffany's
Desolation Angels
♫ I wan
wake up in a city that doesn't sleep
JACK KER
I SOUGHT THE CITY OUT IN WRITING FROM THE LOST GENERATION TO THE BEATNIKS, FROM THE JAZZ AGE TO THE HARLEM RENAISSANCE, FROM NORA EPHRON'S ROM-COMS TO BOLLYWOOD'S MORE FAMILY-ORIENTED ITERATIONS.
MY OWN PROCLIVITY FOR ALL THINGS WESTERN IS NOT BLAMELESS HERE, BUT THE MESSAGE SEEMED TO BE CONSISTENT FROM CULTURE TO ECONOMICS. AMERICA WAS THE PLACE TO BE. THE PLACE WHERE ALL THE INNOVATION WAS HAPPENING, WHERE ART WAS BOOMING, WHERE POSSIBILITIES LOOMED LARGE.
a novel
Teju Cole
The New York Stories
met your mother
the CATCHER in the RYE
a novel by J.D. Salinger
KAL HO NAA HO

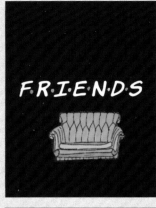

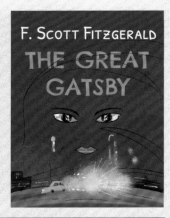

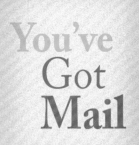

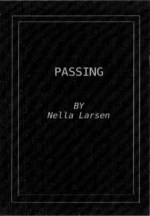

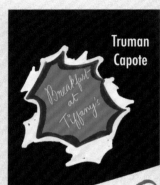

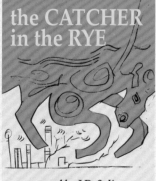

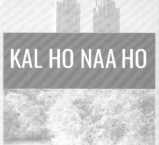

"Ami Chini Go Chini"
by Rabindranath Tagore

আমি   চিনি গো চিনি   তোমারে অগো বিদেশিনী ।
তুমি   থাক সিন্ধুপারে   ওগো বিদেশিনী ॥
তোমায়   দেখেছি শারদপ্রাতে,   তোমায়   দেখেছি মাধবী রাতে,
তোমায়   দেখেছি হৃদি-মাঝারে   ওগো বিদেশিনী ।
আমি   আকাশে পাতিয়া কান   শুনেছি   শুনেছি তোমারি গান,
আমি   তোমারে সঁপেছি প্রাণ   ওগো বিদেশিনী ।
        ভুবন ভ্রমিয়া শেষে   আমি   এসেছি নূতন দেশে,
আমি   অতিথি তোমারি দ্বারে   ওগো বিদেশিনী ॥

SOMETIMES, IF I FOUND MYSELF HAVING TO
STRUGGLE A LITTLE TOO HARD TO READ TAGORE
IN BENGALI (I SPEAK BENGALI FLUENTLY, BUT IT'S
AMAZING HOW FAST A LANGUAGE WILL FALL OUT
OF YOUR CONSCIOUSNESS IF YOU ARE NOT
USING IT REGULARLY)...

...I THOUGHT OF WHO I MIGHT HAVE BECOME IF I HAD NOT
GROWN UP IN A POSTCOLONIAL NATION TRYING TO FIND
ITSELF. IF THE MEDIUM OF INSTRUCTION AT MY SCHOOL
AND COLLEGE HAD BEEN MY MOTHER TONGUE AND IF
WESTERN CULTURE HAD NOT MADE SUCH AN INDELIBLE
MARK ON THE INDIAN SOCIO-CULTURAL FABRIC.

INDIA'S NEW CRIMINAL LAW PUTS SYMBOLISM ABOVE GOOD SENSE

If there's one thing that India's government likes to say it stands for, it's "decolonization."...
Prime Minister Narendra Modi spoke of his time in power as a liberation from a "thousand
years" of slavery to external powers and of how he was laying the foundation for a
thousand year state that would "return" India to its past golden age.

The Washington Post, August 17, 2023

MODI'S POLITICAL PARTY HAS WEAPONIZED BOLLYWOOD

The Washington Post, June 20, 2023

INDIAN GOVERNMENT ACCUSED OF REWRITING HISTORY AFTER EDITS TO SCHOOLBOOKS

The Guardian, April 6, 2023

IT WAS A THOUGHT ROOTED IN A DESIRE FOR DECOLONIZATION, BUT IT WAS QUICKLY WEAPONIZED BY THE RIGHT.

BY 2014, THE PERIOD OF RAPID WESTERNIZATION IN MY CHILDHOOD SAW MASSIVE BACKLASH IN THE FORM
OF THE BHARATIYA JANATA PARTY (BJP), A RIGHT-WING POLITICAL PARTY PRONE TO ETHNONATIONALISM.
THEY CAME TO POWER BY APPEALING TO THE OLD COLONIAL STRATEGY OF DIVIDE AND RULE: PITCHING
HINDU MAJORITY AGAINST MUSLIM MINORITY, BRAINWASHING THE RURAL POOR AND THE STRUGGLING
URBAN YOUTH INTO BELIEVING THAT THEIR SUFFERING WAS SOLELY DUE TO WESTERN INFLUENCE,
MODERNIZATION, AND ERASURE OF HINDU CULTURE, SHIFTING THE BLAME FROM THE LACK OF
SOCIAL SAFETY NETS IN THE CURRENT ECONOMIC SYSTEM.

THEY STAUNCHLY ADVOCATED AGAINST INDIA'S PLURALISTIC ETHOS AND ATTEMPTED
TO REPLACE ONE HEGEMONY WITH ANOTHER, ZEALOUSLY PURSUING THE IDEA OF
A HINDU NATION IN A CONSTITUTIONALLY SECULAR COUNTRY.

UNDER HINDU NATIONALIST LEADERS, SECTARIAN VIOLENCE FLARES IN INDIA

The New York Times, August 1, 2023

NEW INDIAN TEXTBOOKS PURGED OF MUSLIM HISTORY AND HINDU EXTREMISM

The New York Times, April 6, 2023

HOW SOME HINDU NATIONALISTS ARE REWRITING CASTE HISTORY IN THE NAME OF DECOLONISATION

The Conversation, May 9, 2019

INDIA IS THE NEXT BIG FRONTIER FOR NETFLIX AND AMAZON. NOW, THE GOVERNMENT IS TIGHTENING RULES ON CONTENT

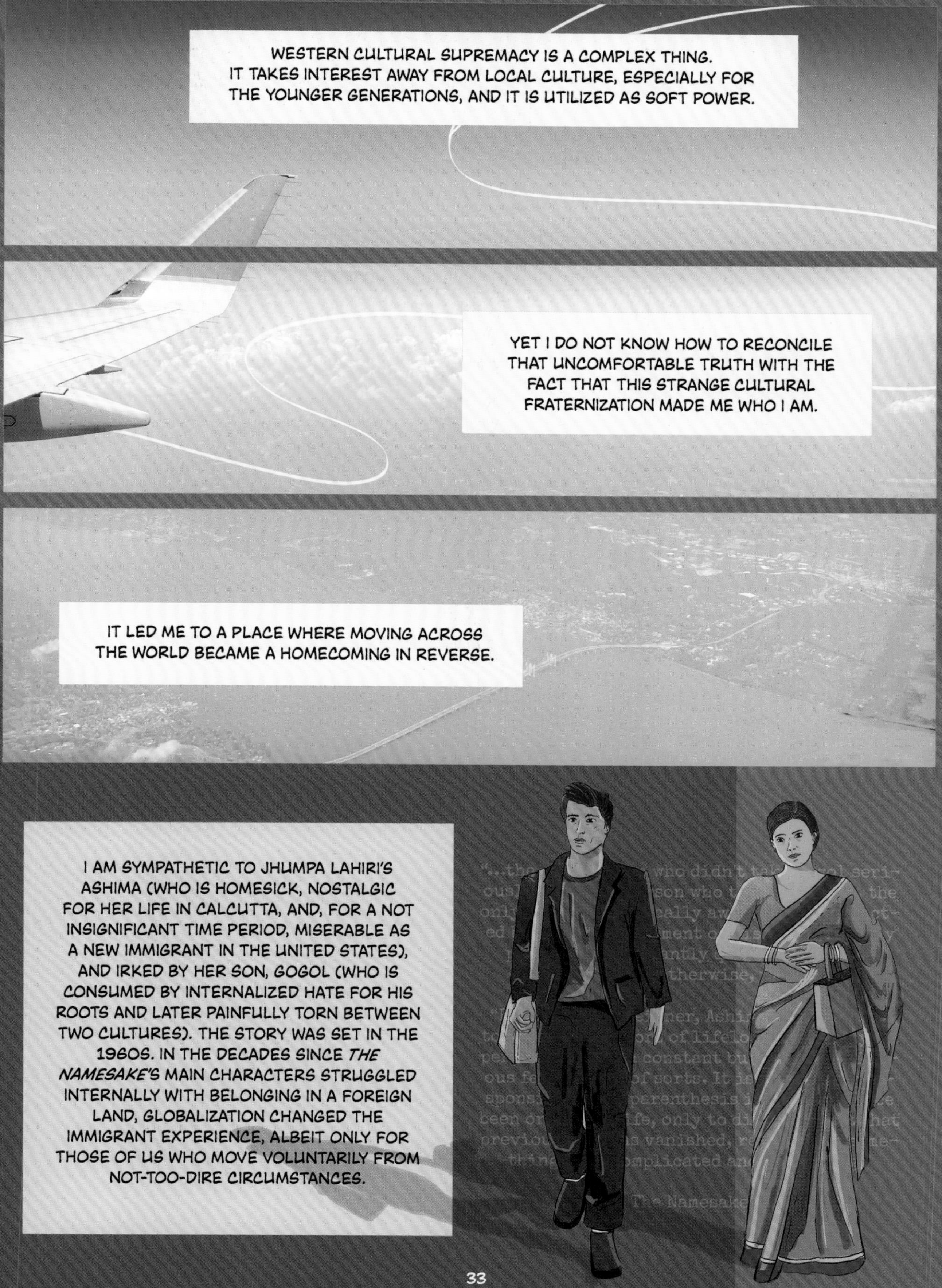

WESTERN CULTURAL SUPREMACY IS A COMPLEX THING. IT TAKES INTEREST AWAY FROM LOCAL CULTURE, ESPECIALLY FOR THE YOUNGER GENERATIONS, AND IT IS UTILIZED AS SOFT POWER.
YET I DO NOT KNOW HOW TO RECONCILE THAT UNCOMFORTABLE TRUTH WITH THE FACT THAT THIS STRANGE CULTURAL FRATERNIZATION MADE ME WHO I AM.
IT LED ME TO A PLACE WHERE MOVING ACROSS THE WORLD BECAME A HOMECOMING IN REVERSE.
I AM SYMPATHETIC TO JHUMPA LAHIRI'S ASHIMA (WHO IS HOMESICK, NOSTALGIC FOR HER LIFE IN CALCUTTA, AND, FOR A NOT INSIGNIFICANT TIME PERIOD, MISERABLE AS A NEW IMMIGRANT IN THE UNITED STATES), AND IRKED BY HER SON, GOGOL (WHO IS CONSUMED BY INTERNALIZED HATE FOR HIS ROOTS AND LATER PAINFULLY TORN BETWEEN TWO CULTURES). THE STORY WAS SET IN THE 1960S. IN THE DECADES SINCE *THE NAMESAKE'S* MAIN CHARACTERS STRUGGLED INTERNALLY WITH BELONGING IN A FOREIGN LAND, GLOBALIZATION CHANGED THE IMMIGRANT EXPERIENCE, ALBEIT ONLY FOR THOSE OF US WHO MOVE VOLUNTARILY FROM NOT-TOO-DIRE CIRCUMSTANCES.
The Namesake

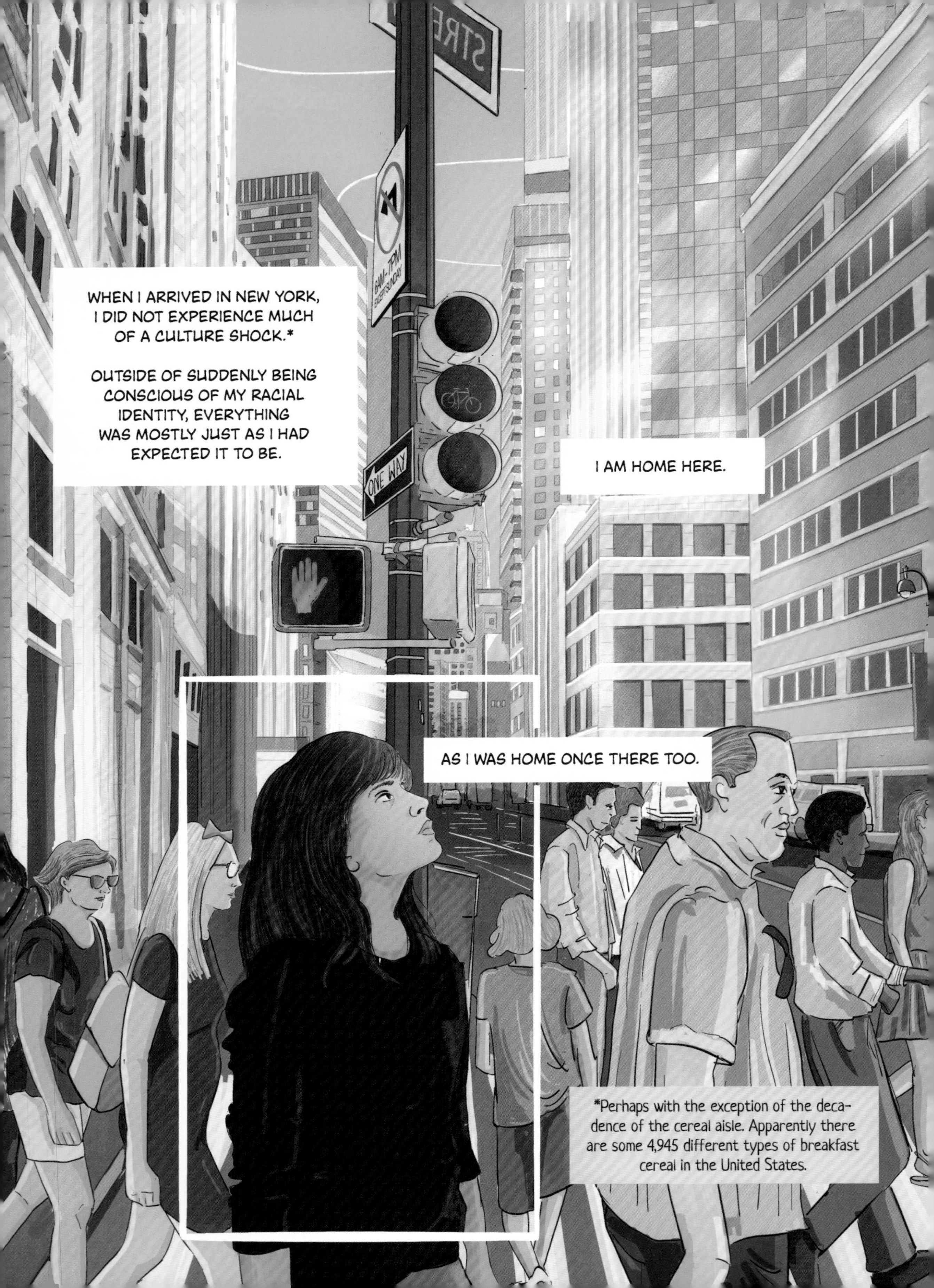
WHEN I ARRIVED IN NEW YORK, I DID NOT EXPERIENCE MUCH OF A CULTURE SHOCK.*
OUTSIDE OF SUDDENLY BEING CONSCIOUS OF MY RACIAL IDENTITY, EVERYTHING WAS MOSTLY JUST AS I HAD EXPECTED IT TO BE.
I AM HOME HERE.
AS I WAS HOME ONCE THERE TOO.
*Perhaps with the exception of the decadence of the cereal aisle. Apparently there are some 4,945 different types of breakfast cereal in the United States.

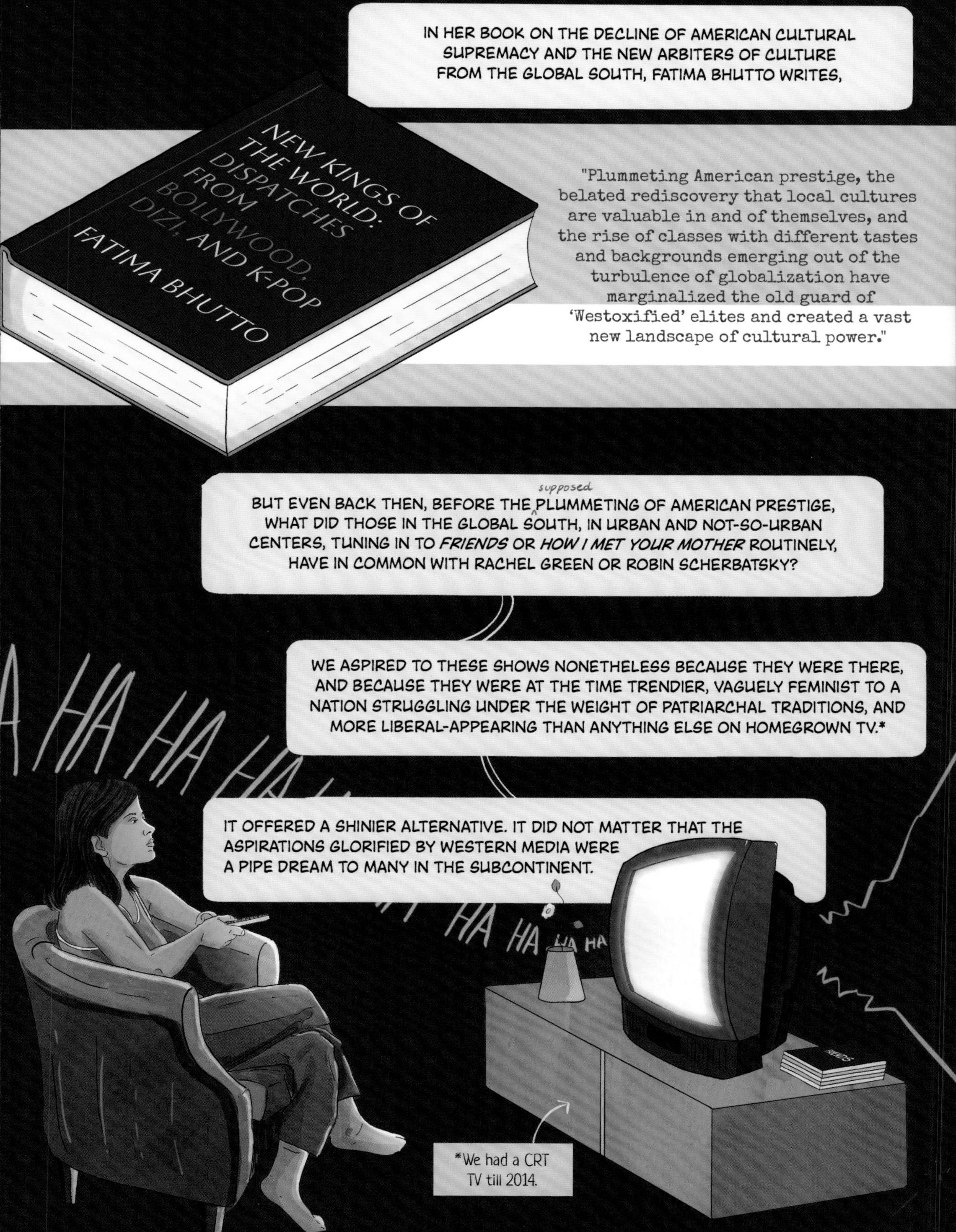
IN HER BOOK ON THE DECLINE OF AMERICAN CULTURAL SUPREMACY AND THE NEW ARBITERS OF CULTURE FROM THE GLOBAL SOUTH, FATIMA BHUTTO WRITES,
NEW KINGS OF THE WORLD: DISPATCHES FROM BOLLYWOOD, DIZI, AND K-POP
FATIMA BHUTTO
"Plummeting American prestige, the belated rediscovery that local cultures are valuable in and of themselves, and the rise of classes with different tastes and backgrounds emerging out of the turbulence of globalization have marginalized the old guard of 'Westoxified' elites and created a vast new landscape of cultural power."
BUT EVEN BACK THEN, BEFORE THE supposed PLUMMETING OF AMERICAN PRESTIGE, WHAT DID THOSE IN THE GLOBAL SOUTH, IN URBAN AND NOT-SO-URBAN CENTERS, TUNING IN TO *FRIENDS* OR *HOW I MET YOUR MOTHER* ROUTINELY, HAVE IN COMMON WITH RACHEL GREEN OR ROBIN SCHERBATSKY?
WE ASPIRED TO THESE SHOWS NONETHELESS BECAUSE THEY WERE THERE, AND BECAUSE THEY WERE AT THE TIME TRENDIER, VAGUELY FEMINIST TO A NATION STRUGGLING UNDER THE WEIGHT OF PATRIARCHAL TRADITIONS, AND MORE LIBERAL-APPEARING THAN ANYTHING ELSE ON HOMEGROWN TV.*
HA HA HA HA
IT OFFERED A SHINIER ALTERNATIVE. IT DID NOT MATTER THAT THE ASPIRATIONS GLORIFIED BY WESTERN MEDIA WERE A PIPE DREAM TO MANY IN THE SUBCONTINENT.
HA HA HA HA
*We had a CRT TV till 2014.

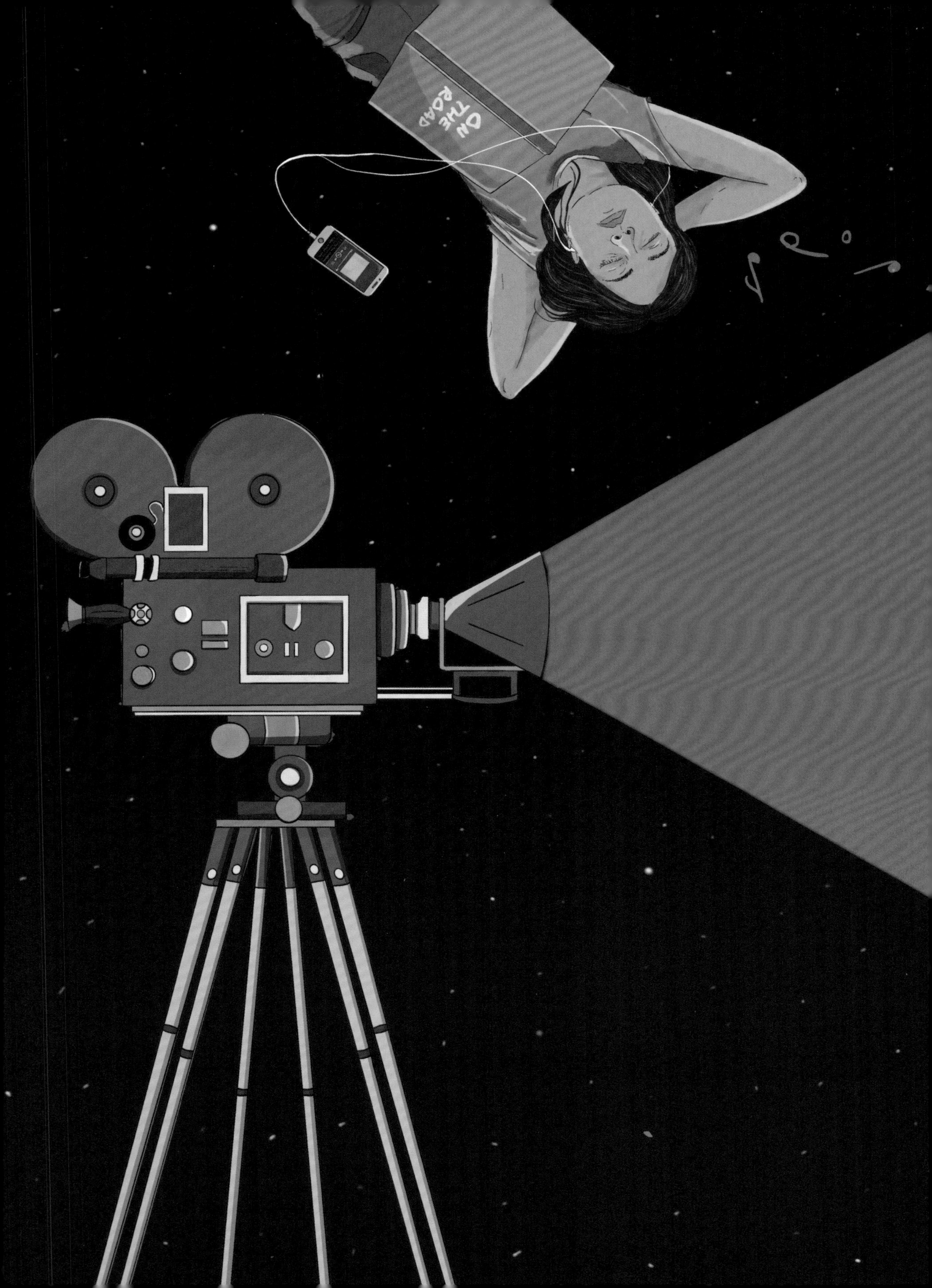
ON THE ROAD

**CULTURE IS AN INDUSTRY.
IT MANUFACTURES DREAMS, DESIRES, AND AESTHETICS.**

IN THE 1990S AND EARLY 2000S, WITH THE ADVENT OF CABLE TV,
STAR MOVIES, MTV, VH1, NICKELODEON, AND CARTOON NETWORK
CAME TO OUR HOMES. AMERICAN POPULAR CULTURE WAS
PREDOMINANT AND INESCAPABLE.

ITS ONLY COMPETITION IN THE SUBCONTINENT WAS **BOLLYWOOD**
(A CONTENTIOUS TERM FOR THE INDIAN HINDI FILM INDUSTRY, OWING
TO ITS DERIVATION FROM ITS WESTERN COUNTERPART). IT IS THE
BIGGEST FILM INDUSTRY IN THE WORLD, PRODUCING MORE THAN
A THOUSAND FILMS EVERY YEAR.

BOLLYWOOD CONCOCTED ITS OWN HYBRID GENRES BEYOND
ROM-COMS, ACTION, THRILLERS, OR DRAMAS. THE BLOCKBUSTERS
HAD IT ALL: ROMANCE, COMEDY, SOCIAL DRAMA IN A PREDICTABLE
SEQUENCE, OFTEN WITH SPECTACULAR MUSICAL PERFORMANCES
THROWN IN FOR GOOD MEASURE.

BUT EVEN HINDI CINEMA WAS ENAMORED WITH THE WEST. ONCE TOO
MELODRAMATIC AND GAUCHE TO THE POINT OF BEING RIDICULOUS
(ESPECIALLY IN THE EIGHTIES WHEN YASH CHOPRA'S SOPHISTICATED
ROMANCES WERE LOSING GROUND TO KITSCHY, OVER-THE-TOP
ACTION FLICKS), IN THE NINETIES, BOLLYWOOD WAS REINVENTING
ITSELF TO CATER TO A YOUNGER INDIA AND, TO A CERTAIN EXTENT,
THE MILLIONS OF INDIANS LIVING ABROAD.

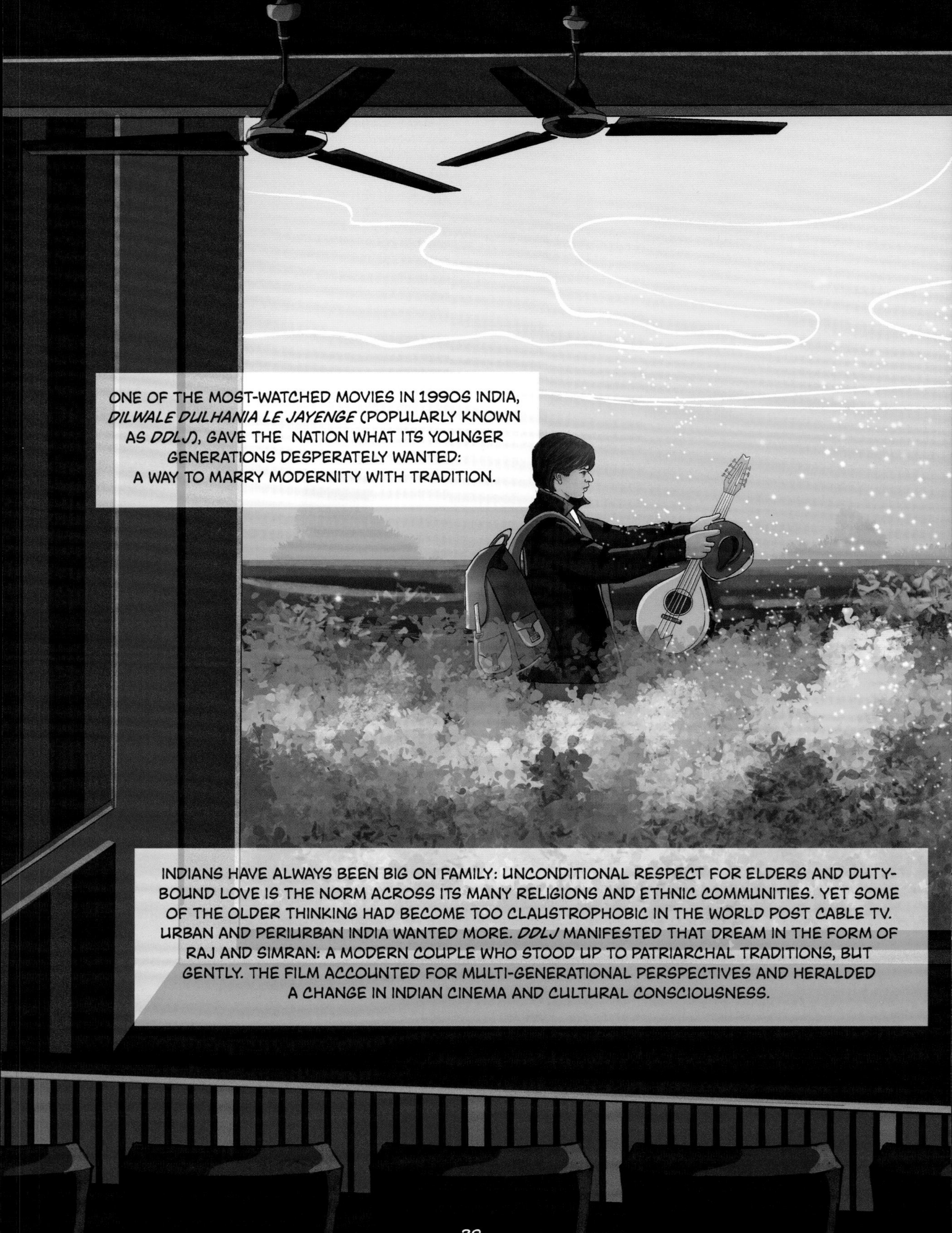
ONE OF THE MOST-WATCHED MOVIES IN 1990S INDIA, *DILWALE DULHANIA LE JAYENGE* (POPULARLY KNOWN AS *DDLJ*), GAVE THE NATION WHAT ITS YOUNGER GENERATIONS DESPERATELY WANTED: A WAY TO MARRY MODERNITY WITH TRADITION.
INDIANS HAVE ALWAYS BEEN BIG ON FAMILY: UNCONDITIONAL RESPECT FOR ELDERS AND DUTY-BOUND LOVE IS THE NORM ACROSS ITS MANY RELIGIONS AND ETHNIC COMMUNITIES. YET SOME OF THE OLDER THINKING HAD BECOME TOO CLAUSTROPHOBIC IN THE WORLD POST CABLE TV. URBAN AND PERIURBAN INDIA WANTED MORE. *DDLJ* MANIFESTED THAT DREAM IN THE FORM OF RAJ AND SIMRAN: A MODERN COUPLE WHO STOOD UP TO PATRIARCHAL TRADITIONS, BUT GENTLY. THE FILM ACCOUNTED FOR MULTI-GENERATIONAL PERSPECTIVES AND HERALDED A CHANGE IN INDIAN CINEMA AND CULTURAL CONSCIOUSNESS.

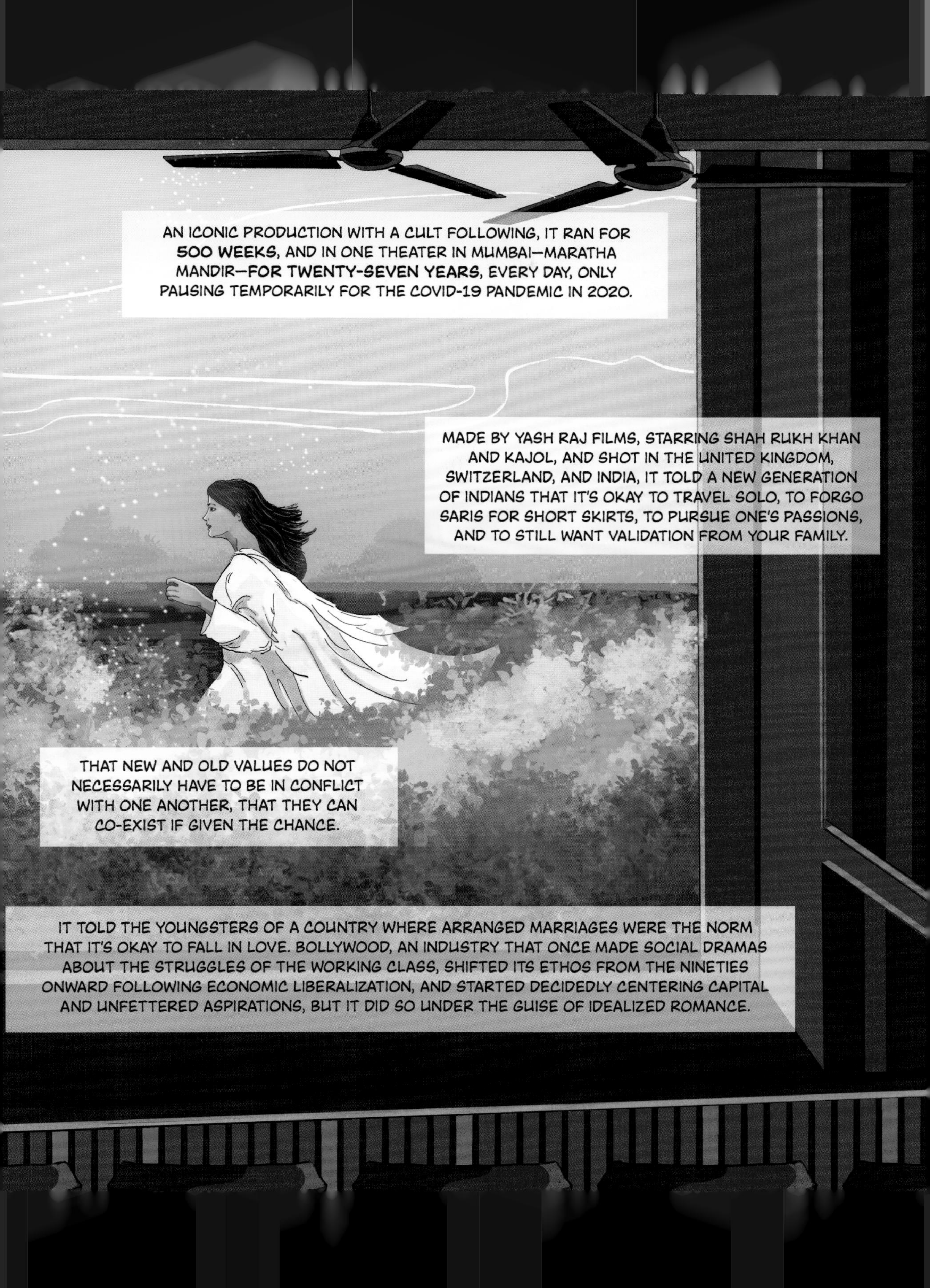
AN ICONIC PRODUCTION WITH A CULT FOLLOWING, IT RAN FOR 500 WEEKS, AND IN ONE THEATER IN MUMBAI—MARATHA MANDIR—FOR TWENTY-SEVEN YEARS, EVERY DAY, ONLY PAUSING TEMPORARILY FOR THE COVID-19 PANDEMIC IN 2020.
MADE BY YASH RAJ FILMS, STARRING SHAH RUKH KHAN AND KAJOL, AND SHOT IN THE UNITED KINGDOM, SWITZERLAND, AND INDIA, IT TOLD A NEW GENERATION OF INDIANS THAT IT'S OKAY TO TRAVEL SOLO, TO FORGO SARIS FOR SHORT SKIRTS, TO PURSUE ONE'S PASSIONS, AND TO STILL WANT VALIDATION FROM YOUR FAMILY.
THAT NEW AND OLD VALUES DO NOT NECESSARILY HAVE TO BE IN CONFLICT WITH ONE ANOTHER, THAT THEY CAN CO-EXIST IF GIVEN THE CHANCE.
IT TOLD THE YOUNGSTERS OF A COUNTRY WHERE ARRANGED MARRIAGES WERE THE NORM THAT IT'S OKAY TO FALL IN LOVE. BOLLYWOOD, AN INDUSTRY THAT ONCE MADE SOCIAL DRAMAS ABOUT THE STRUGGLES OF THE WORKING CLASS, SHIFTED ITS ETHOS FROM THE NINETIES ONWARD FOLLOWING ECONOMIC LIBERALIZATION, AND STARTED DECIDEDLY CENTERING CAPITAL AND UNFETTERED ASPIRATIONS, BUT IT DID SO UNDER THE GUISE OF IDEALIZED ROMANCE.

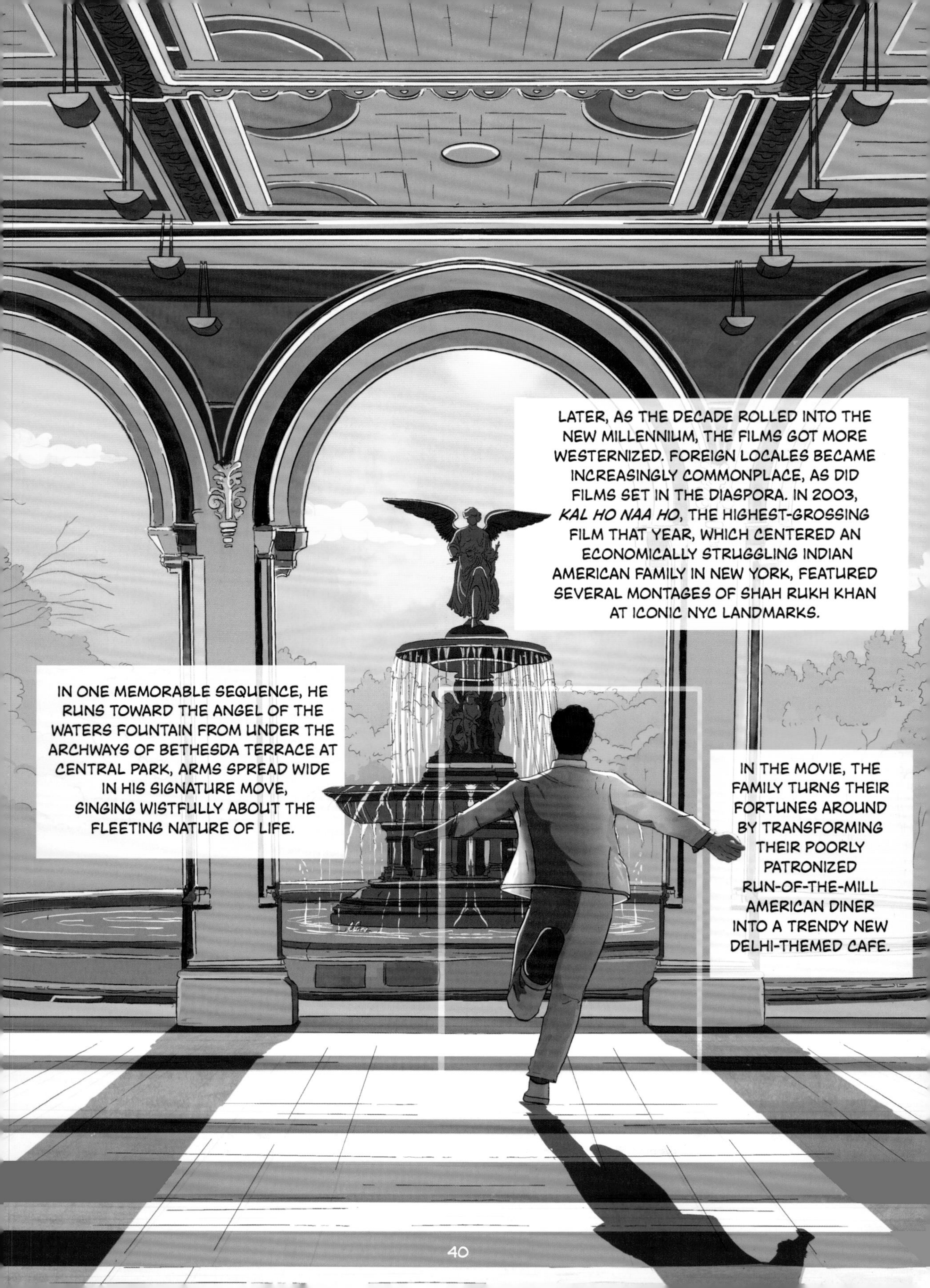
LATER, AS THE DECADE ROLLED INTO THE NEW MILLENNIUM, THE FILMS GOT MORE WESTERNIZED. FOREIGN LOCALES BECAME INCREASINGLY COMMONPLACE, AS DID FILMS SET IN THE DIASPORA. IN 2003, *KAL HO NAA HO*, THE HIGHEST-GROSSING FILM THAT YEAR, WHICH CENTERED AN ECONOMICALLY STRUGGLING INDIAN AMERICAN FAMILY IN NEW YORK, FEATURED SEVERAL MONTAGES OF SHAH RUKH KHAN AT ICONIC NYC LANDMARKS.
IN ONE MEMORABLE SEQUENCE, HE RUNS TOWARD THE ANGEL OF THE WATERS FOUNTAIN FROM UNDER THE ARCHWAYS OF BETHESDA TERRACE AT CENTRAL PARK, ARMS SPREAD WIDE IN HIS SIGNATURE MOVE, SINGING WISTFULLY ABOUT THE FLEETING NATURE OF LIFE.
IN THE MOVIE, THE FAMILY TURNS THEIR FORTUNES AROUND BY TRANSFORMING THEIR POORLY PATRONIZED RUN-OF-THE-MILL AMERICAN DINER INTO A TRENDY NEW DELHI-THEMED CAFE.

BY THEN, BOLLYWOOD HAD PERFECTED THE TROPE OF COMBINING THE BEST OF THE EAST AND THE WEST, OF TRADITION AND MODERNITY, OF THE OLD AND NEW WORLD. **SHAH RUKH KHAN**, A MUSLIM ACTOR IN A HINDU-MAJORITY COUNTRY, BECAME A HEARTTHROB, AN ARBITER OF CULTURE, A POSTER BOY FOR SECULAR INDIA, AN ICON OF ITS LIBERAL ASPIRATIONS, AND THE GREATEST SUPERSTAR THE COUNTRY HAS EVER SEEN.

HE CAME FROM A SQUARELY LOWER-MIDDLE-CLASS FAMILY AND LOST BOTH HIS PARENTS BY HIS EARLY TWENTIES. HE SPENT HIS COLLEGE DAYS DOING THEATER IN DELHI AND ONE DAY, AT AROUND TWENTY-FIVE, JUMPED ON A PLANE TO MUMBAI.

BY THIRTY, HE WAS A STAR; BY FORTY, ON THE COVER OF *TIME* MAGAZINE, AND BY FIFTY, THE SECOND RICHEST ACTOR IN THE WORLD ACCORDING TO *FORBES* AND A RECIPIENT OF THE HIGHEST CIVILIAN AWARD—THE LEGION OF HONOUR—FROM THE GOVERNMENT OF FRANCE FOR HIS CONTRIBUTION TO GLOBAL CULTURAL DIVERSITY.

HIS HOME "MANNAT," WHICH ROUGHLY TRANSLATES AS "A PRAYER OR A WISH FULFILLED," BECAME AN URBAN PILGRIMAGE OF SORTS OVER THE YEARS—A SIGN THAT HOPE STILL LINGERS IN THE CITY OF DREAMS, AMID THE INEQUALITY AND THE CHAOS AND AGAINST ALL ODDS.

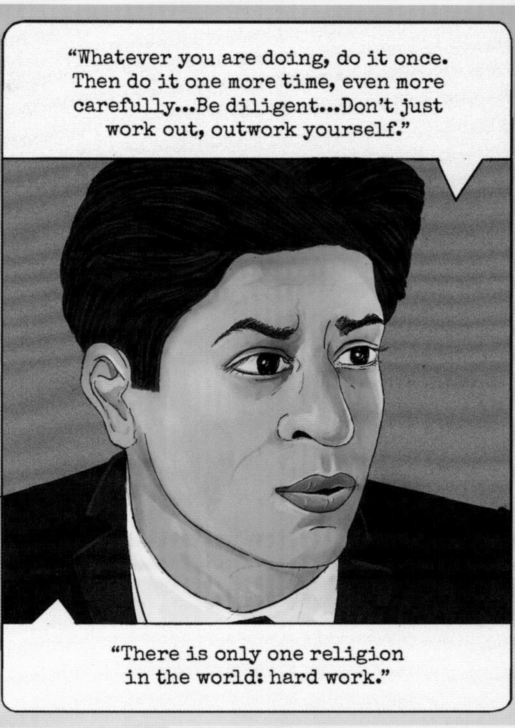
"Whatever you are doing, do it once. Then do it one more time, even more carefully...Be diligent...Don't just work out, outwork yourself."
"There is only one religion in the world: hard work."

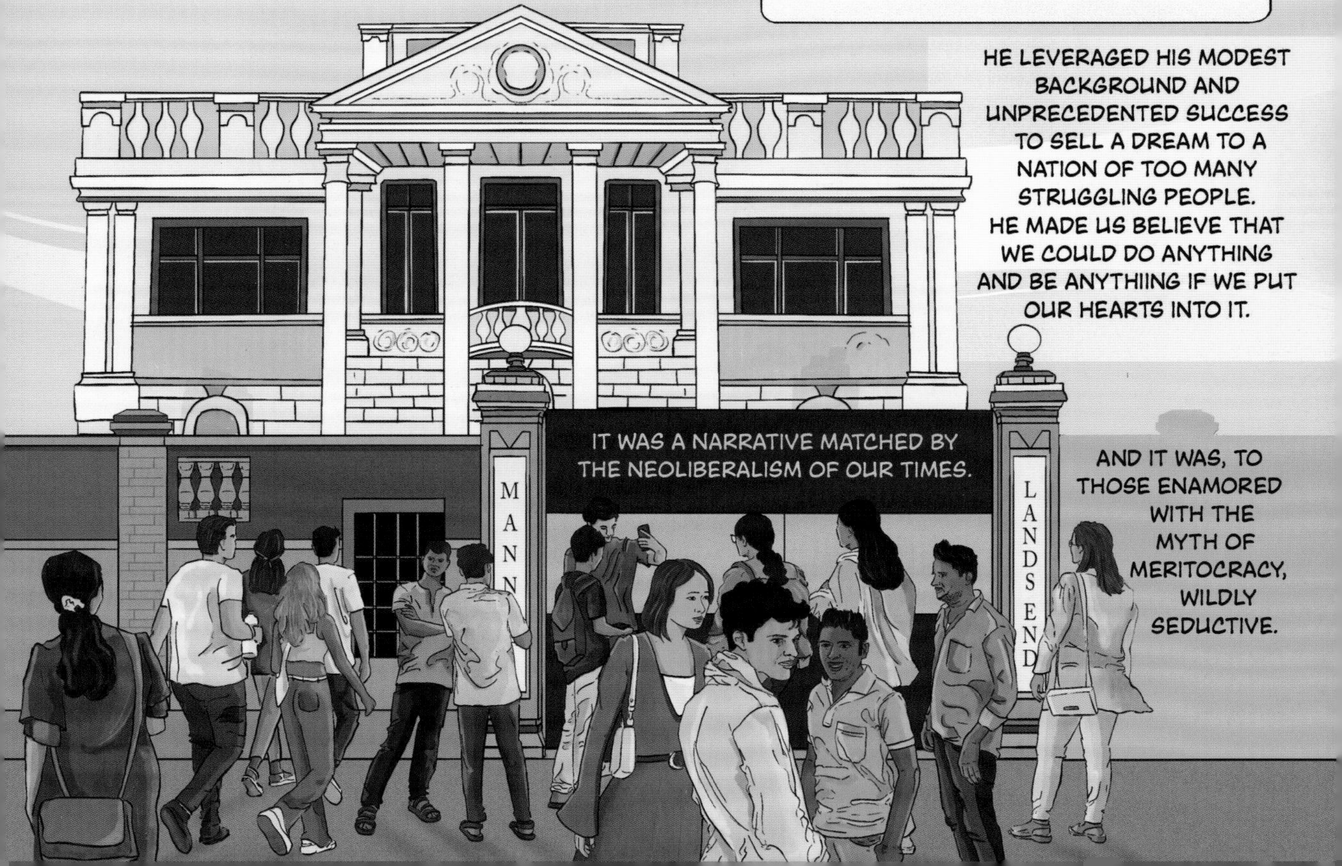
HE LEVERAGED HIS MODEST BACKGROUND AND UNPRECEDENTED SUCCESS TO SELL A DREAM TO A NATION OF TOO MANY STRUGGLING PEOPLE. HE MADE US BELIEVE THAT WE COULD DO ANYTHING AND BE ANYTHIING IF WE PUT OUR HEARTS INTO IT.
IT WAS A NARRATIVE MATCHED BY THE NEOLIBERALISM OF OUR TIMES.
MANN
LANDS END
AND IT WAS, TO THOSE ENAMORED WITH THE MYTH OF MERITOCRACY, WILDLY SEDUCTIVE.

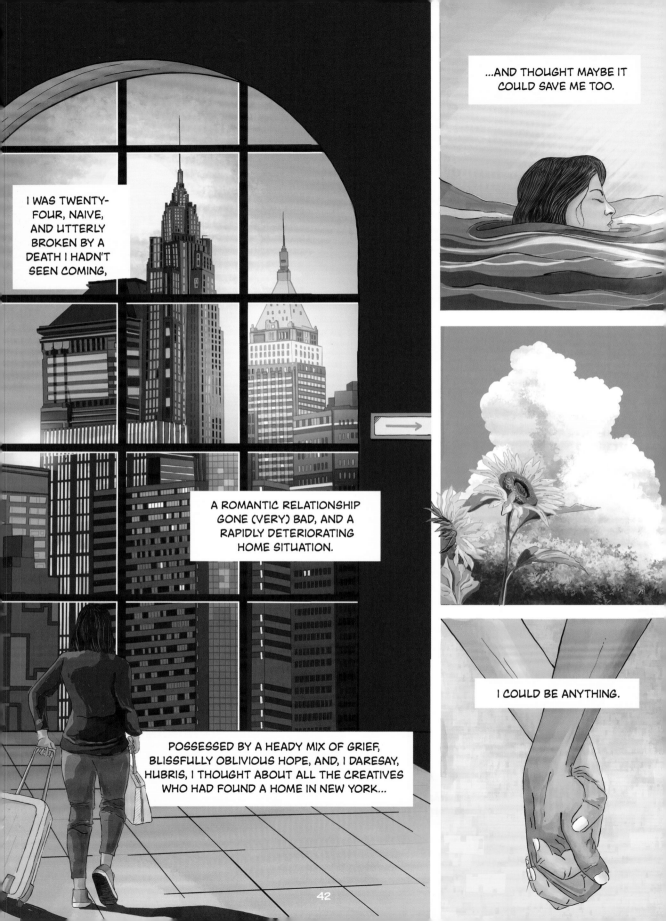

I WAS TWENTY-FOUR, NAIVE, AND UTTERLY BROKEN BY A DEATH I HADN'T SEEN COMING,

A ROMANTIC RELATIONSHIP GONE (VERY) BAD, AND A RAPIDLY DETERIORATING HOME SITUATION.

POSSESSED BY A HEADY MIX OF GRIEF, BLISSFULLY OBLIVIOUS HOPE, AND, I DARESAY, HUBRIS, I THOUGHT ABOUT ALL THE CREATIVES WHO HAD FOUND A HOME IN NEW YORK...

...AND THOUGHT MAYBE IT COULD SAVE ME TOO.

I COULD BE ANYTHING.

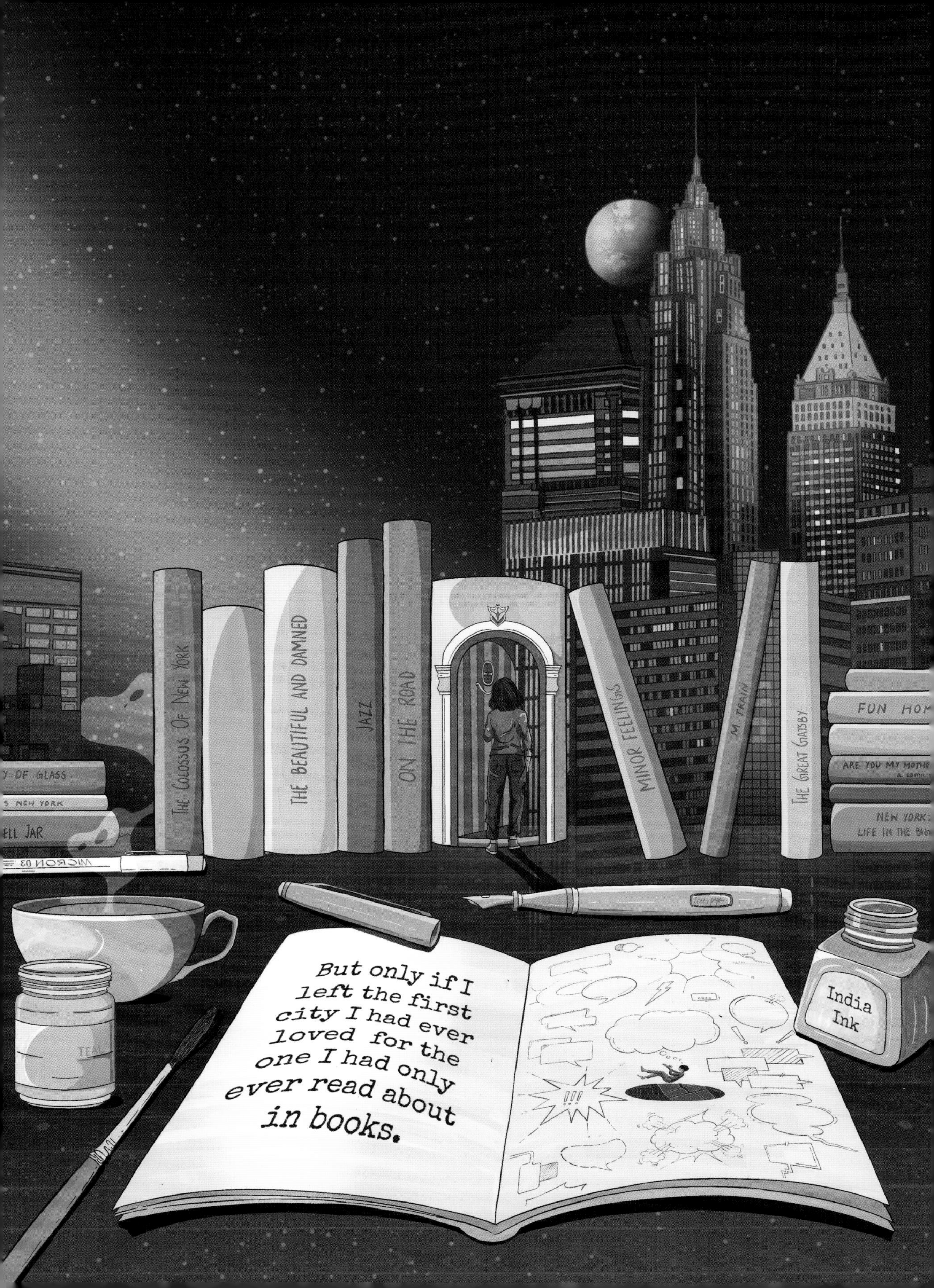

THE COLOSSUS OF NEW YORK
THE BEAUTIFUL AND DAMNED
JAZZ
ON THE ROAD
MINOR FEELINGS
M TRAIN
THE GREAT GATSBY
MICRON 03
India Ink
TEAL
But only if I left the first city I had ever loved for the one I had only ever read about in books.

CLEMENTINES,

Because in Bengali, We Do Not Say, "I Love You"

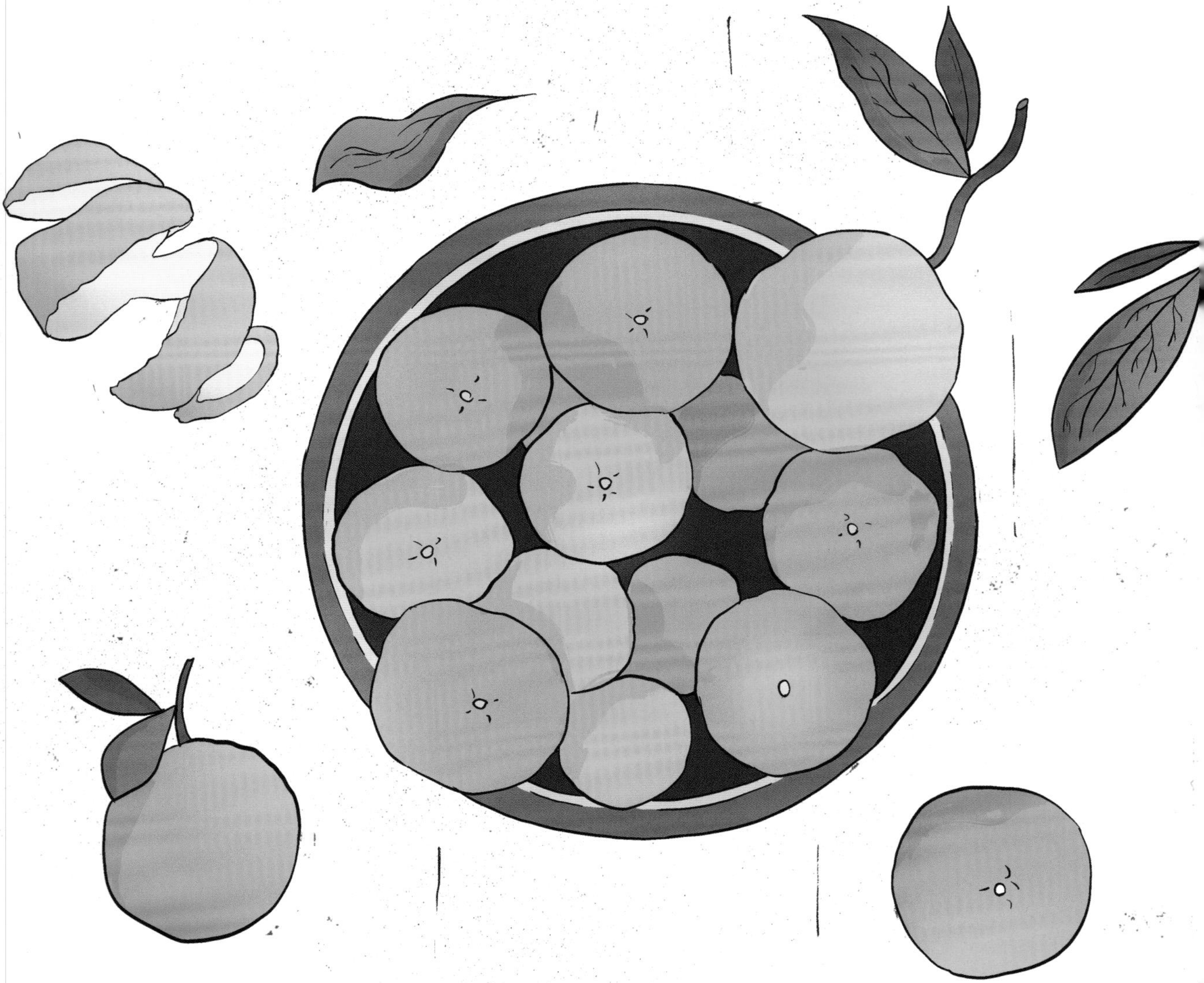

IN A RAPIDLY CHANGING SOCIO-CULTURAL LANDSCAPE, THE ONE THING THAT REMAINED CONSTANT IN MY CHILDHOOD WAS OUR RELATIONSHIP TO FOOD. ON SUN-KISSED WINTER AFTERNOONS, MY GRANDMOTHER USED TO MAKE A RITUAL OUT OF PEELING CLEMENTINES—

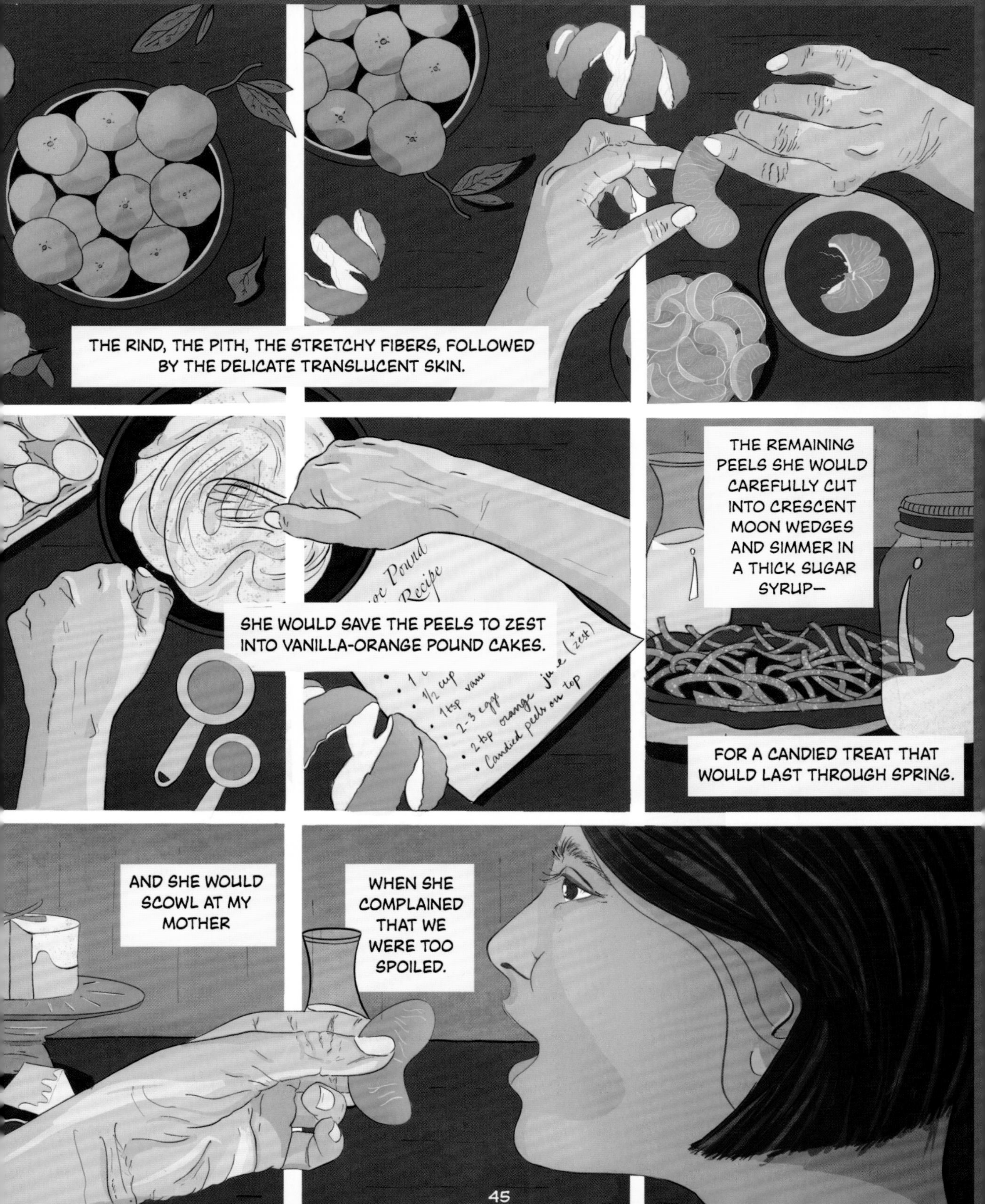
THE RIND, THE PITH, THE STRETCHY FIBERS, FOLLOWED BY THE DELICATE TRANSLUCENT SKIN.
SHE WOULD SAVE THE PEELS TO ZEST INTO VANILLA-ORANGE POUND CAKES.
Recipe
2-3 eggs
2 tsp orange juice (+ zest)
Candied peels on top
THE REMAINING PEELS SHE WOULD CAREFULLY CUT INTO CRESCENT MOON WEDGES AND SIMMER IN A THICK SUGAR SYRUP—
FOR A CANDIED TREAT THAT WOULD LAST THROUGH SPRING.
AND SHE WOULD SCOWL AT MY MOTHER
WHEN SHE COMPLAINED THAT WE WERE TOO SPOILED.

DURING THE LONG SUMMERS, SHE MADE KULFI ICE CREAM WITH CRUSHED PISTACHIOS AND BITS OF CARDAMOM

AND COLD AAM PANNA WITH UNRIPE MANGO AND MINT LEAVES.

ON OUR BIRTHDAYS, SHE MADE PAYESH FOR DESSERT, A SWEET RICE PUDDING MADE BY SIMMERING MILK, SUGAR, AND SHORT-GRAIN RICE* OVER A LOW FLAME, TOPPED WITH RAISINS AND CASHEWS ROASTED IN CLARIFIED BUTTER.

IT WAS SWEET, STICKY, AND BELIEVED TO BE AUSPICIOUS.

*(usually made with Gobindobhog, a fragrant variety mostly cultivated in Bengal)

SHE MADE FRIES OUT OF POTATO SKINS TO GO WITH LENTILS OVER RICE,

AND HOMEMADE YOGURT WITH LEFTOVER MILK*, USING THE DAY'S BATCH AS A STARTER FOR THE NEXT.

*(called doi in Bengali households or curd in the subcontinent)

SHE MADE OUR SCHOOL LUNCHES WITH A LITTLE BIT OF EVERYTHING IN VARIOUS COMBINATIONS, EVERY DAY TILL WE GRADUATED FROM HIGH SCHOOL.

SHE MADE A THREE-INGREDIENT STIR FRY THAT TOOK MORE PATIENCE THAN MATERIALS.

HER SIGNATURE KORAISHUTIR KOCHURI* BECAME SO POPULAR AMONG MY FRIENDS THAT SHE OFTEN RESORTED TO SENDING ME TO SCHOOL WITH EXTRA.

*(flatbread stuffed with spiced peas)

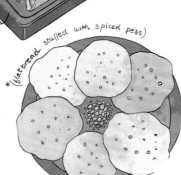

SHE FED US WITH HER OWN HANDS, LET US MAKE OUTRAGEOUS REQUESTS FOR DINNER, AND SURPRISED US WITH HOMEMADE TREATS WITH PREDICTABLE FREQUENCY. STILL, INDULGENCE NOTWITHSTANDING, FOOD WAS ALSO PRECIOUS. SACRED. WE WERE NEVER TO WASTE IT. WE WERE TO NEVER TAKE IT FOR GRANTED. NOT IN A COUNTRY WHERE, AT THE TIME, IN THE NINETIES, 200 MILLION PEOPLE WENT TO BED HUNGRY EVERY NIGHT. NOT IN A FAMILY THAT WAS JUST BEGINNING TO ENJOY THE SMALL, OFTEN SHAKY, COMFORTS OF THE NEWLY MIDDLE CLASS.

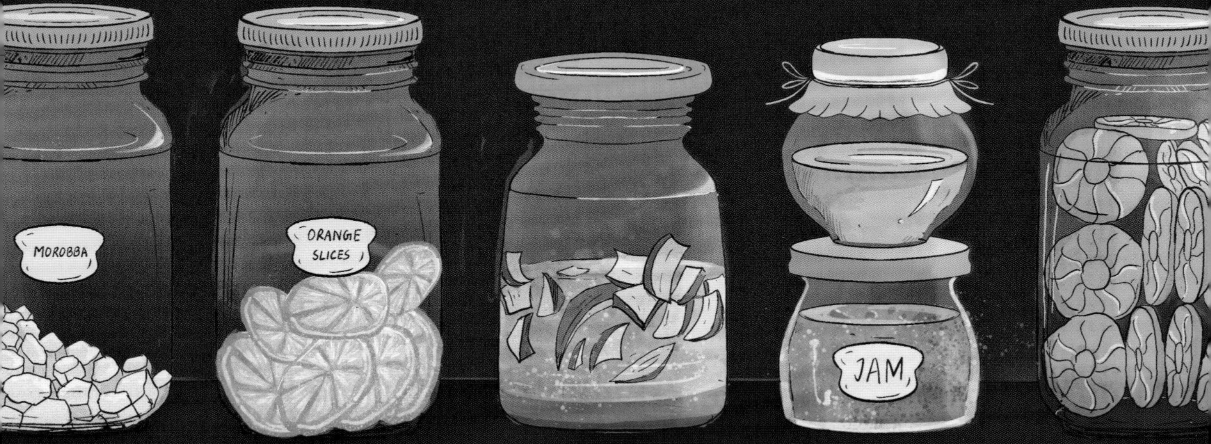
MOROBBA
ORANGE SLICES
JAM

SHE FELL IN LOVE WITH MY GRANDFATHER IN HIGH SCHOOL, AND BY NINETEEN, THEY WERE ALREADY MARRI

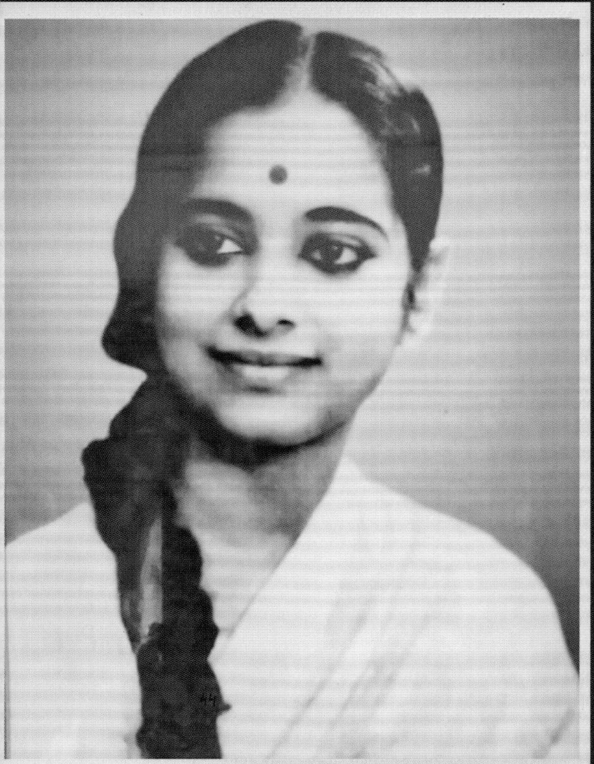

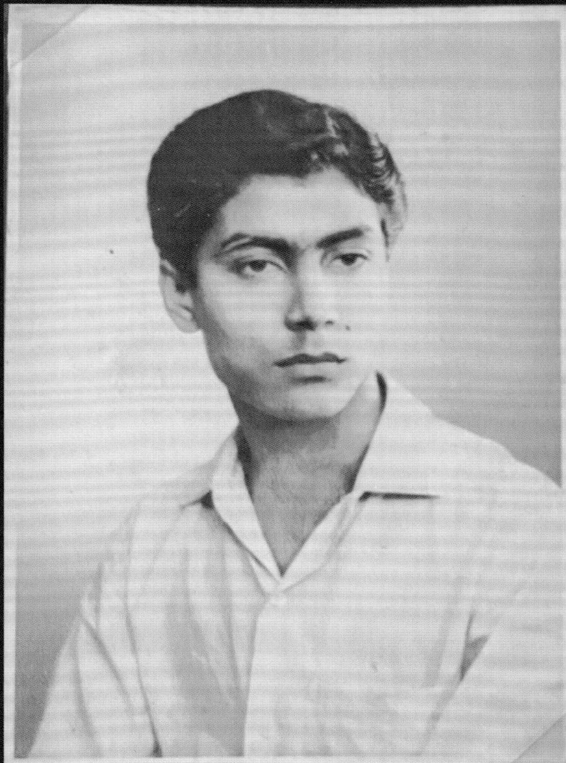

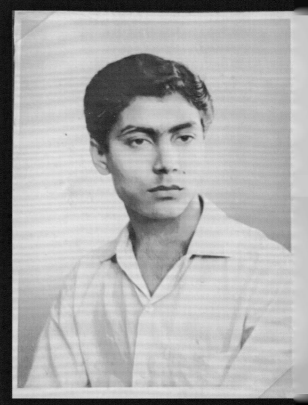

TOGETHER, THEY MOVED OUT OF THE CITY TO A QUIET TOWN IN THE OUTSKIRTS AND RAISED THREE CHILDREN ON A SINGLE INCOME IN A SMALL TWO-BEDROOM RENTAL BEFORE THEY

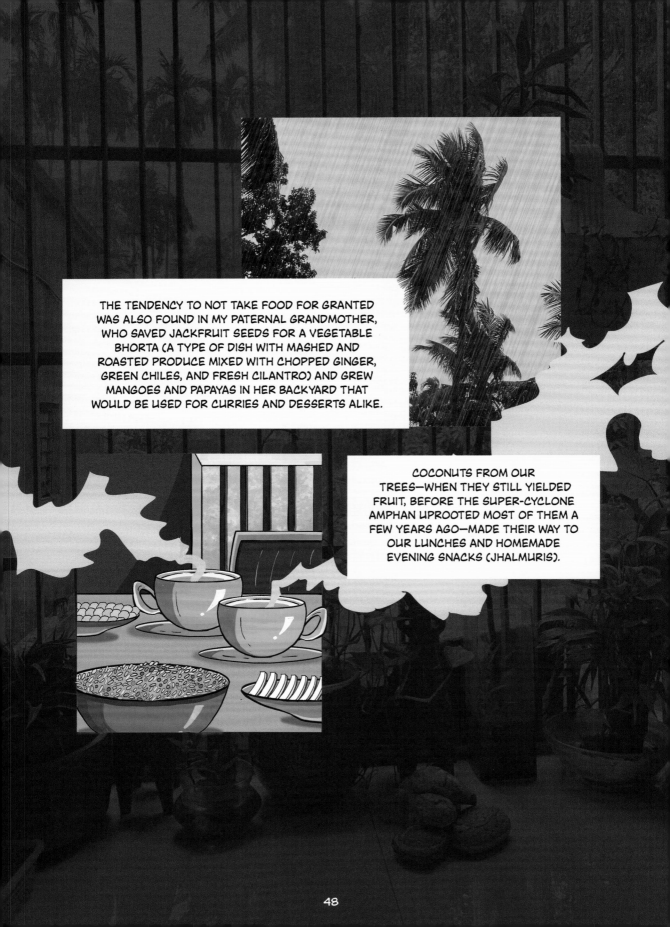

THE TENDENCY TO NOT TAKE FOOD FOR GRANTED WAS ALSO FOUND IN MY PATERNAL GRANDMOTHER, WHO SAVED JACKFRUIT SEEDS FOR A VEGETABLE BHORTA (A TYPE OF DISH WITH MASHED AND ROASTED PRODUCE MIXED WITH CHOPPED GINGER, GREEN CHILES, AND FRESH CILANTRO) AND GREW MANGOES AND PAPAYAS IN HER BACKYARD THAT WOULD BE USED FOR CURRIES AND DESSERTS ALIKE.

COCONUTS FROM OUR TREES—WHEN THEY STILL YIELDED FRUIT, BEFORE THE SUPER-CYCLONE AMPHAN UPROOTED MOST OF THEM A FEW YEARS AGO—MADE THEIR WAY TO OUR LUNCHES AND HOMEMADE EVENING SNACKS (JHALMURIS).

MY MOTHER HAD A KNACK FOR TURNING FLOWERS INTO FOOD. KUMRO PHOOL (SQUASH BLOSSOMS) DIPPED IN GRAM FLOUR BECAME CRISPY-EDGED GOLDEN FRITTERS. HER STIR-FRIED SOJNE PHOOL (MORINGA BLOSSOMS) WITH SHREDDED COCONUT AND MUSTARD, SAVORY AND SWEET, MADE FOR A DELICIOUS SIDE WITH LENTILS.

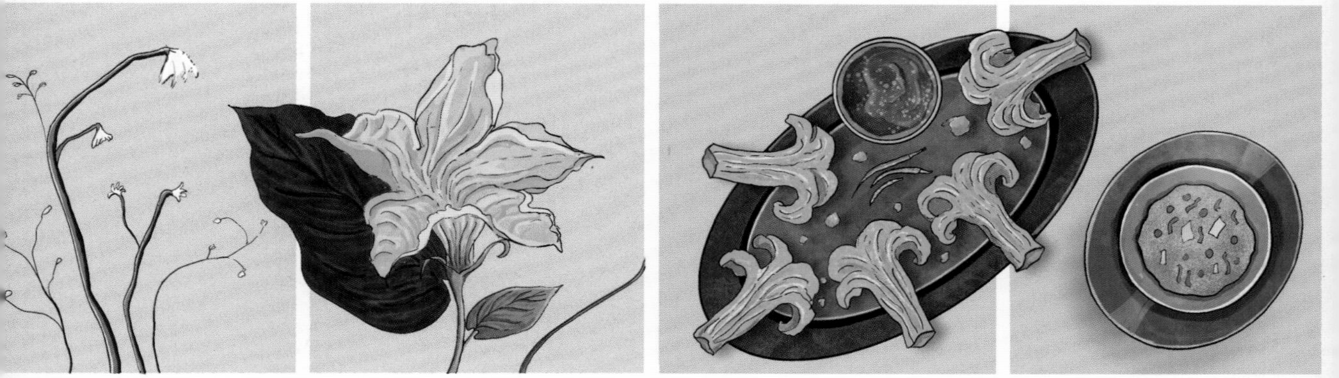

WE HAD VARYING PREPARATIONS OF FISH MONDAY THROUGH FRIDAY—RANGING FROM MALAIKARIS AND KOFTA TO A SIMPLE STEW.

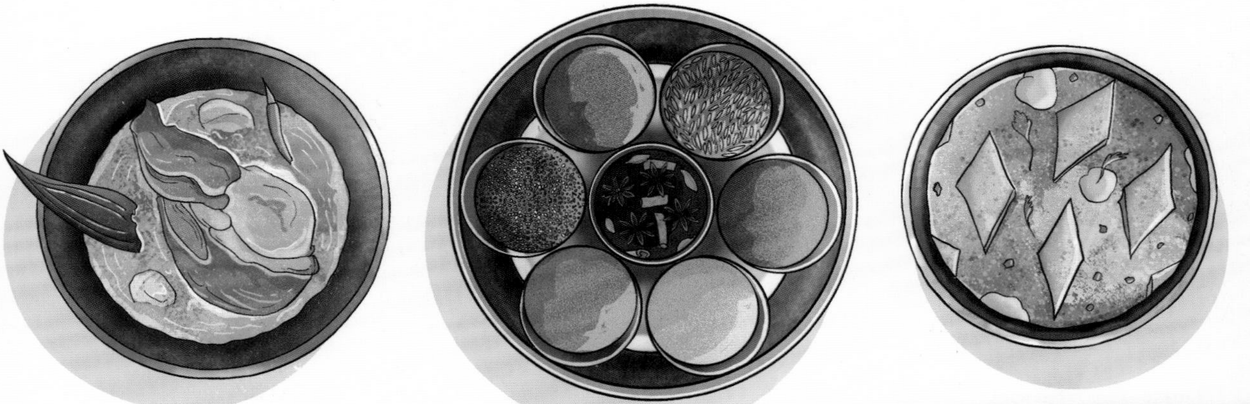

WE ONLY ATE VEGETARIAN FOOD ON SATURDAYS.

AND ON SUNDAYS, TOO MANY ADULTS—MUM, GRANDMUM, GRANDFATHER, PAPA, MAMI—GATHERED IN THE KITCHEN TO MAKE A SPECIAL CHICKEN CURRY WITH PULAO.

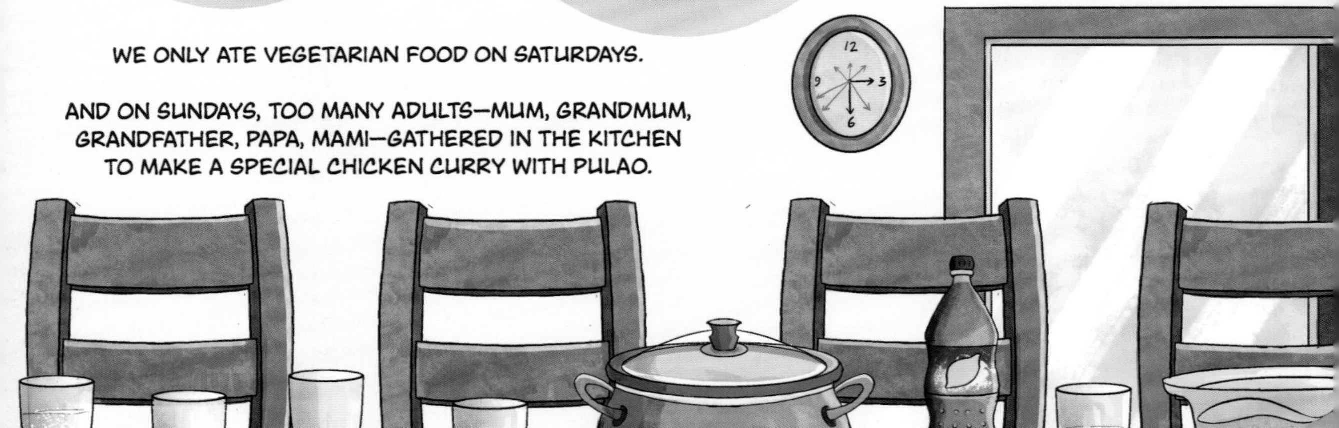
12
9
3
6

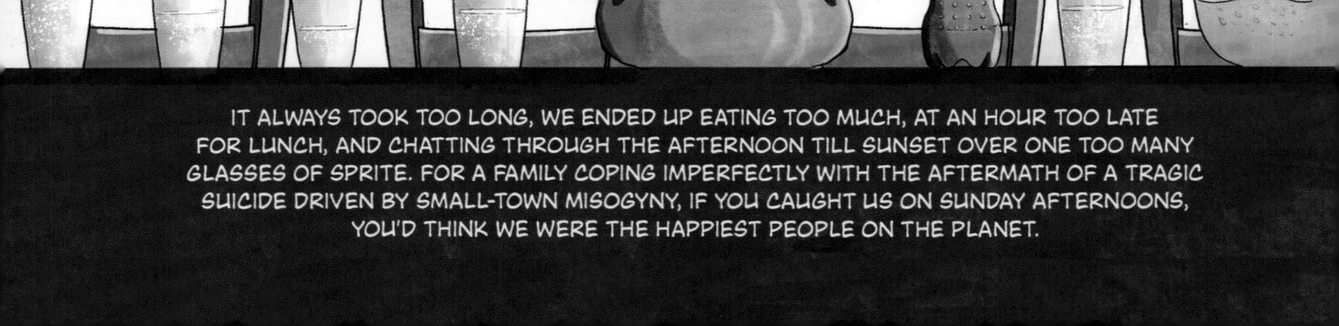

IT ALWAYS TOOK TOO LONG, WE ENDED UP EATING TOO MUCH, AT AN HOUR TOO LATE FOR LUNCH, AND CHATTING THROUGH THE AFTERNOON TILL SUNSET OVER ONE TOO MANY GLASSES OF SPRITE. FOR A FAMILY COPING IMPERFECTLY WITH THE AFTERMATH OF A TRAGIC SUICIDE DRIVEN BY SMALL-TOWN MISOGYNY, IF YOU CAUGHT US ON SUNDAY AFTERNOONS, YOU'D THINK WE WERE THE HAPPIEST PEOPLE ON THE PLANET.

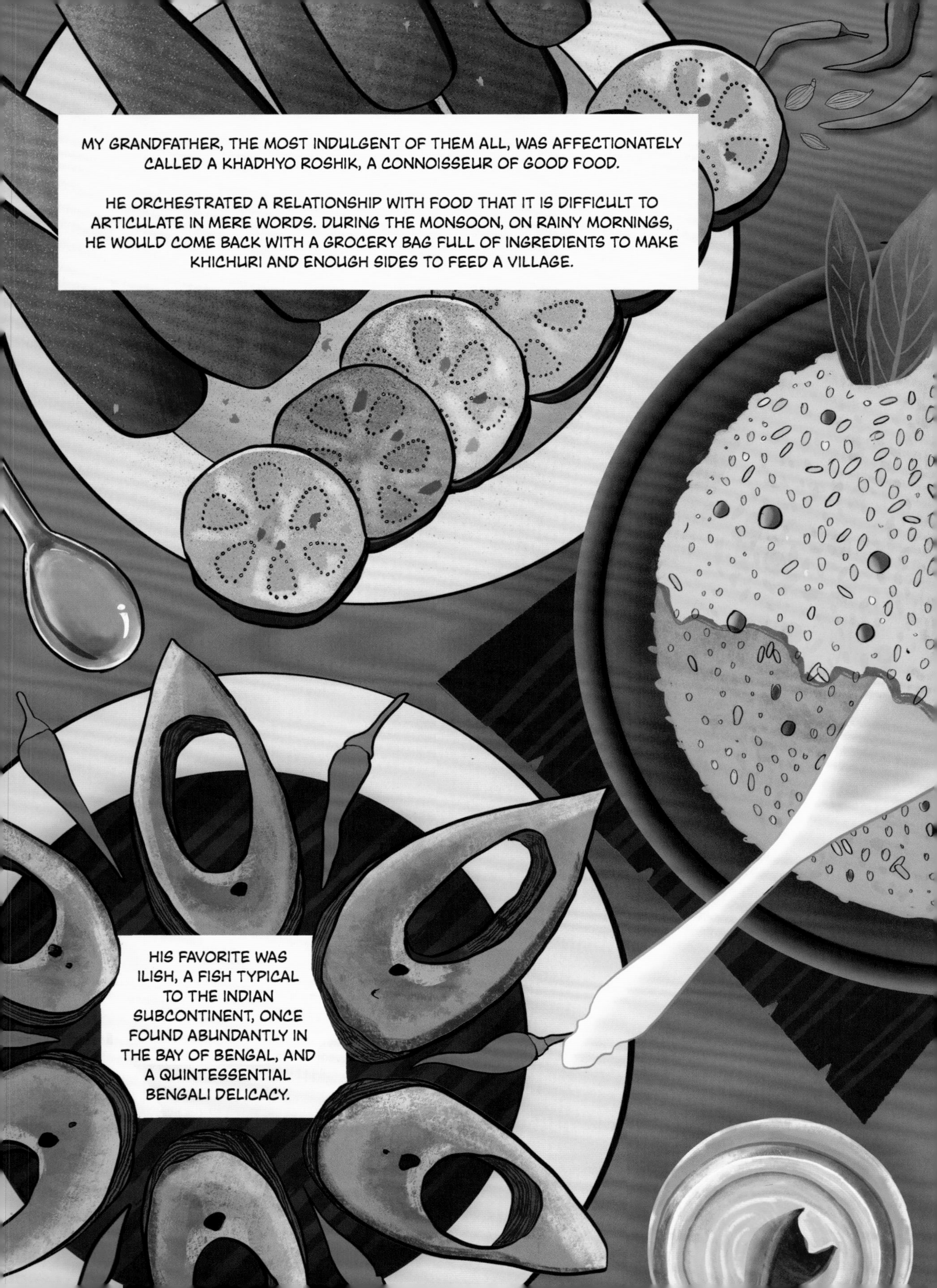
MY GRANDFATHER, THE MOST INDULGENT OF THEM ALL, WAS AFFECTIONATELY CALLED A KHADHYO ROSHIK, A CONNOISSEUR OF GOOD FOOD.
HE ORCHESTRATED A RELATIONSHIP WITH FOOD THAT IT IS DIFFICULT TO ARTICULATE IN MERE WORDS. DURING THE MONSOON, ON RAINY MORNINGS, HE WOULD COME BACK WITH A GROCERY BAG FULL OF INGREDIENTS TO MAKE KHICHURI AND ENOUGH SIDES TO FEED A VILLAGE.
HIS FAVORITE WAS ILISH, A FISH TYPICAL TO THE INDIAN SUBCONTINENT, ONCE FOUND ABUNDANTLY IN THE BAY OF BENGAL, AND A QUINTESSENTIAL BENGALI DELICACY.

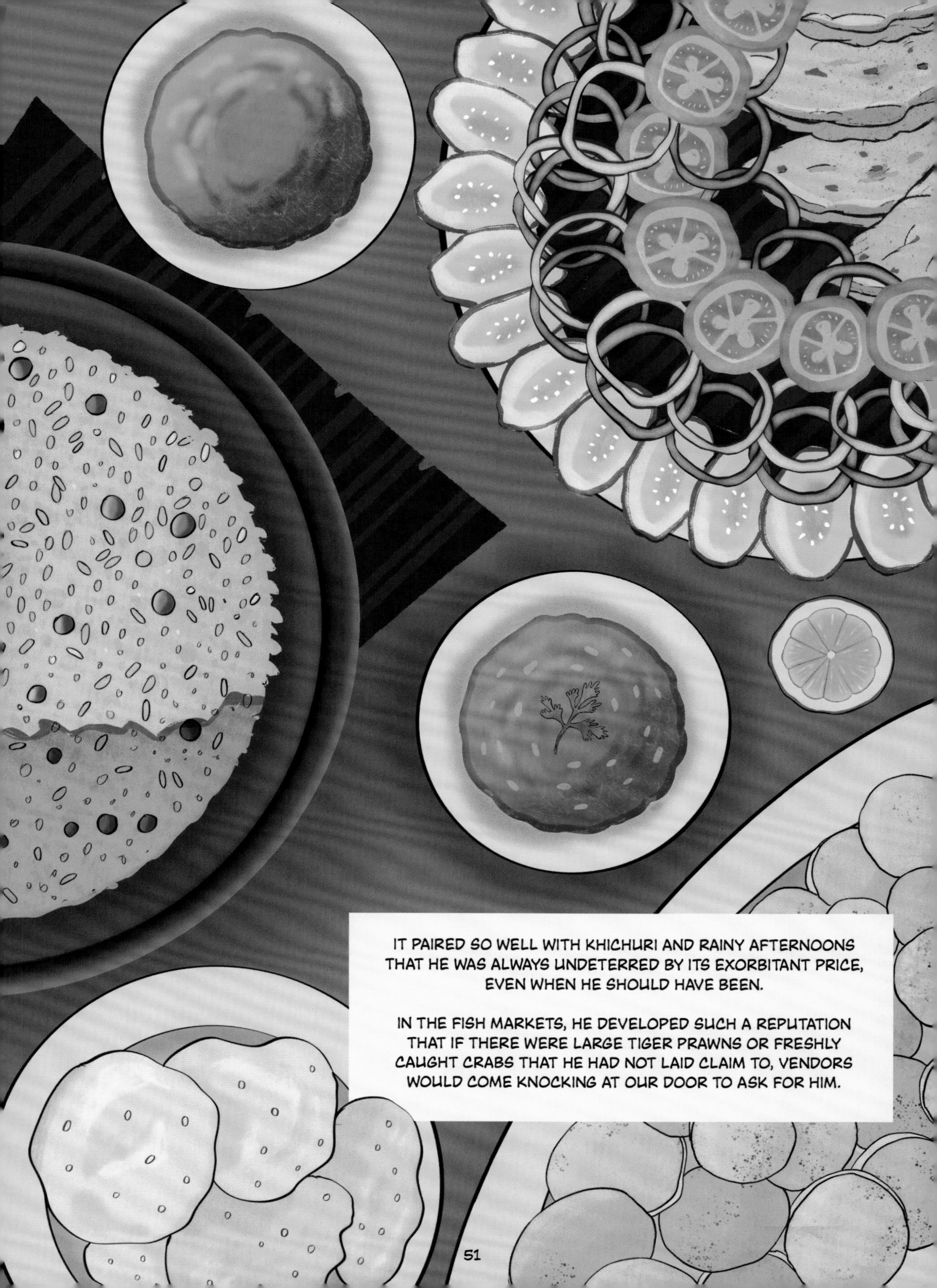
IT PAIRED SO WELL WITH KHICHURI AND RAINY AFTERNOONS THAT HE WAS ALWAYS UNDETERRED BY ITS EXORBITANT PRICE, EVEN WHEN HE SHOULD HAVE BEEN.
IN THE FISH MARKETS, HE DEVELOPED SUCH A REPUTATION THAT IF THERE WERE LARGE TIGER PRAWNS OR FRESHLY CAUGHT CRABS THAT HE HAD NOT LAID CLAIM TO, VENDORS WOULD COME KNOCKING AT OUR DOOR TO ASK FOR HIM.

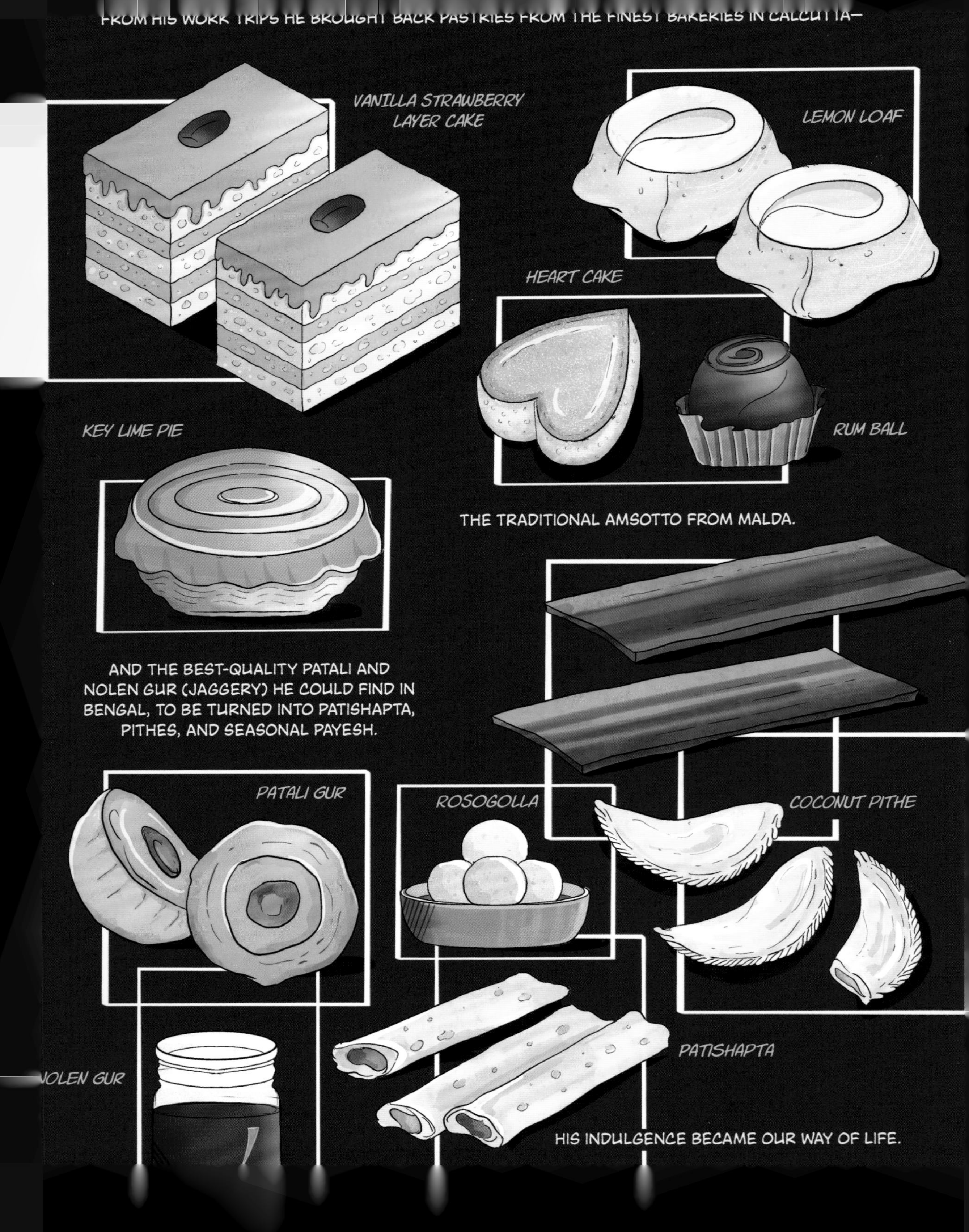
FROM HIS WORK TRIPS HE BROUGHT BACK PASTRIES FROM THE FINEST BAKERIES IN CALCUTTA—
VANILLA STRAWBERRY LAYER CAKE
LEMON LOAF
HEART CAKE
RUM BALL
KEY LIME PIE
THE TRADITIONAL AMSOTTO FROM MALDA.
AND THE BEST-QUALITY PATALI AND NOLEN GUR (JAGGERY) HE COULD FIND IN BENGAL, TO BE TURNED INTO PATISHAPTA, PITHES, AND SEASONAL PAYESH.
PATALI GUR
ROSOGOLLA
COCONUT PITHE
NOLEN GUR
PATISHAPTA
HIS INDULGENCE BECAME OUR WAY OF LIFE.

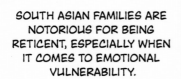

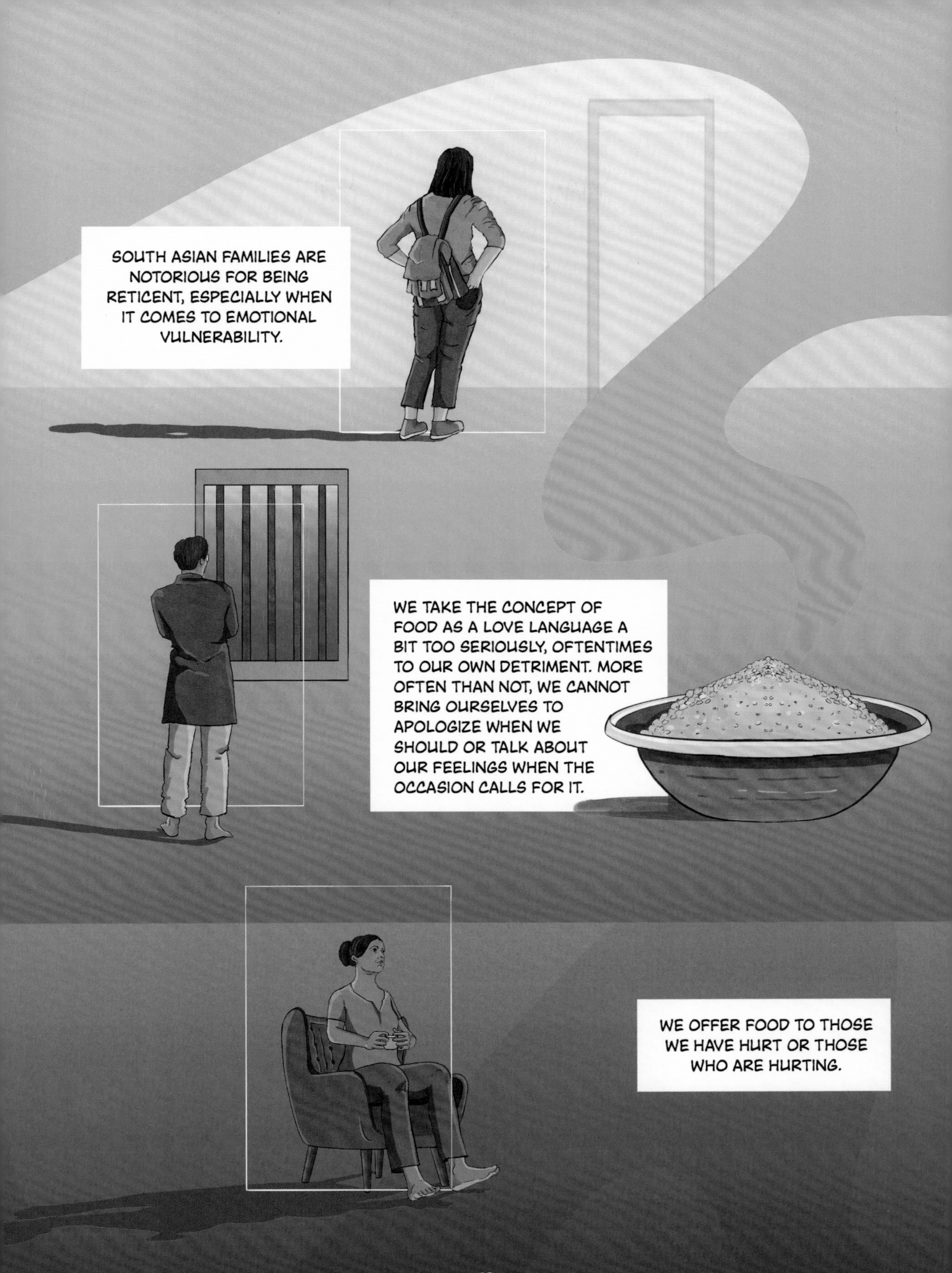

SOUTH ASIAN FAMILIES ARE NOTORIOUS FOR BEING RETICENT, ESPECIALLY WHEN IT COMES TO EMOTIONAL VULNERABILITY.

WE TAKE THE CONCEPT OF FOOD AS A LOVE LANGUAGE A BIT TOO SERIOUSLY, OFTENTIMES TO OUR OWN DETRIMENT. MORE OFTEN THAN NOT, WE CANNOT BRING OURSELVES TO APOLOGIZE WHEN WE SHOULD OR TALK ABOUT OUR FEELINGS WHEN THE OCCASION CALLS FOR IT.

WE OFFER FOOD TO THOSE WE HAVE HURT OR THOSE WHO ARE HURTING.

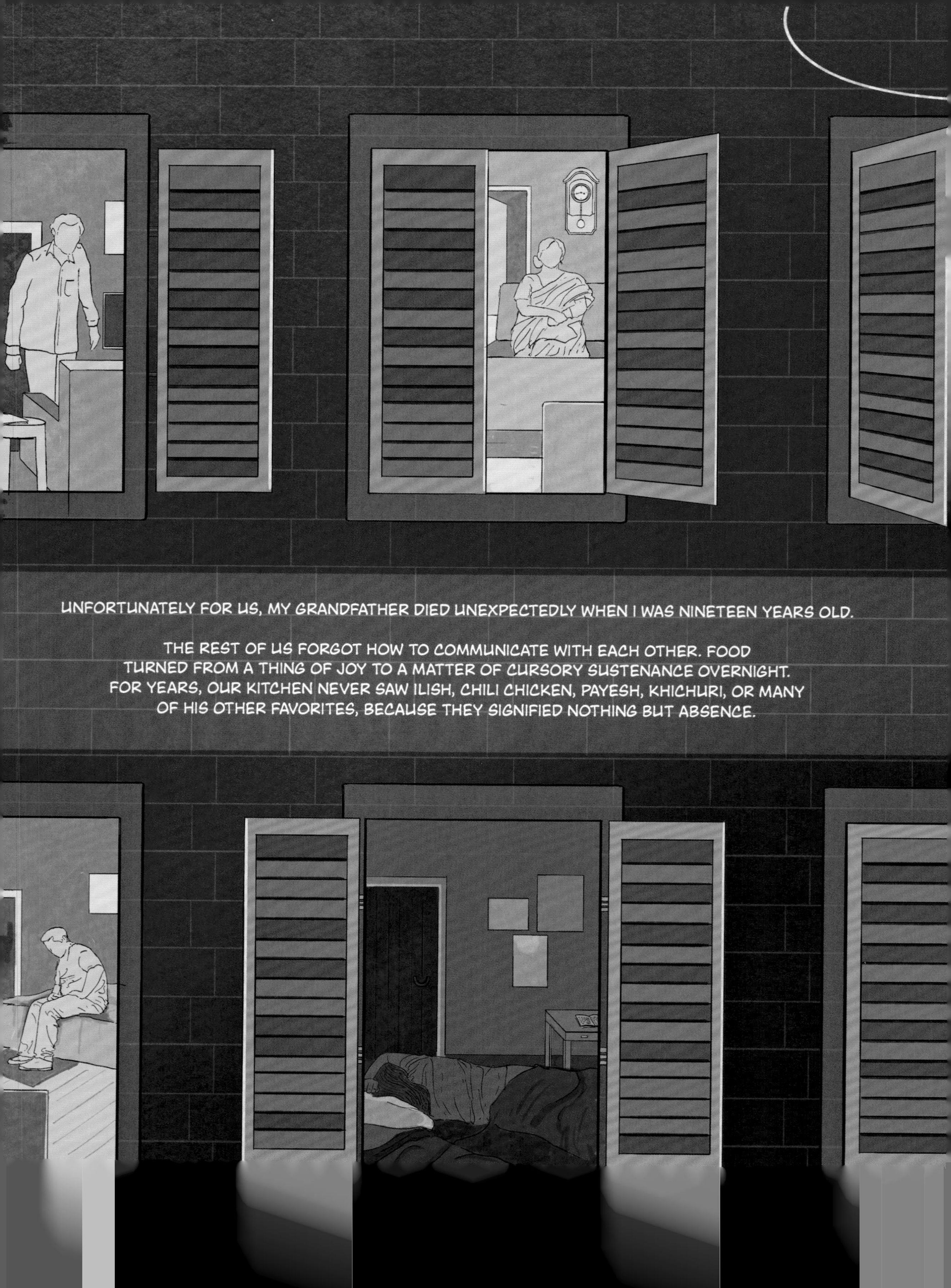
UNFORTUNATELY FOR US, MY GRANDFATHER DIED UNEXPECTEDLY WHEN I WAS NINETEEN YEARS OLD.
THE REST OF US FORGOT HOW TO COMMUNICATE WITH EACH OTHER. FOOD TURNED FROM A THING OF JOY TO A MATTER OF CURSORY SUSTENANCE OVERNIGHT. FOR YEARS, OUR KITCHEN NEVER SAW ILISH, CHILI CHICKEN, PAYESH, KHICHURI, OR MANY OF HIS OTHER FAVORITES, BECAUSE THEY SIGNIFIED NOTHING BUT ABSENCE.

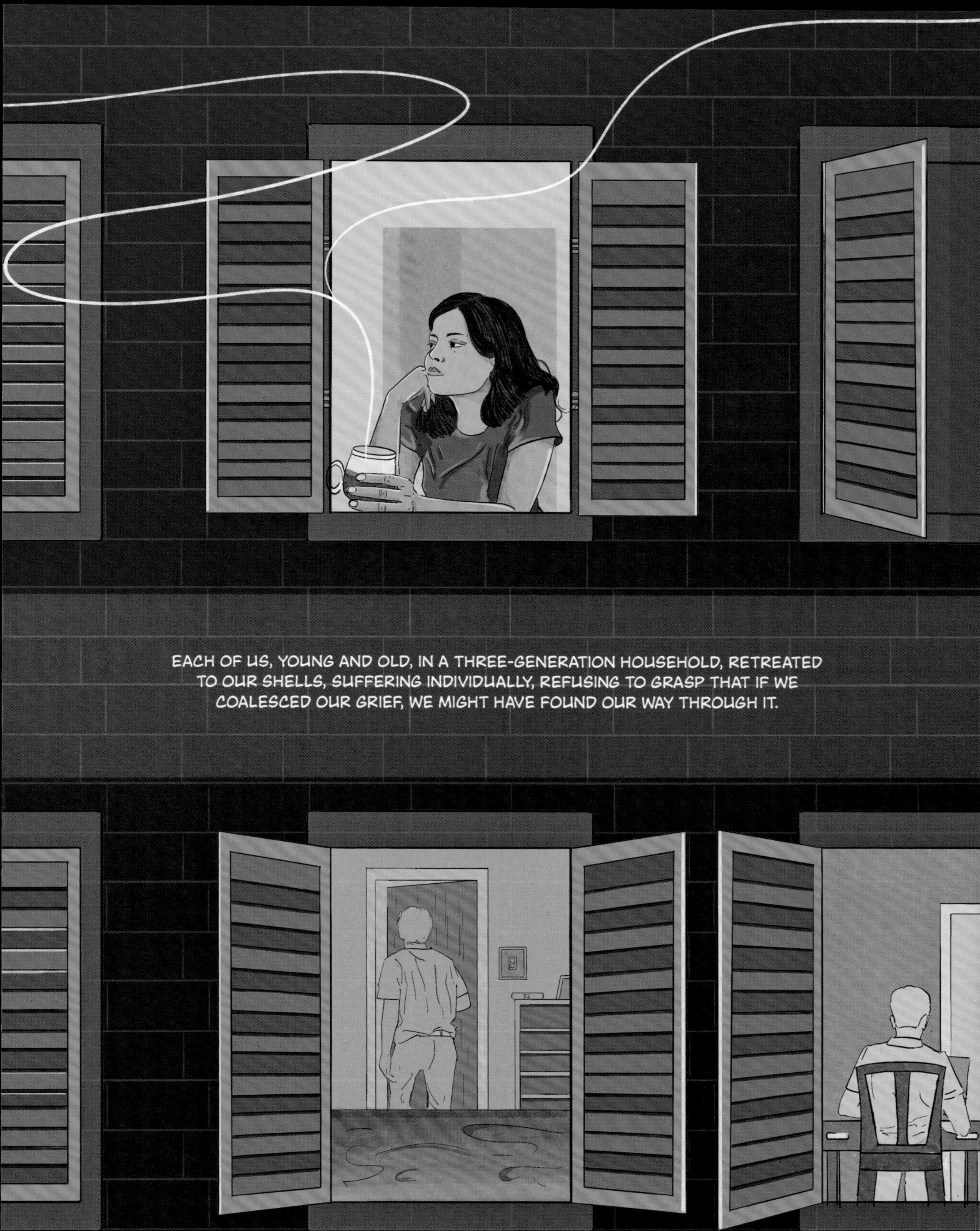
EACH OF US, YOUNG AND OLD, IN A THREE-GENERATION HOUSEHOLD, RETREATED TO OUR SHELLS, SUFFERING INDIVIDUALLY, REFUSING TO GRASP THAT IF WE COALESCED OUR GRIEF, WE MIGHT HAVE FOUND OUR WAY THROUGH IT.

THE HARDEST PART WAS THAT MERE MONTHS BEFORE HIS PASSING, DADAMONI WAS RUNNING A BUSINESS, TRAVELING FOR WORK, LIVING A FULL LIFE, HOLDING OUR FAMILY TOGETHER—AND THEN SUDDENLY HE WASN'T.

HE DIED JUST BEFORE SMARTPHONES WITH THE GOOD CAMERAS BECAME UBIQUITOUS. THE WEEK BEFORE HIS SURGERY HE ASKED ME IF I WANTED THE NEW IPHONE. IT MUST HAVE BEEN THE FIFTH IN THE SERIES, AND I REMEMBER SAYING IT WAS TOO MUCH.

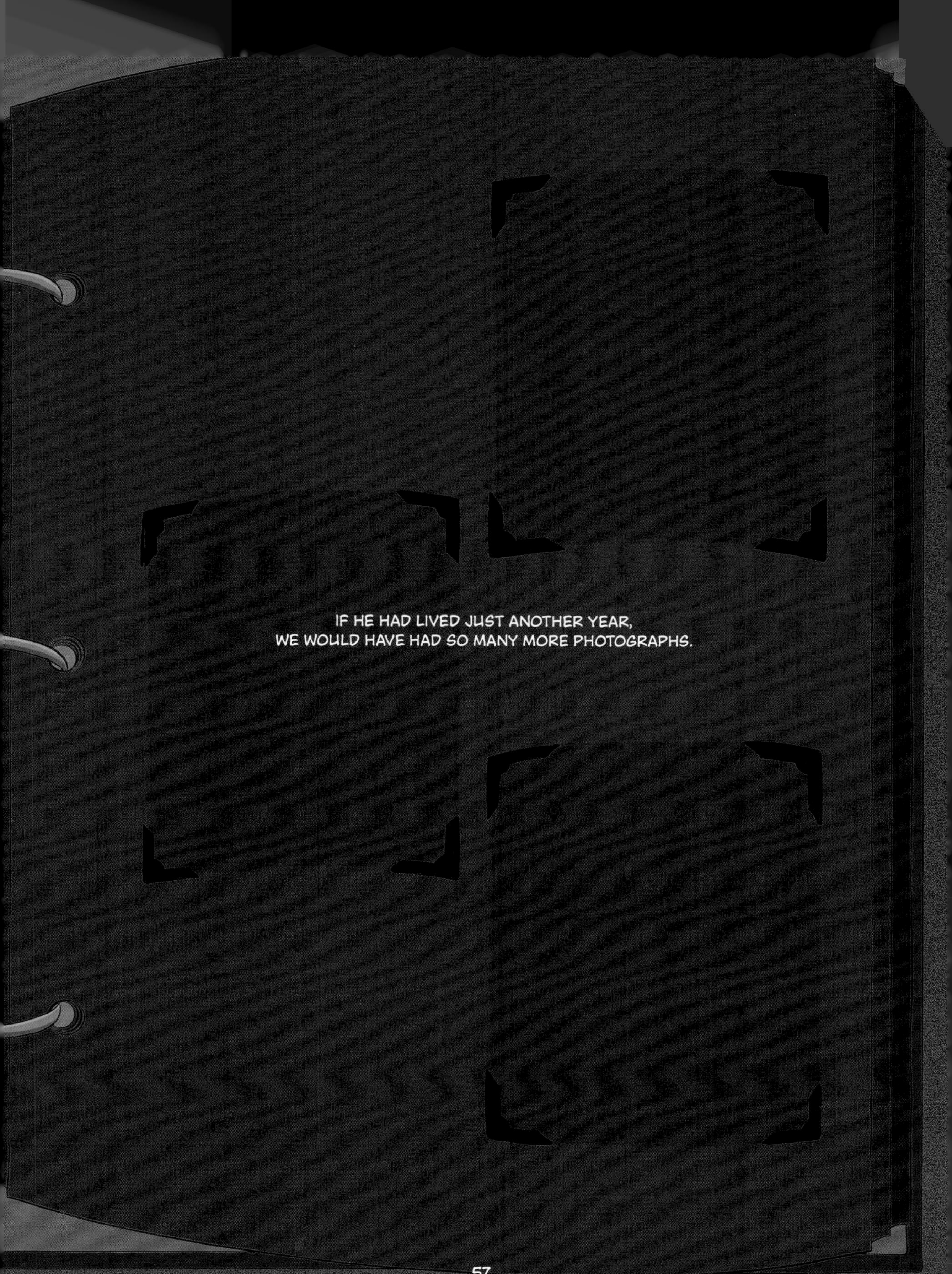
IF HE HAD LIVED JUST ANOTHER YEAR,
WE WOULD HAVE HAD SO MANY MORE PHOTOGRAPHS.

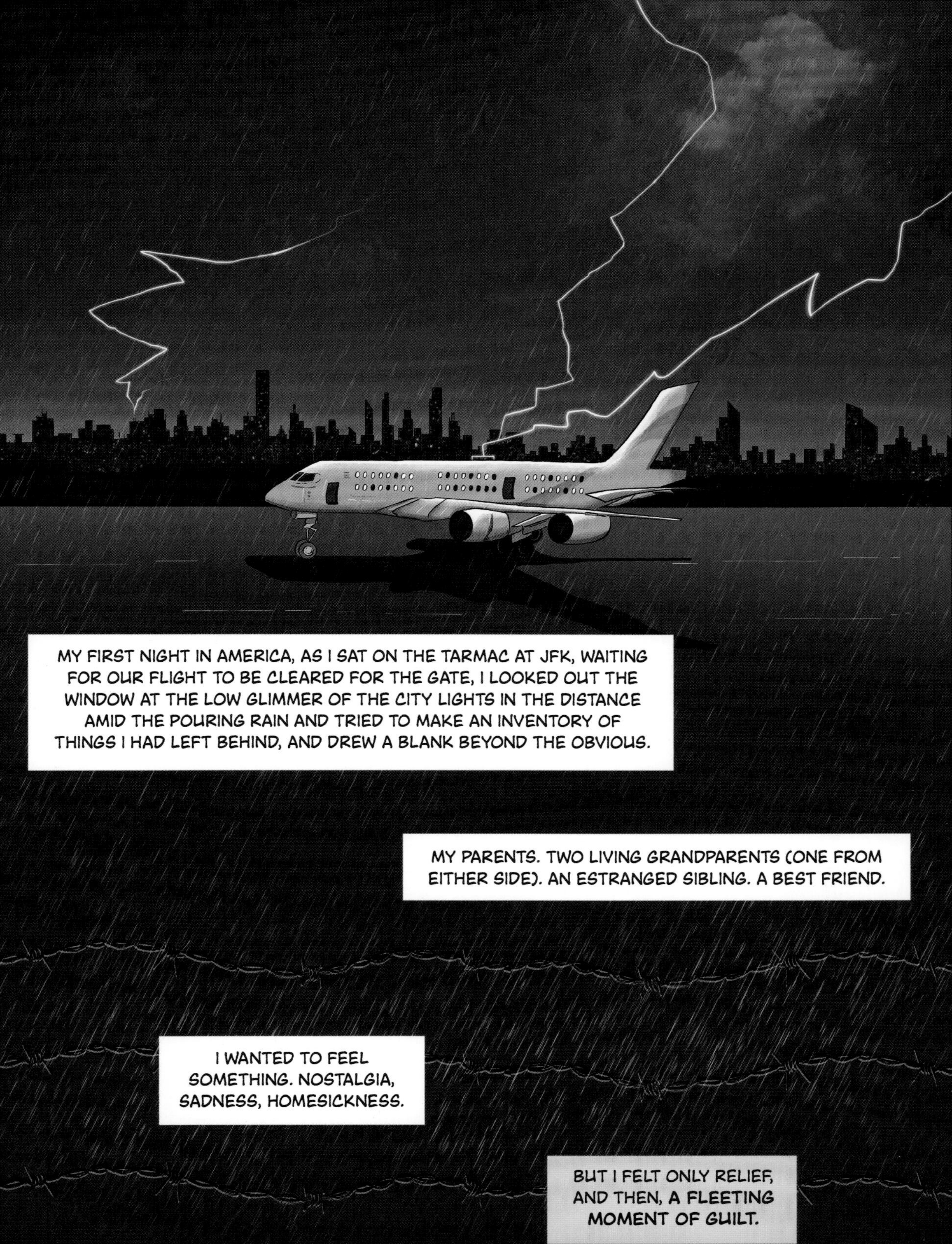
MY FIRST NIGHT IN AMERICA, AS I SAT ON THE TARMAC AT JFK, WAITING FOR OUR FLIGHT TO BE CLEARED FOR THE GATE, I LOOKED OUT THE WINDOW AT THE LOW GLIMMER OF THE CITY LIGHTS IN THE DISTANCE AMID THE POURING RAIN AND TRIED TO MAKE AN INVENTORY OF THINGS I HAD LEFT BEHIND, AND DREW A BLANK BEYOND THE OBVIOUS.
MY PARENTS. TWO LIVING GRANDPARENTS (ONE FROM EITHER SIDE). AN ESTRANGED SIBLING. A BEST FRIEND.
I WANTED TO FEEL SOMETHING. NOSTALGIA, SADNESS, HOMESICKNESS.
BUT I FELT ONLY RELIEF, AND THEN, A FLEETING MOMENT OF GUILT.

A DEATH AND A DISAPPEARING ACT

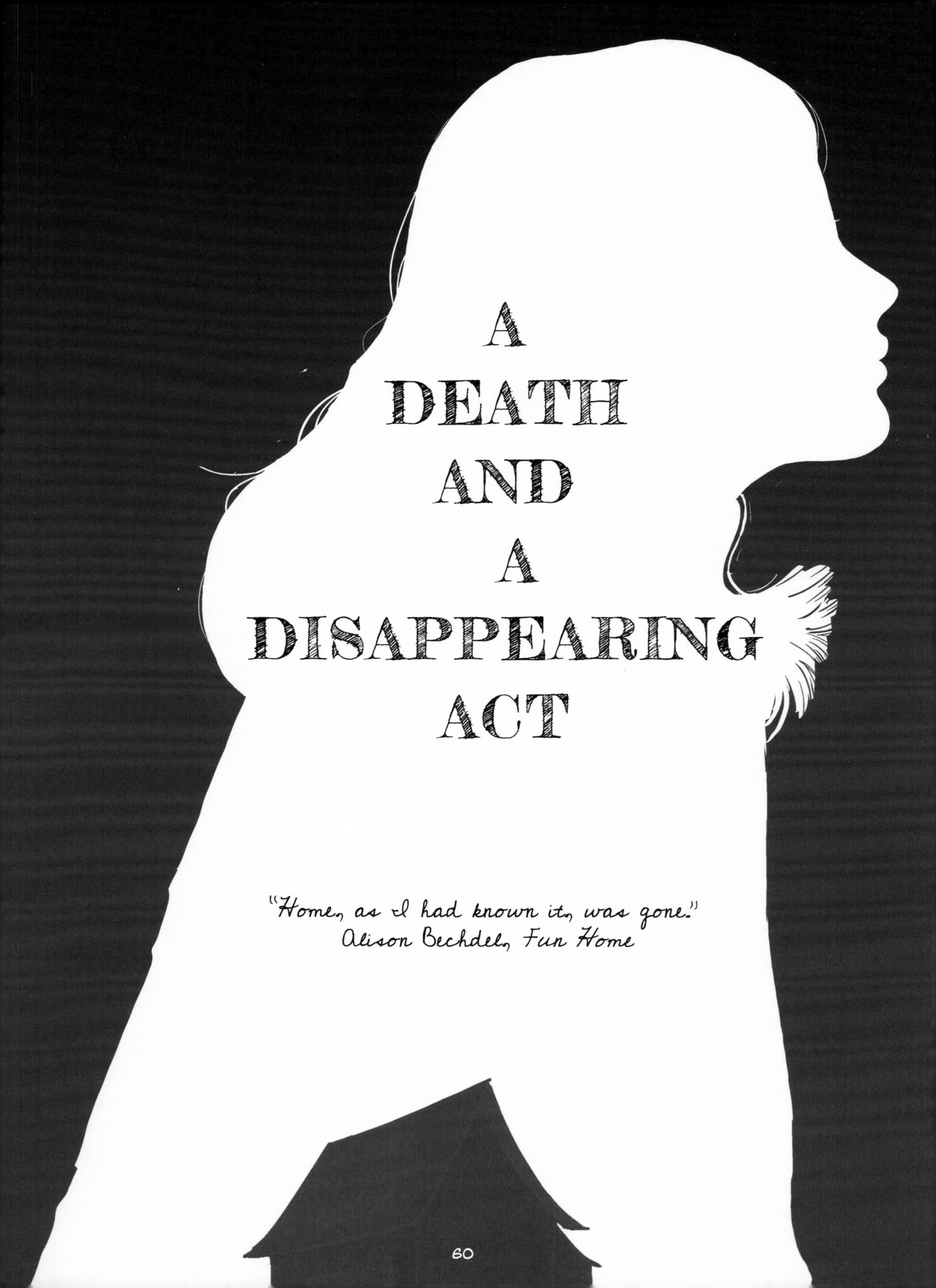

"Home, as I had known it, was gone."
Alison Bechdel, *Fun Home*

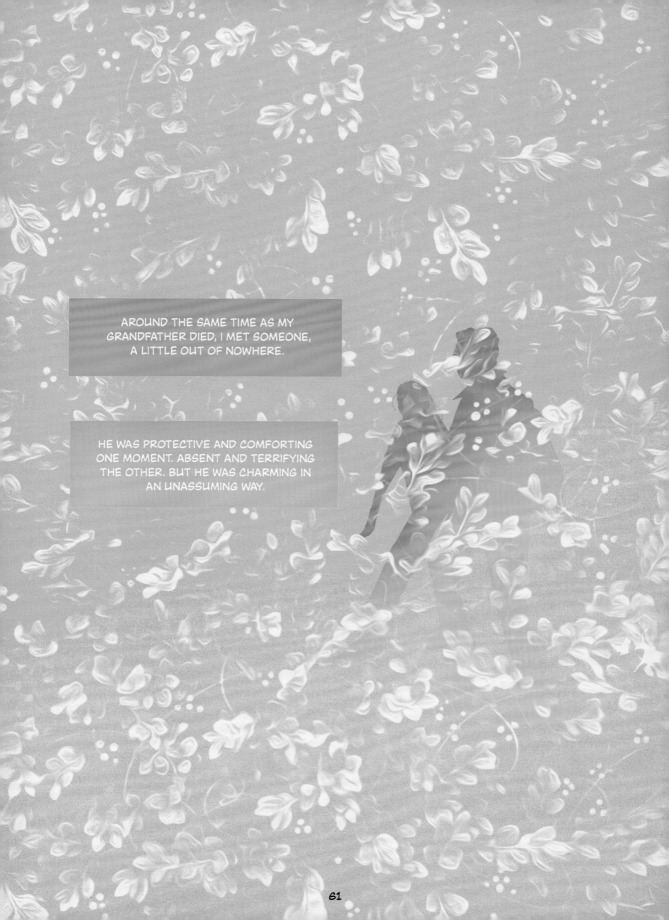

AROUND THE SAME TIME AS MY
GRANDFATHER DIED, I MET SOMEONE,
A LITTLE OUT OF NOWHERE.

HE WAS PROTECTIVE AND COMFORTING
ONE MOMENT. ABSENT AND TERRIFYING
THE OTHER. BUT HE WAS CHARMING IN
AN UNASSUMING WAY.

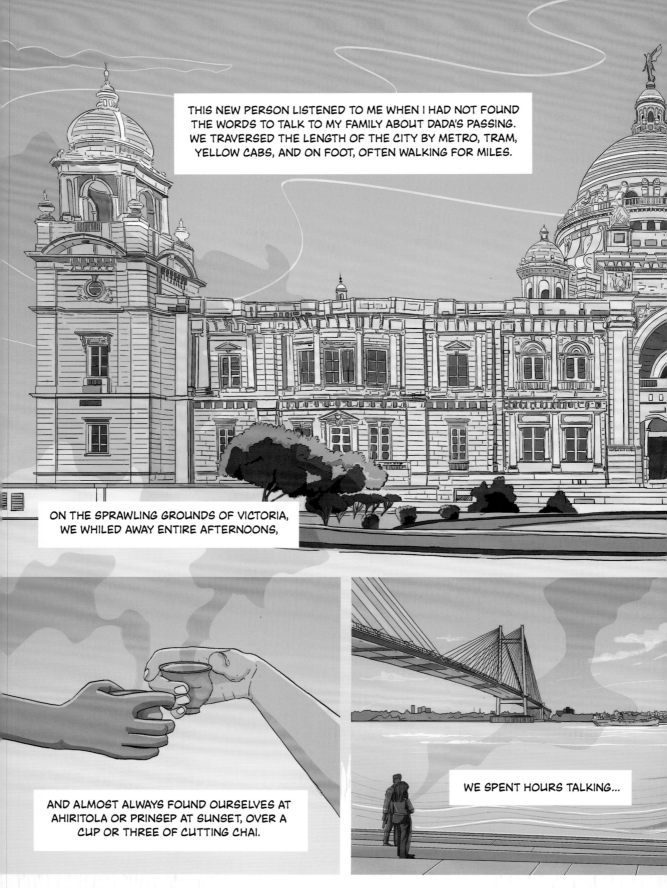

THIS NEW PERSON LISTENED TO ME WHEN I HAD NOT FOUND THE WORDS TO TALK TO MY FAMILY ABOUT DADA'S PASSING. WE TRAVERSED THE LENGTH OF THE CITY BY METRO, TRAM, YELLOW CABS, AND ON FOOT, OFTEN WALKING FOR MILES.

ON THE SPRAWLING GROUNDS OF VICTORIA, WE WHILED AWAY ENTIRE AFTERNOONS,

AND ALMOST ALWAYS FOUND OURSELVES AT AHIRITOLA OR PRINSEP AT SUNSET, OVER A CUP OR THREE OF CUTTING CHAI.

WE SPENT HOURS TALKING...

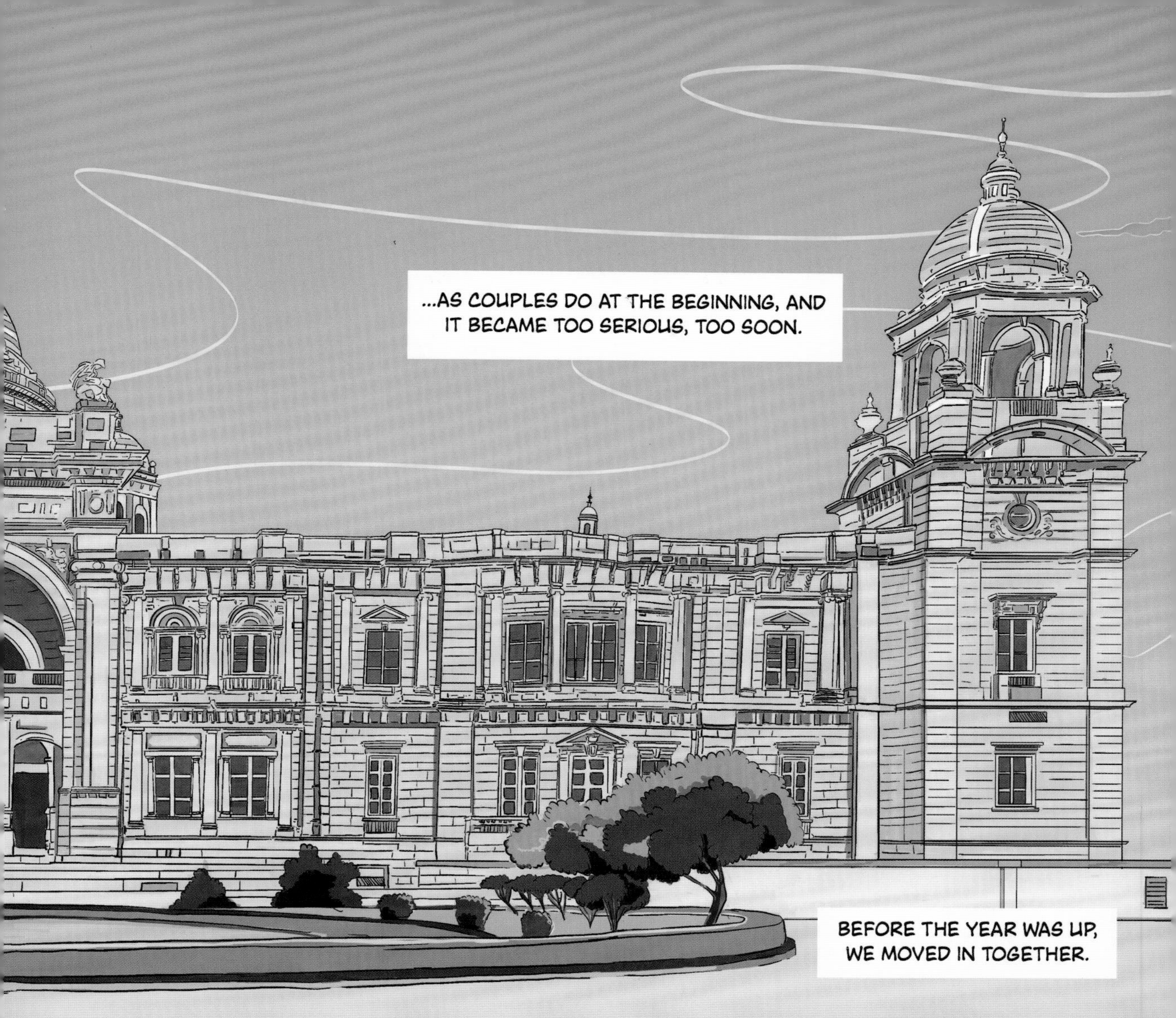
...AS COUPLES DO AT THE BEGINNING, AND IT BECAME TOO SERIOUS, TOO SOON.
BEFORE THE YEAR WAS UP, WE MOVED IN TOGETHER.

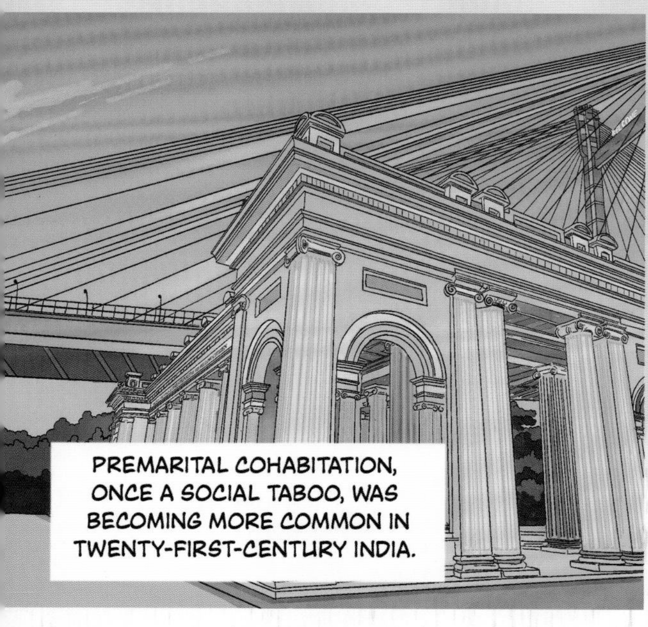
PREMARITAL COHABITATION, ONCE A SOCIAL TABOO, WAS BECOMING MORE COMMON IN TWENTY-FIRST-CENTURY INDIA.

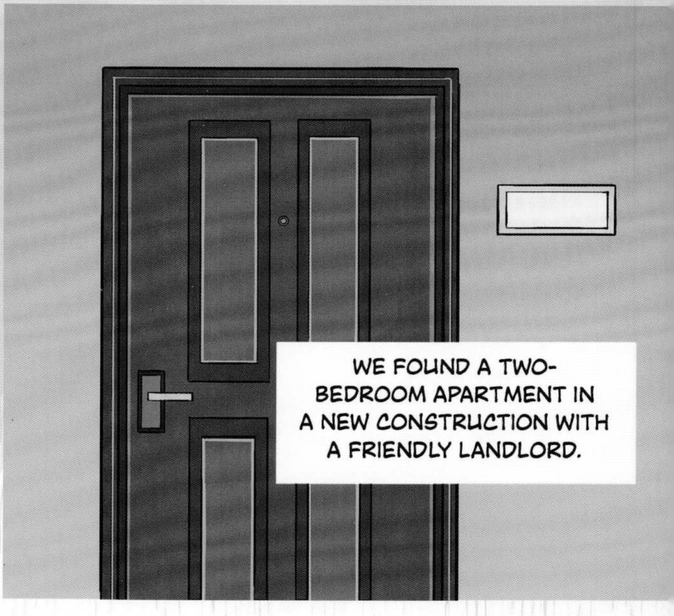
WE FOUND A TWO-BEDROOM APARTMENT IN A NEW CONSTRUCTION WITH A FRIENDLY LANDLORD.

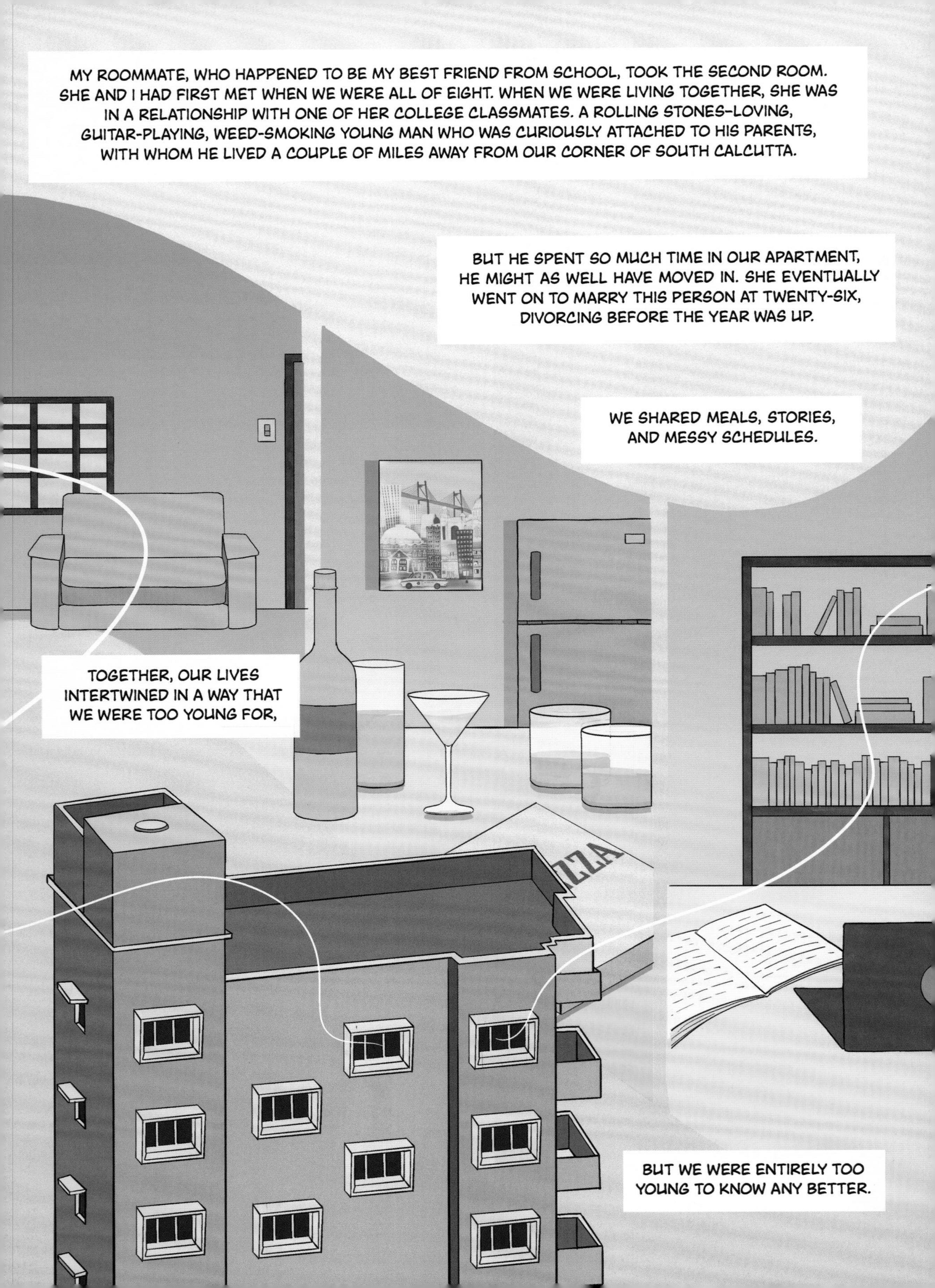
MY ROOMMATE, WHO HAPPENED TO BE MY BEST FRIEND FROM SCHOOL, TOOK THE SECOND ROOM. SHE AND I HAD FIRST MET WHEN WE WERE ALL OF EIGHT. WHEN WE WERE LIVING TOGETHER, SHE WAS IN A RELATIONSHIP WITH ONE OF HER COLLEGE CLASSMATES. A ROLLING STONES–LOVING, GUITAR-PLAYING, WEED-SMOKING YOUNG MAN WHO WAS CURIOUSLY ATTACHED TO HIS PARENTS, WITH WHOM HE LIVED A COUPLE OF MILES AWAY FROM OUR CORNER OF SOUTH CALCUTTA.
BUT HE SPENT SO MUCH TIME IN OUR APARTMENT, HE MIGHT AS WELL HAVE MOVED IN. SHE EVENTUALLY WENT ON TO MARRY THIS PERSON AT TWENTY-SIX, DIVORCING BEFORE THE YEAR WAS UP.
WE SHARED MEALS, STORIES, AND MESSY SCHEDULES.
TOGETHER, OUR LIVES INTERTWINED IN A WAY THAT WE WERE TOO YOUNG FOR,
BUT WE WERE ENTIRELY TOO YOUNG TO KNOW ANY BETTER.

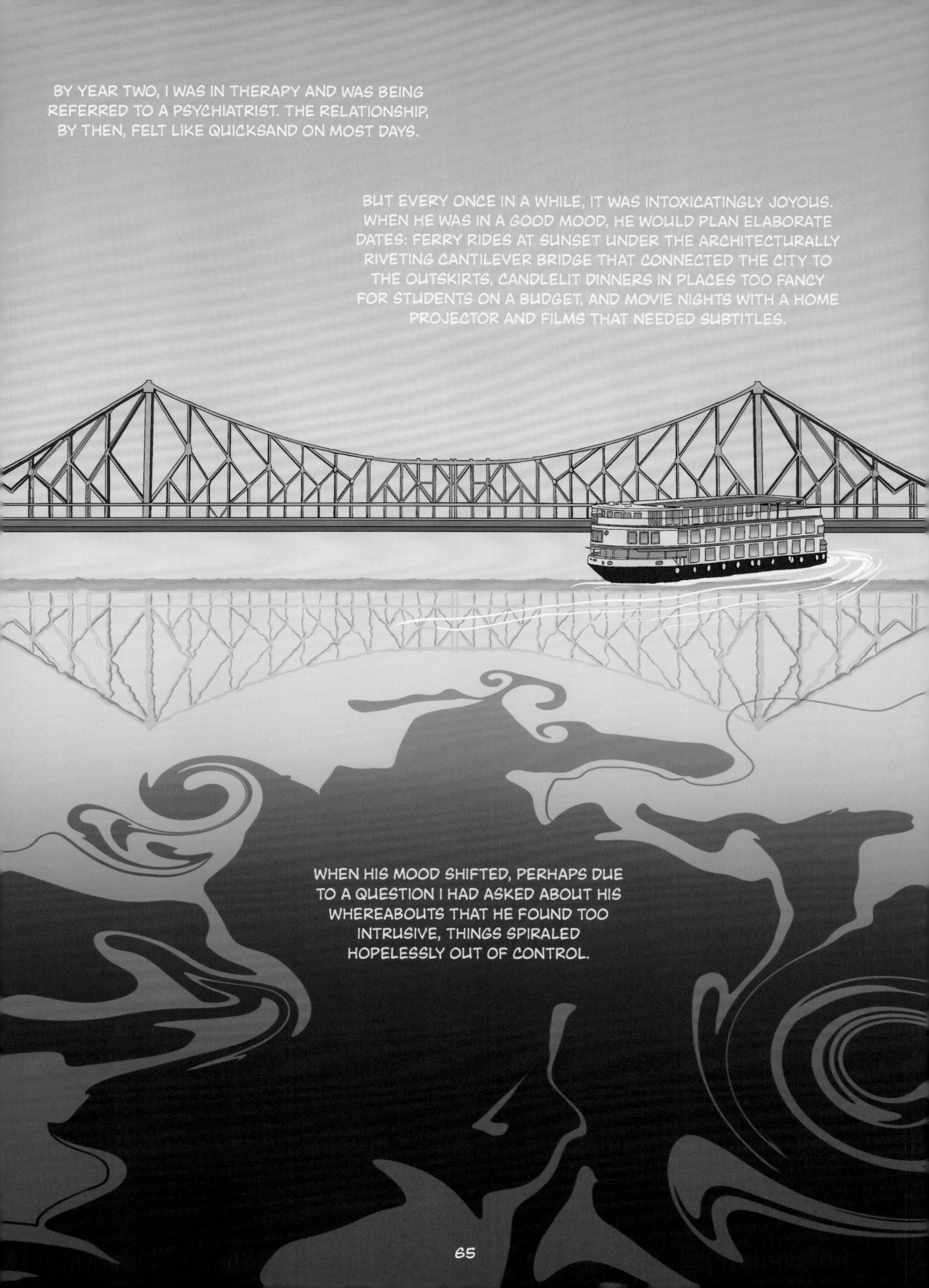
BY YEAR TWO, I WAS IN THERAPY AND WAS BEING REFERRED TO A PSYCHIATRIST. THE RELATIONSHIP, BY THEN, FELT LIKE QUICKSAND ON MOST DAYS.
BUT EVERY ONCE IN A WHILE, IT WAS INTOXICATINGLY JOYOUS. WHEN HE WAS IN A GOOD MOOD, HE WOULD PLAN ELABORATE DATES: FERRY RIDES AT SUNSET UNDER THE ARCHITECTURALLY RIVETING CANTILEVER BRIDGE THAT CONNECTED THE CITY TO THE OUTSKIRTS, CANDLELIT DINNERS IN PLACES TOO FANCY FOR STUDENTS ON A BUDGET, AND MOVIE NIGHTS WITH A HOME PROJECTOR AND FILMS THAT NEEDED SUBTITLES.
WHEN HIS MOOD SHIFTED, PERHAPS DUE TO A QUESTION I HAD ASKED ABOUT HIS WHEREABOUTS THAT HE FOUND TOO INTRUSIVE, THINGS SPIRALED HOPELESSLY OUT OF CONTROL.

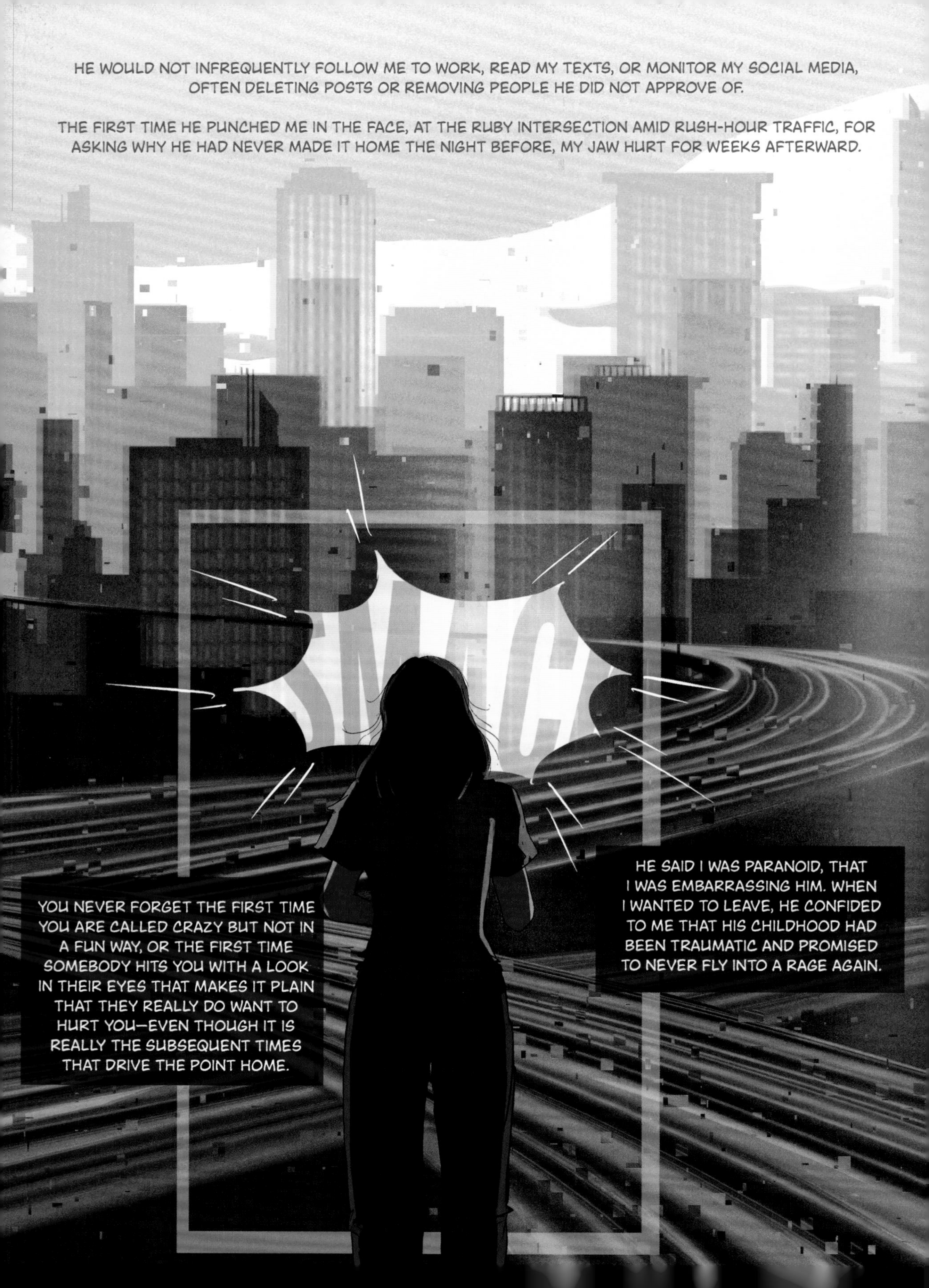
HE WOULD NOT INFREQUENTLY FOLLOW ME TO WORK, READ MY TEXTS, OR MONITOR MY SOCIAL MEDIA, OFTEN DELETING POSTS OR REMOVING PEOPLE HE DID NOT APPROVE OF.
THE FIRST TIME HE PUNCHED ME IN THE FACE, AT THE RUBY INTERSECTION AMID RUSH-HOUR TRAFFIC, FOR ASKING WHY HE HAD NEVER MADE IT HOME THE NIGHT BEFORE, MY JAW HURT FOR WEEKS AFTERWARD.
YOU NEVER FORGET THE FIRST TIME YOU ARE CALLED CRAZY BUT NOT IN A FUN WAY, OR THE FIRST TIME SOMEBODY HITS YOU WITH A LOOK IN THEIR EYES THAT MAKES IT PLAIN THAT THEY REALLY DO WANT TO HURT YOU—EVEN THOUGH IT IS REALLY THE SUBSEQUENT TIMES THAT DRIVE THE POINT HOME.
HE SAID I WAS PARANOID, THAT I WAS EMBARRASSING HIM. WHEN I WANTED TO LEAVE, HE CONFIDED TO ME THAT HIS CHILDHOOD HAD BEEN TRAUMATIC AND PROMISED TO NEVER FLY INTO A RAGE AGAIN.

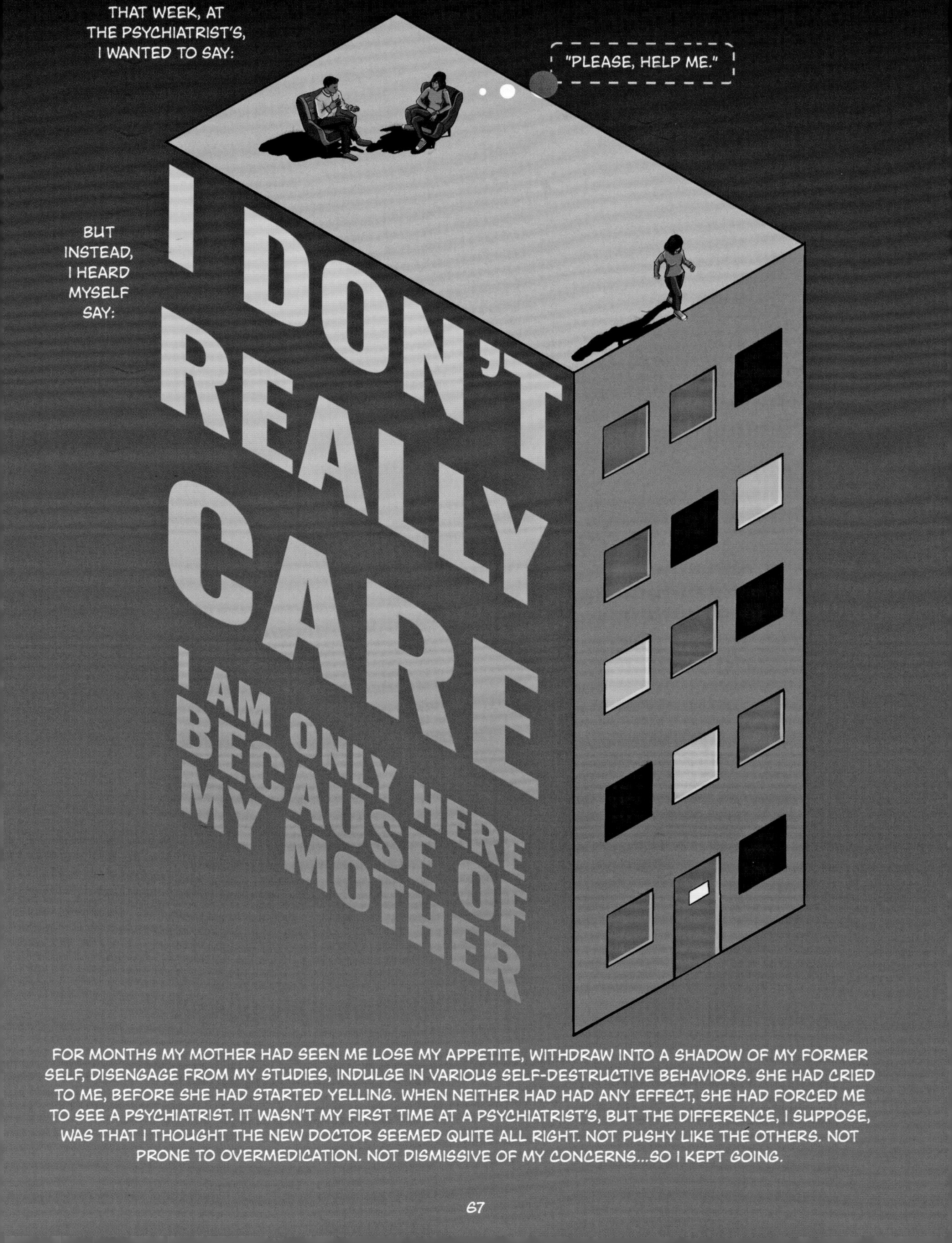
THAT WEEK, AT THE PSYCHIATRIST'S, I WANTED TO SAY:
"PLEASE, HELP ME."
BUT INSTEAD, I HEARD MYSELF SAY:
I DON'T REALLY CARE
I AM ONLY HERE BECAUSE OF MY MOTHER

FOR MONTHS MY MOTHER HAD SEEN ME LOSE MY APPETITE, WITHDRAW INTO A SHADOW OF MY FORMER SELF, DISENGAGE FROM MY STUDIES, INDULGE IN VARIOUS SELF-DESTRUCTIVE BEHAVIORS. SHE HAD CRIED TO ME, BEFORE SHE HAD STARTED YELLING. WHEN NEITHER HAD HAD ANY EFFECT, SHE HAD FORCED ME TO SEE A PSYCHIATRIST. IT WASN'T MY FIRST TIME AT A PSYCHIATRIST'S, BUT THE DIFFERENCE, I SUPPOSE, WAS THAT I THOUGHT THE NEW DOCTOR SEEMED QUITE ALL RIGHT. NOT PUSHY LIKE THE OTHERS. NOT PRONE TO OVERMEDICATION. NOT DISMISSIVE OF MY CONCERNS...SO I KEPT GOING.

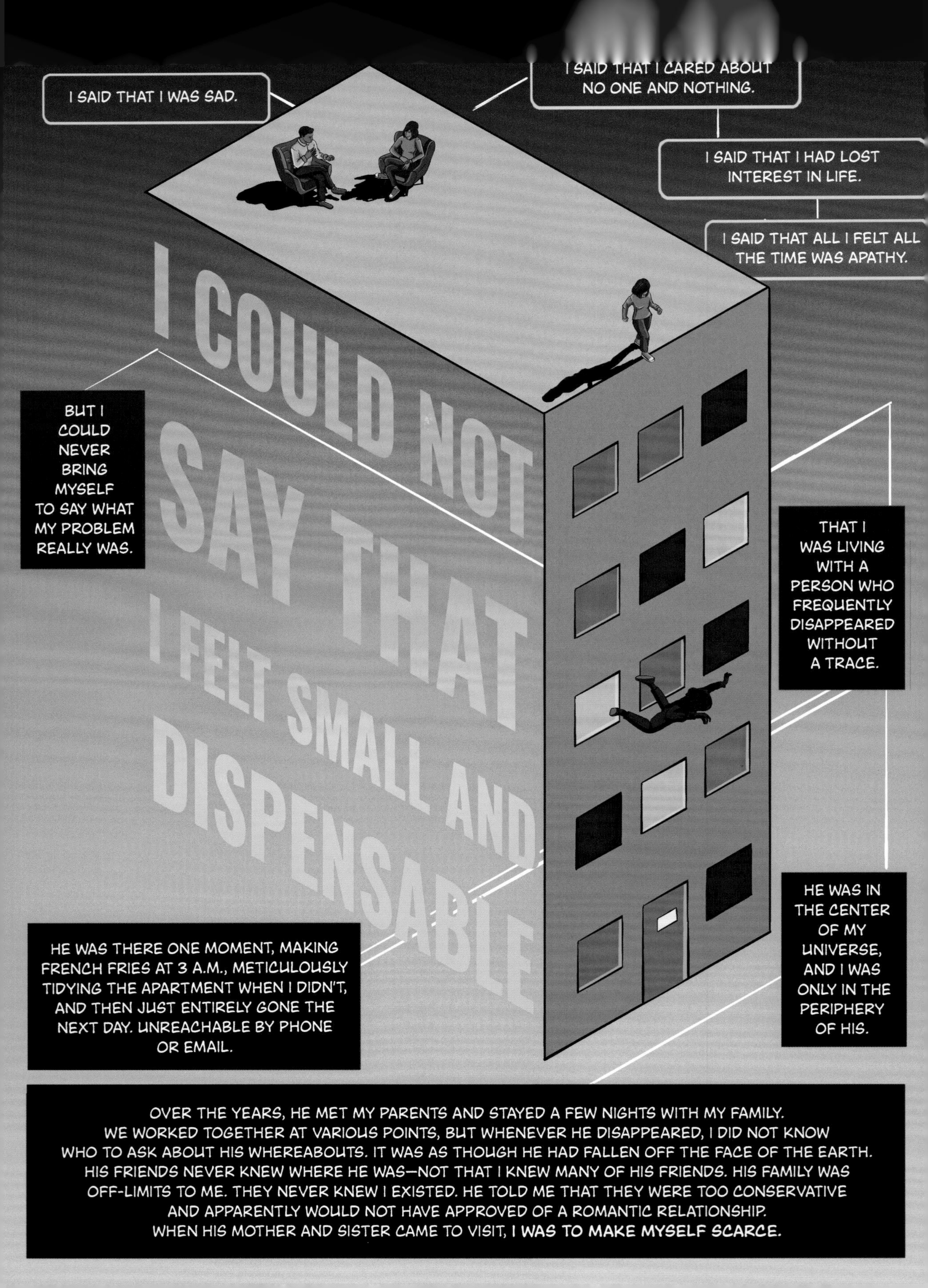
I SAID THAT I WAS SAD.
I SAID THAT I CARED ABOUT NO ONE AND NOTHING.
I SAID THAT I HAD LOST INTEREST IN LIFE.
I SAID THAT ALL I FELT ALL THE TIME WAS APATHY.
BUT I COULD NEVER BRING MYSELF TO SAY WHAT MY PROBLEM REALLY WAS.
I COULD NOT SAY THAT I FELT SMALL AND DISPENSABLE
THAT I WAS LIVING WITH A PERSON WHO FREQUENTLY DISAPPEARED WITHOUT A TRACE.
HE WAS THERE ONE MOMENT, MAKING FRENCH FRIES AT 3 A.M., METICULOUSLY TIDYING THE APARTMENT WHEN I DIDN'T, AND THEN JUST ENTIRELY GONE THE NEXT DAY. UNREACHABLE BY PHONE OR EMAIL.
HE WAS IN THE CENTER OF MY UNIVERSE, AND I WAS ONLY IN THE PERIPHERY OF HIS.
OVER THE YEARS, HE MET MY PARENTS AND STAYED A FEW NIGHTS WITH MY FAMILY. WE WORKED TOGETHER AT VARIOUS POINTS, BUT WHENEVER HE DISAPPEARED, I DID NOT KNOW WHO TO ASK ABOUT HIS WHEREABOUTS. IT WAS AS THOUGH HE HAD FALLEN OFF THE FACE OF THE EARTH. HIS FRIENDS NEVER KNEW WHERE HE WAS—NOT THAT I KNEW MANY OF HIS FRIENDS. HIS FAMILY WAS OFF-LIMITS TO ME. THEY NEVER KNEW I EXISTED. HE TOLD ME THAT THEY WERE TOO CONSERVATIVE AND APPARENTLY WOULD NOT HAVE APPROVED OF A ROMANTIC RELATIONSHIP. WHEN HIS MOTHER AND SISTER CAME TO VISIT, I WAS TO MAKE MYSELF SCARCE.

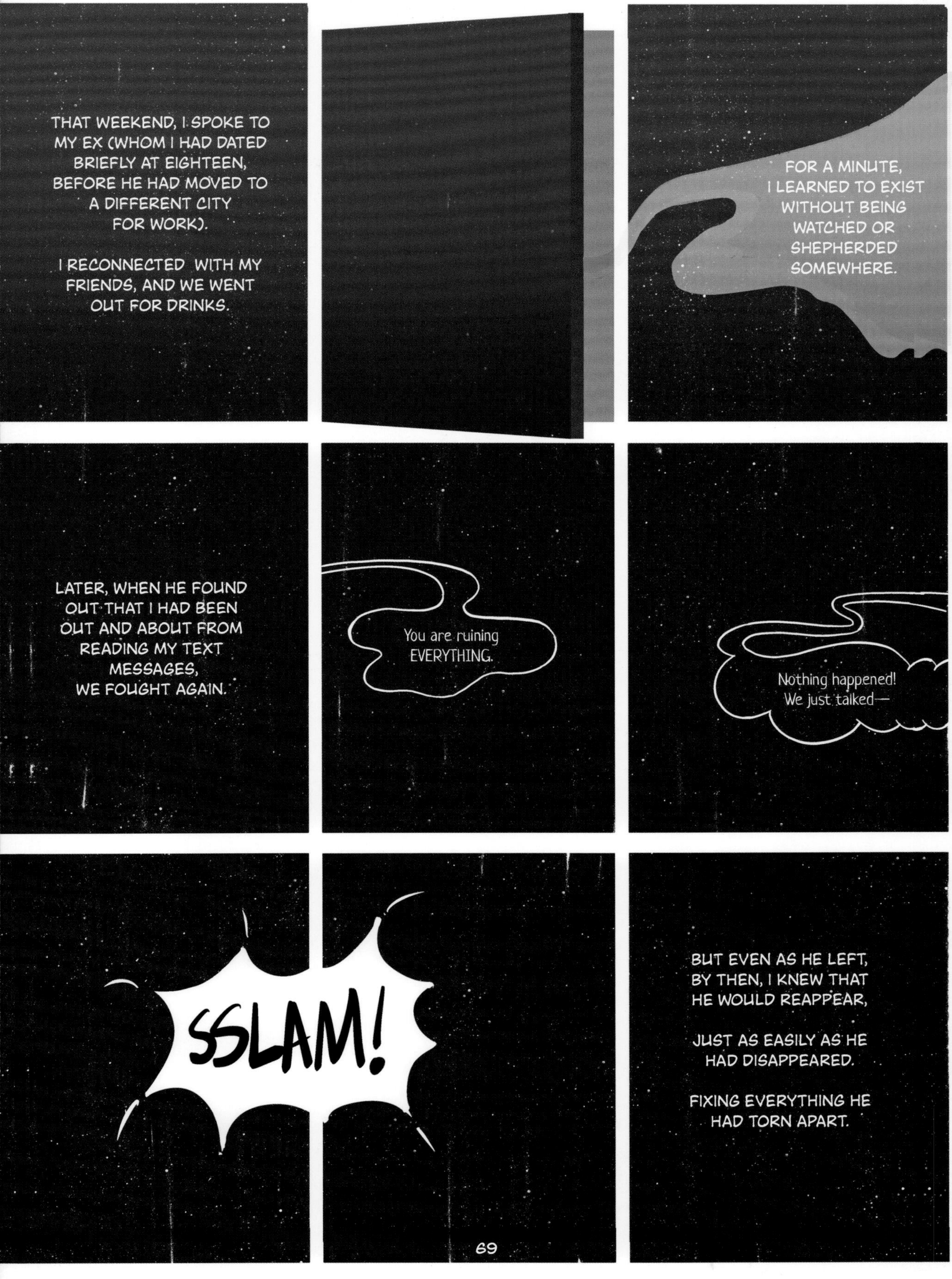
THAT WEEKEND, I SPOKE TO MY EX (WHOM I HAD DATED BRIEFLY AT EIGHTEEN, BEFORE HE HAD MOVED TO A DIFFERENT CITY FOR WORK).
I RECONNECTED WITH MY FRIENDS, AND WE WENT OUT FOR DRINKS.
FOR A MINUTE, I LEARNED TO EXIST WITHOUT BEING WATCHED OR SHEPHERDED SOMEWHERE.
LATER, WHEN HE FOUND OUT THAT I HAD BEEN OUT AND ABOUT FROM READING MY TEXT MESSAGES, WE FOUGHT AGAIN.
You are ruining EVERYTHING.
Nothing happened! We just talked—
SSLAM!
BUT EVEN AS HE LEFT, BY THEN, I KNEW THAT HE WOULD REAPPEAR,
JUST AS EASILY AS HE HAD DISAPPEARED.
FIXING EVERYTHING HE HAD TORN APART.

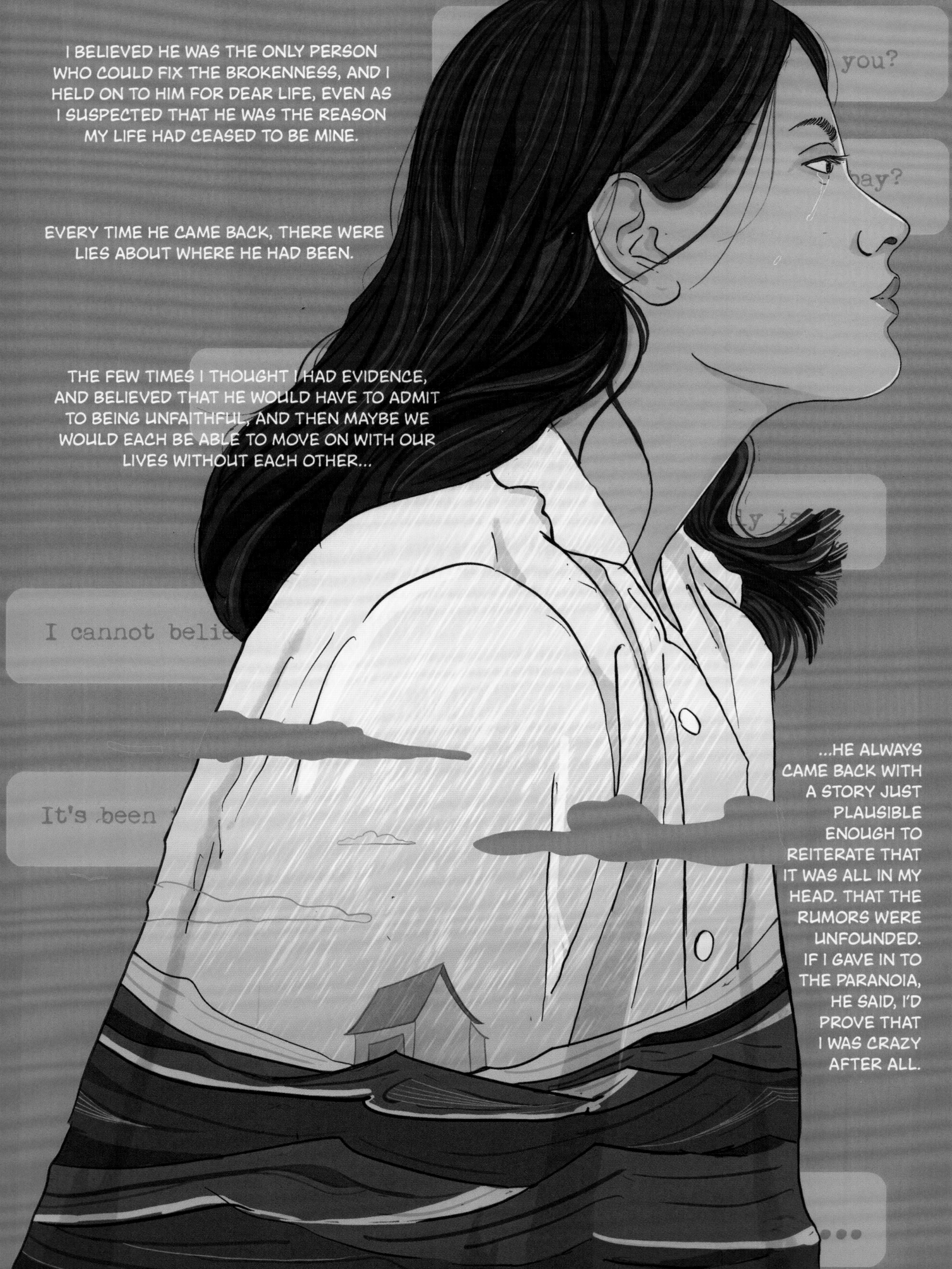
I BELIEVED HE WAS THE ONLY PERSON WHO COULD FIX THE BROKENNESS, AND I HELD ON TO HIM FOR DEAR LIFE, EVEN AS I SUSPECTED THAT HE WAS THE REASON MY LIFE HAD CEASED TO BE MINE.
you?
EVERY TIME HE CAME BACK, THERE WERE LIES ABOUT WHERE HE HAD BEEN.
THE FEW TIMES I THOUGHT I HAD EVIDENCE, AND BELIEVED THAT HE WOULD HAVE TO ADMIT TO BEING UNFAITHFUL, AND THEN MAYBE WE WOULD EACH BE ABLE TO MOVE ON WITH OUR LIVES WITHOUT EACH OTHER...
I cannot belie
It's been
...HE ALWAYS CAME BACK WITH A STORY JUST PLAUSIBLE ENOUGH TO REITERATE THAT IT WAS ALL IN MY HEAD. THAT THE RUMORS WERE UNFOUNDED. IF I GAVE IN TO THE PARANOIA, HE SAID, I'D PROVE THAT I WAS CRAZY AFTER ALL.

MY FRIENDS WOULD SOMETIMES TRY TO INTERVENE. THEY DID NOT SEE THE WHOLE PICTURE BUT SAW ME SAD ENOUGH TIMES TO KNOW WHATEVER WAS GOING ON WAS NOT NORMAL BY ANY STRETCH OF THE IMAGINATION. BUT I WAS ADAMANT ABOUT THEIR ONE-SIDED PERCEPTION OF THE SITUATION.

I TOLD MYSELF THAT THEY DIDN'T REALLY KNOW HIM LIKE I DID. THAT THEY DID NOT SEE THE GOOD PARTS. I COULD NOT SEE THAT I HAD FALLEN FOR THIS PERSON WHEN I HAD BEEN NEWLY GRIEVING THE DEATH OF A LOVED ONE. I DID NOT SEE THAT I HAD FALLEN FOR HIM AT A TIME OF DEEP EMOTIONAL VULNERABILITY, WHEN I HAD BEEN PARTICULARLY SUSCEPTIBLE TO ABUSE.

I COULD NOT IMAGINE WHAT THE RIPPLE EFFECTS OF ONE'S MEMORY AND SENSE OF REALITY BEING QUESTIONED ONE TOO MANY TIMES COULD BE IN THE LONG RUN.

BUT YEARS HAD GONE BY AND I WAS TIRED.

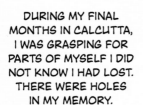

DURING MY FINAL MONTHS IN CALCUTTA, I WAS GRASPING FOR PARTS OF MYSELF I DID NOT KNOW I HAD LOST. THERE WERE HOLES IN MY MEMORY.

I WAS LIED TO OVER AND OVER AGAIN, TO THE EXTENT THAT THE BOUNDARY BETWEEN LIES AND TRUTH HAD BECOME POROUS, AND, IF YOU ASKED ME, I COULD NOT TELL WHAT WAS REAL ANYMORE.

I ONLY KNEW THAT I HAD SPENT MOST OF MY ADULT LIFE UNTIL THEN IN A TURBULENT RELATIONSHIP WITH A PERSON WHO HAD DISAPPEARED ONE TOO MANY TIMES.

WHOSE INNATE TENDERNESS WAS ONLY MATCHED BY HIS UNPREDICTABLE RAGE, WHICH SPILLED INTO OUR TURQUOISE-WALLED APARTMENT UNTIL THE WALLS CLOSED IN ON ME.

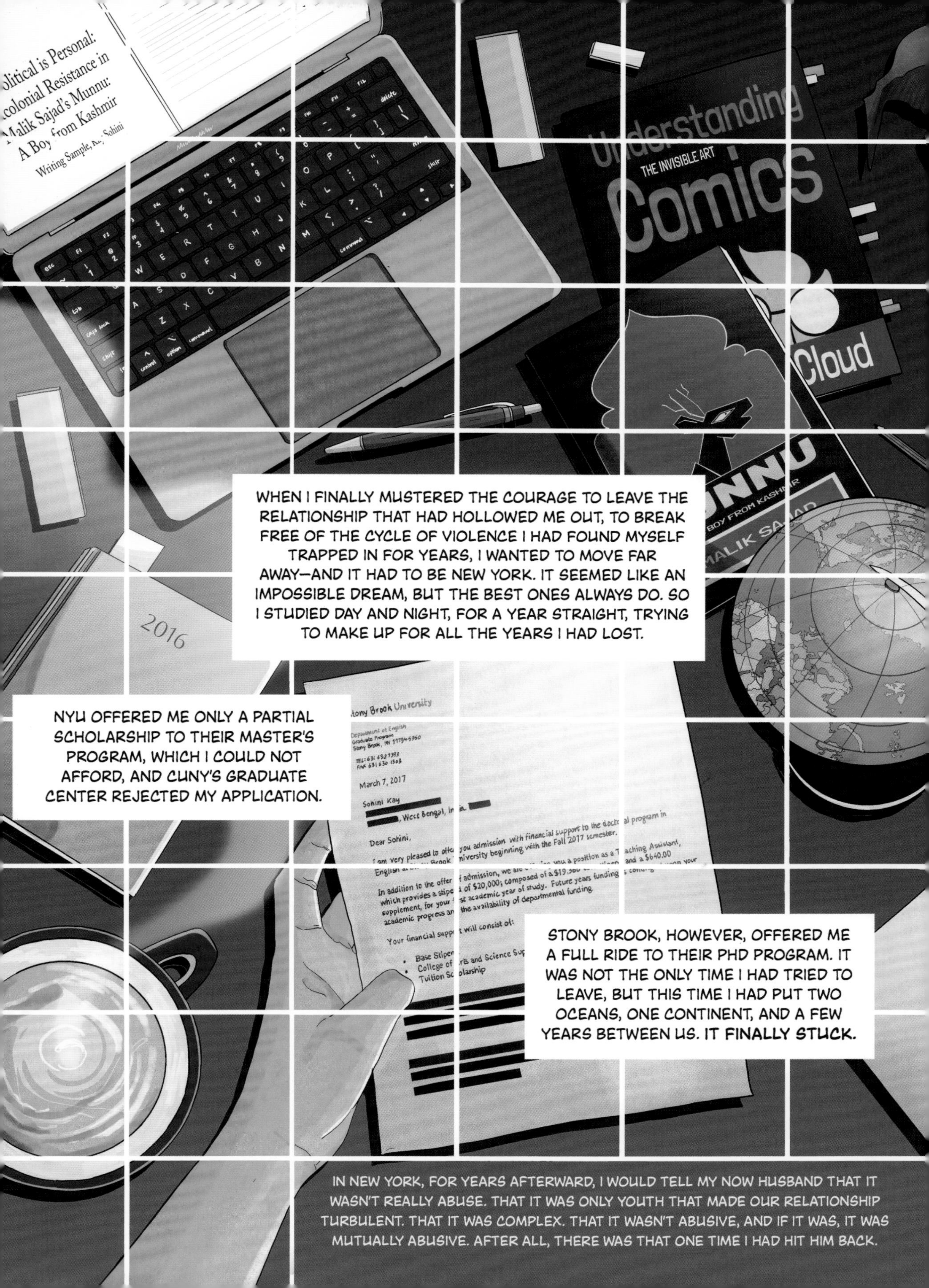
Understanding Comics
THE INVISIBLE ART
Cloud
2016
WHEN I FINALLY MUSTERED THE COURAGE TO LEAVE THE RELATIONSHIP THAT HAD HOLLOWED ME OUT, TO BREAK FREE OF THE CYCLE OF VIOLENCE I HAD FOUND MYSELF TRAPPED IN FOR YEARS, I WANTED TO MOVE FAR AWAY—AND IT HAD TO BE NEW YORK. IT SEEMED LIKE AN IMPOSSIBLE DREAM, BUT THE BEST ONES ALWAYS DO. SO I STUDIED DAY AND NIGHT, FOR A YEAR STRAIGHT, TRYING TO MAKE UP FOR ALL THE YEARS I HAD LOST.
NYU OFFERED ME ONLY A PARTIAL SCHOLARSHIP TO THEIR MASTER'S PROGRAM, WHICH I COULD NOT AFFORD, AND CUNY'S GRADUATE CENTER REJECTED MY APPLICATION.
March 7, 2017
Sohini Kay
Dear Sohini,
STONY BROOK, HOWEVER, OFFERED ME A FULL RIDE TO THEIR PHD PROGRAM. IT WAS NOT THE ONLY TIME I HAD TRIED TO LEAVE, BUT THIS TIME I HAD PUT TWO OCEANS, ONE CONTINENT, AND A FEW YEARS BETWEEN US. IT FINALLY STUCK.
IN NEW YORK, FOR YEARS AFTERWARD, I WOULD TELL MY NOW HUSBAND THAT IT WASN'T REALLY ABUSE. THAT IT WAS ONLY YOUTH THAT MADE OUR RELATIONSHIP TURBULENT. THAT IT WAS COMPLEX. THAT IT WASN'T ABUSIVE, AND IF IT WAS, IT WAS MUTUALLY ABUSIVE. AFTER ALL, THERE WAS THAT ONE TIME I HAD HIT HIM BACK.

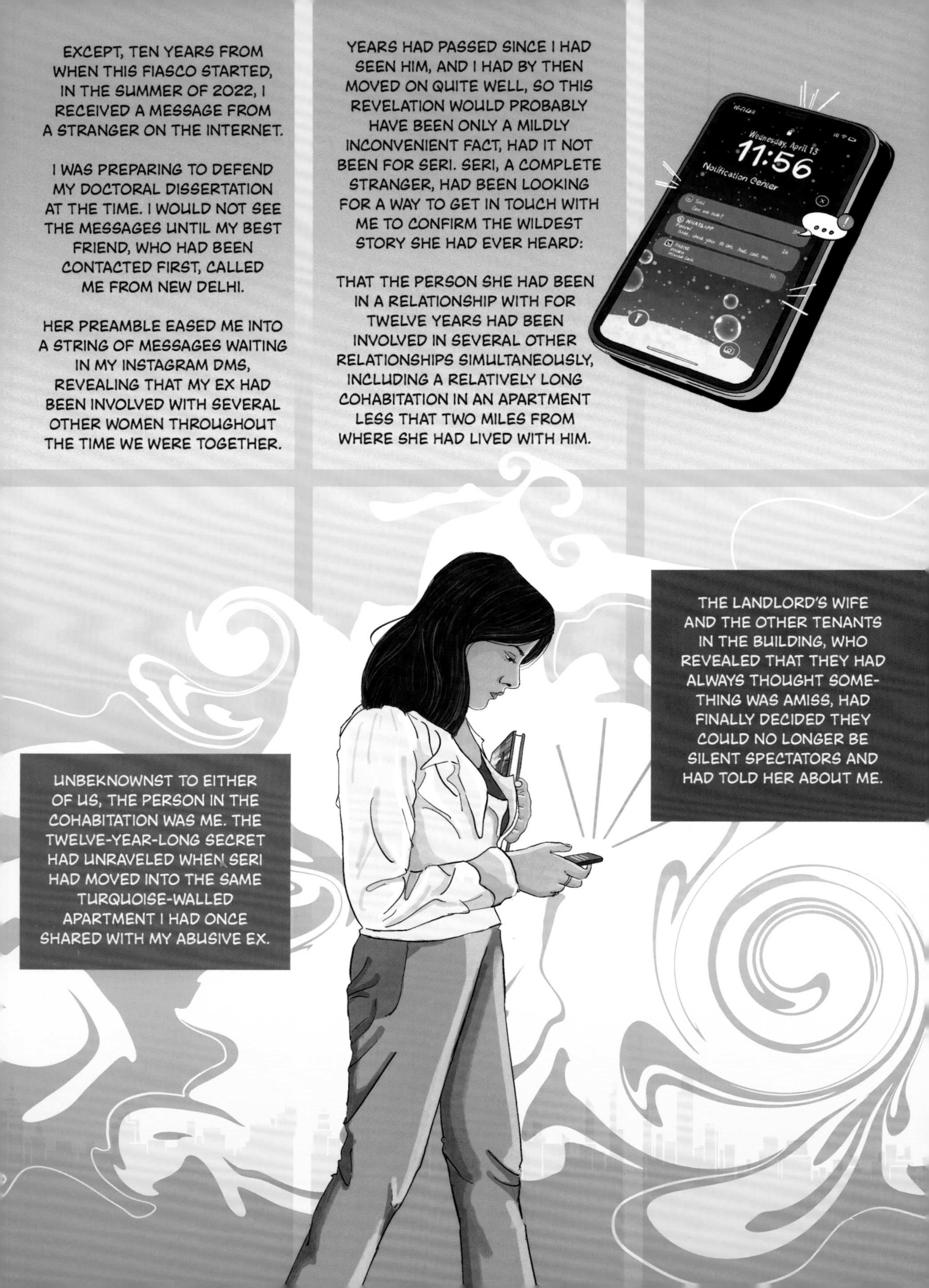
EXCEPT, TEN YEARS FROM WHEN THIS FIASCO STARTED, IN THE SUMMER OF 2022, I RECEIVED A MESSAGE FROM A STRANGER ON THE INTERNET.
I WAS PREPARING TO DEFEND MY DOCTORAL DISSERTATION AT THE TIME. I WOULD NOT SEE THE MESSAGES UNTIL MY BEST FRIEND, WHO HAD BEEN CONTACTED FIRST, CALLED ME FROM NEW DELHI.
HER PREAMBLE EASED ME INTO A STRING OF MESSAGES WAITING IN MY INSTAGRAM DMS, REVEALING THAT MY EX HAD BEEN INVOLVED WITH SEVERAL OTHER WOMEN THROUGHOUT THE TIME WE WERE TOGETHER.
YEARS HAD PASSED SINCE I HAD SEEN HIM, AND I HAD BY THEN MOVED ON QUITE WELL, SO THIS REVELATION WOULD PROBABLY HAVE BEEN ONLY A MILDLY INCONVENIENT FACT, HAD IT NOT BEEN FOR SERI. SERI, A COMPLETE STRANGER, HAD BEEN LOOKING FOR A WAY TO GET IN TOUCH WITH ME TO CONFIRM THE WILDEST STORY SHE HAD EVER HEARD:
THAT THE PERSON SHE HAD BEEN IN A RELATIONSHIP WITH FOR TWELVE YEARS HAD BEEN INVOLVED IN SEVERAL OTHER RELATIONSHIPS SIMULTANEOUSLY, INCLUDING A RELATIVELY LONG COHABITATION IN AN APARTMENT LESS THAT TWO MILES FROM WHERE SHE HAD LIVED WITH HIM.
Wednesday, April 13
11:56
Notification Center
UNBEKNOWNST TO EITHER OF US, THE PERSON IN THE COHABITATION WAS ME. THE TWELVE-YEAR-LONG SECRET HAD UNRAVELED WHEN SERI HAD MOVED INTO THE SAME TURQUOISE-WALLED APARTMENT I HAD ONCE SHARED WITH MY ABUSIVE EX.
THE LANDLORD'S WIFE AND THE OTHER TENANTS IN THE BUILDING, WHO REVEALED THAT THEY HAD ALWAYS THOUGHT SOME-THING WAS AMISS, HAD FINALLY DECIDED THEY COULD NO LONGER BE SILENT SPECTATORS AND HAD TOLD HER ABOUT ME.

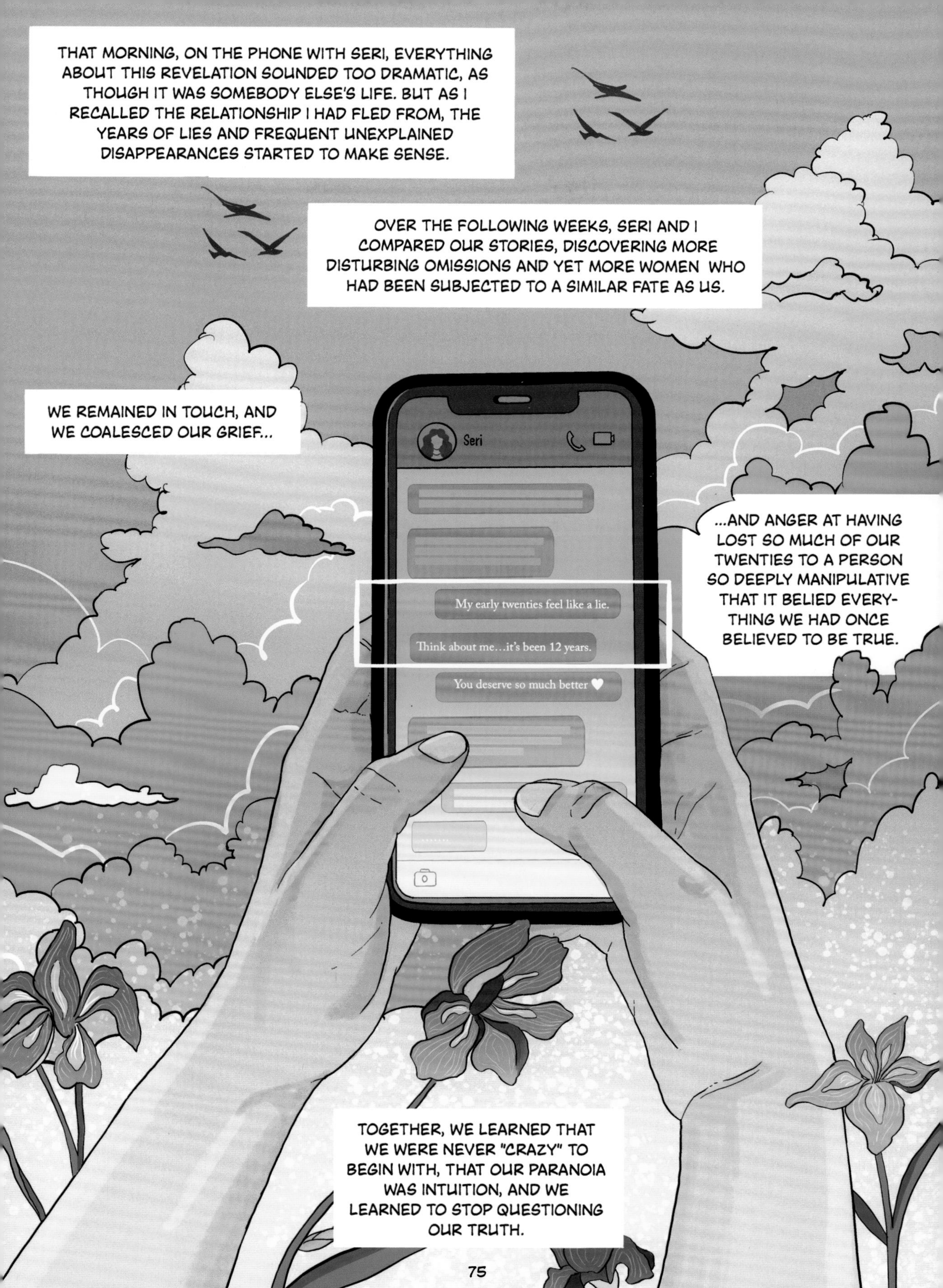

THAT MORNING, ON THE PHONE WITH SERI, EVERYTHING ABOUT THIS REVELATION SOUNDED TOO DRAMATIC, AS THOUGH IT WAS SOMEBODY ELSE'S LIFE. BUT AS I RECALLED THE RELATIONSHIP I HAD FLED FROM, THE YEARS OF LIES AND FREQUENT UNEXPLAINED DISAPPEARANCES STARTED TO MAKE SENSE.
OVER THE FOLLOWING WEEKS, SERI AND I COMPARED OUR STORIES, DISCOVERING MORE DISTURBING OMISSIONS AND YET MORE WOMEN WHO HAD BEEN SUBJECTED TO A SIMILAR FATE AS US.
WE REMAINED IN TOUCH, AND WE COALESCED OUR GRIEF...
Seri
My early twenties feel like a lie.
Think about me…it's been 12 years.
You deserve so much better ♥
...AND ANGER AT HAVING LOST SO MUCH OF OUR TWENTIES TO A PERSON SO DEEPLY MANIPULATIVE THAT IT BELIED EVERYTHING WE HAD ONCE BELIEVED TO BE TRUE.
TOGETHER, WE LEARNED THAT WE WERE NEVER "CRAZY" TO BEGIN WITH, THAT OUR PARANOIA WAS INTUITION, AND WE LEARNED TO STOP QUESTIONING OUR TRUTH.

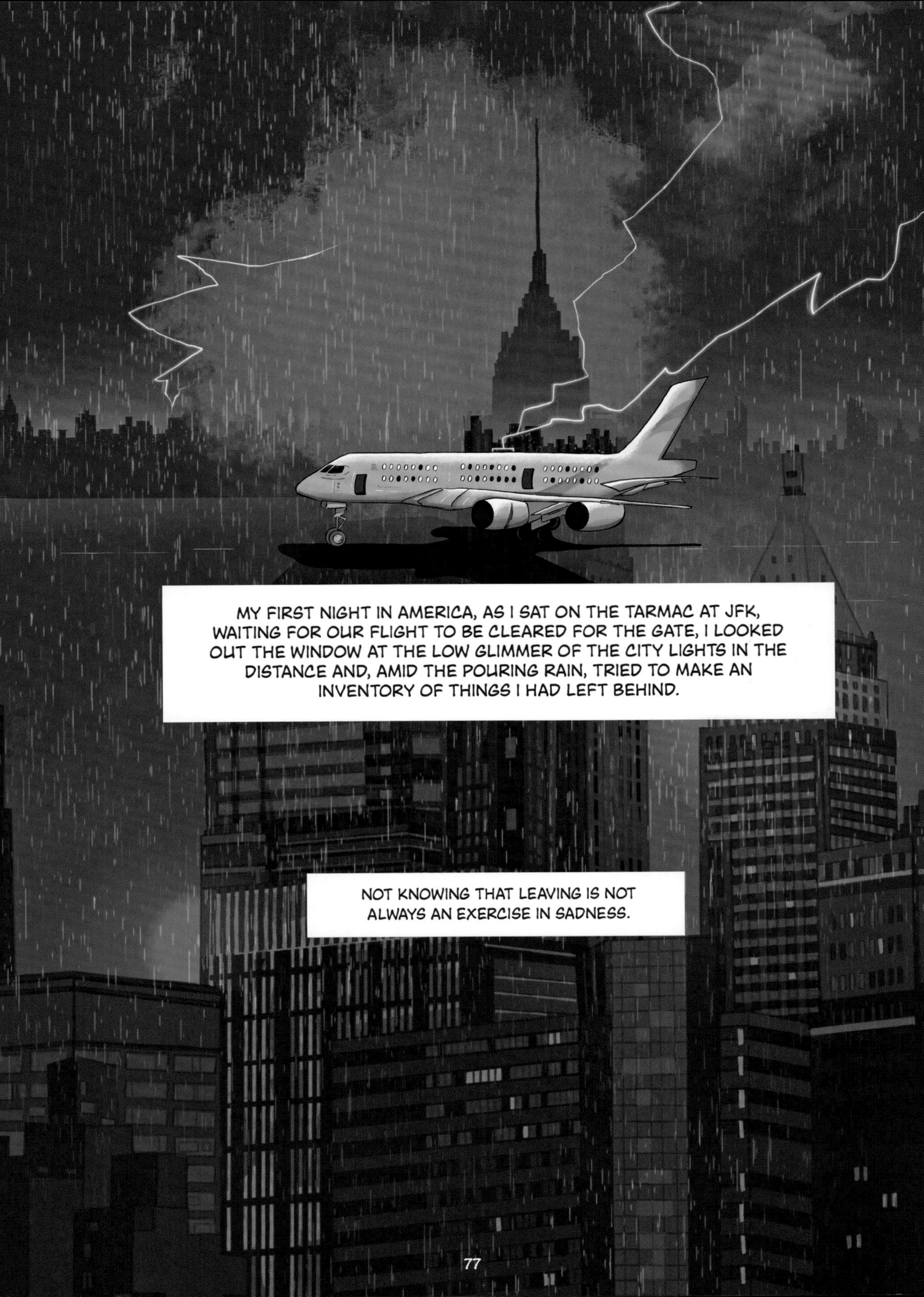
MY FIRST NIGHT IN AMERICA, AS I SAT ON THE TARMAC AT JFK, WAITING FOR OUR FLIGHT TO BE CLEARED FOR THE GATE, I LOOKED OUT THE WINDOW AT THE LOW GLIMMER OF THE CITY LIGHTS IN THE DISTANCE AND, AMID THE POURING RAIN, TRIED TO MAKE AN INVENTORY OF THINGS I HAD LEFT BEHIND.
NOT KNOWING THAT LEAVING IS NOT ALWAYS AN EXERCISE IN SADNESS.

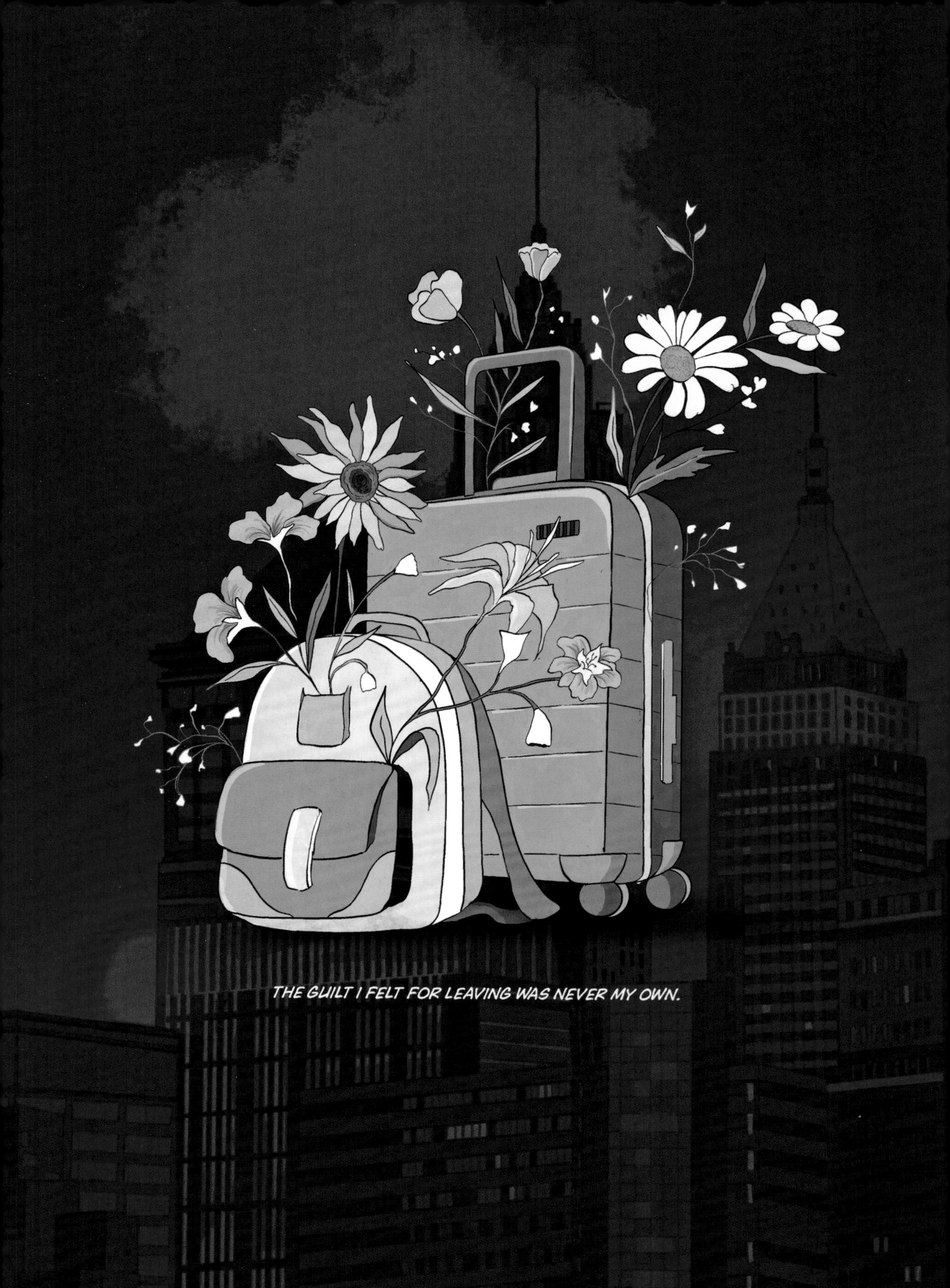
THE GUILT I FELT FOR LEAVING WAS NEVER MY OWN.

NEW YORK, NEW YORK

"I believe in New Yorkers. Whether they've ever questioned the dream in which they live, I wouldn't know, because I won't ever dare ask that question."

Dylan Thomas

YOU'D HAVE TO BE A LITTLE MAD TO LOVE NEW YORK

A CONTRADICTION, A TOURIST TRAP, A BILLIONAIRE'S ROW, A CENTER FOR THE ARTS, A CULTURAL CAPITAL, A FINANCIAL DISTRICT, AN EXPERIMENTAL KITCHEN OF ALL THE WORLD'S CUISINES, A PORTAL TO THE NEW WORLD, A MELTING POT, A BASTION OF PROGRESSIVE IDEALS, AN IMPERFECT SANCTUARY CITY WITH A SERIES OF UNFORTUNATE MAYORAL PICKS, A SPIRITED SELLER OF IMPOSSIBLE DREAMS, ALL ROLLED INTO ONE AND A QUARTER ISLANDS, AND ~~FOUR~~ FIVE (I KEEP FORGETTING ABOUT STATEN ISLAND) BOROUGHS.

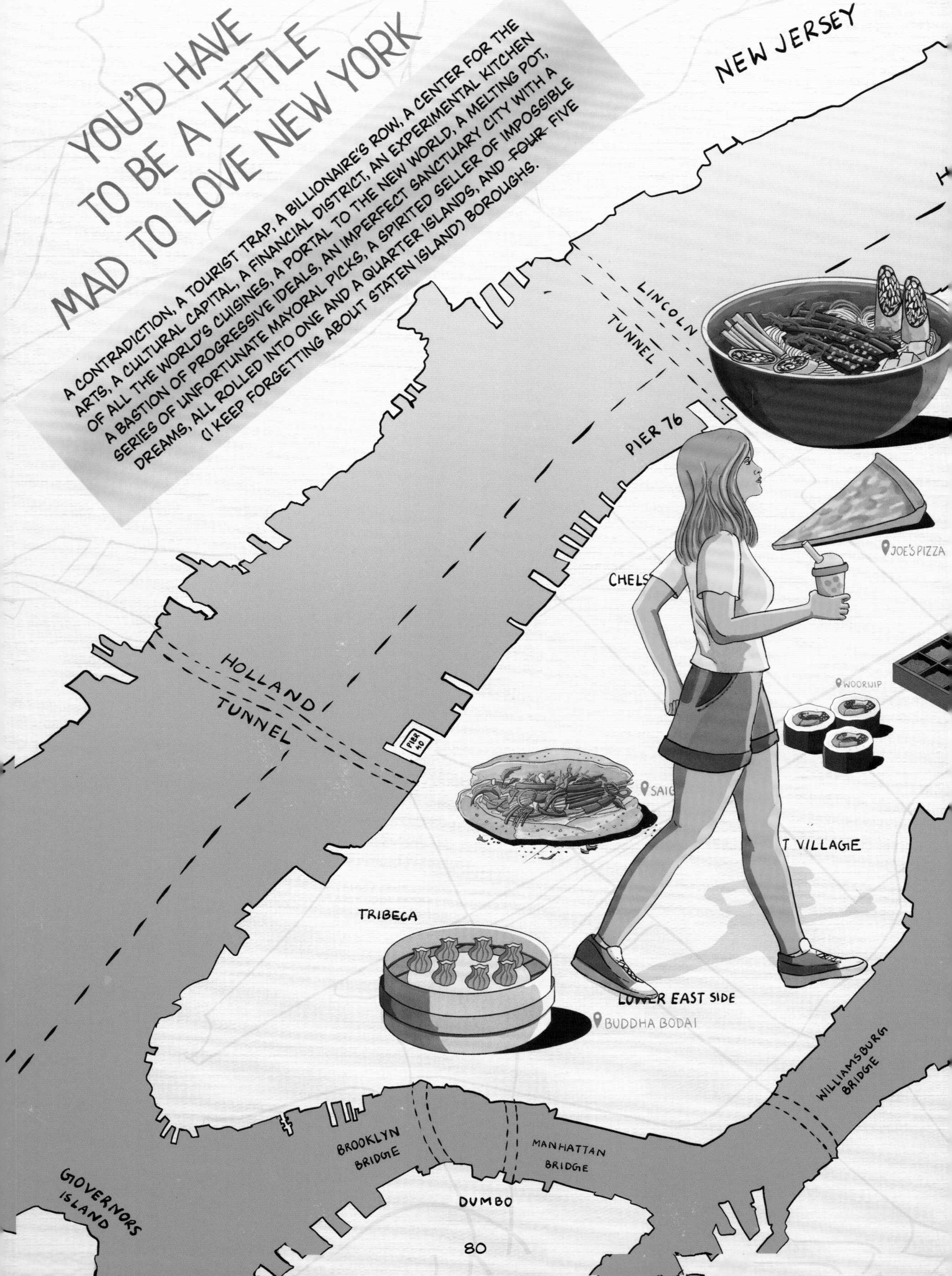

NEW JERSEY
LINCOLN TUNNEL
PIER 76
JOE'S PIZZA
CHELS
WOORIJIP
HOLLAND TUNNEL
PIER 40
SAIG
T VILLAGE
TRIBECA
LOWER EAST SIDE
BUDDHA BODAI
WILLIAMSBURG BRIDGE
BROOKLYN BRIDGE
MANHATTAN BRIDGE
DUMBO
GOVERNORS ISLAND

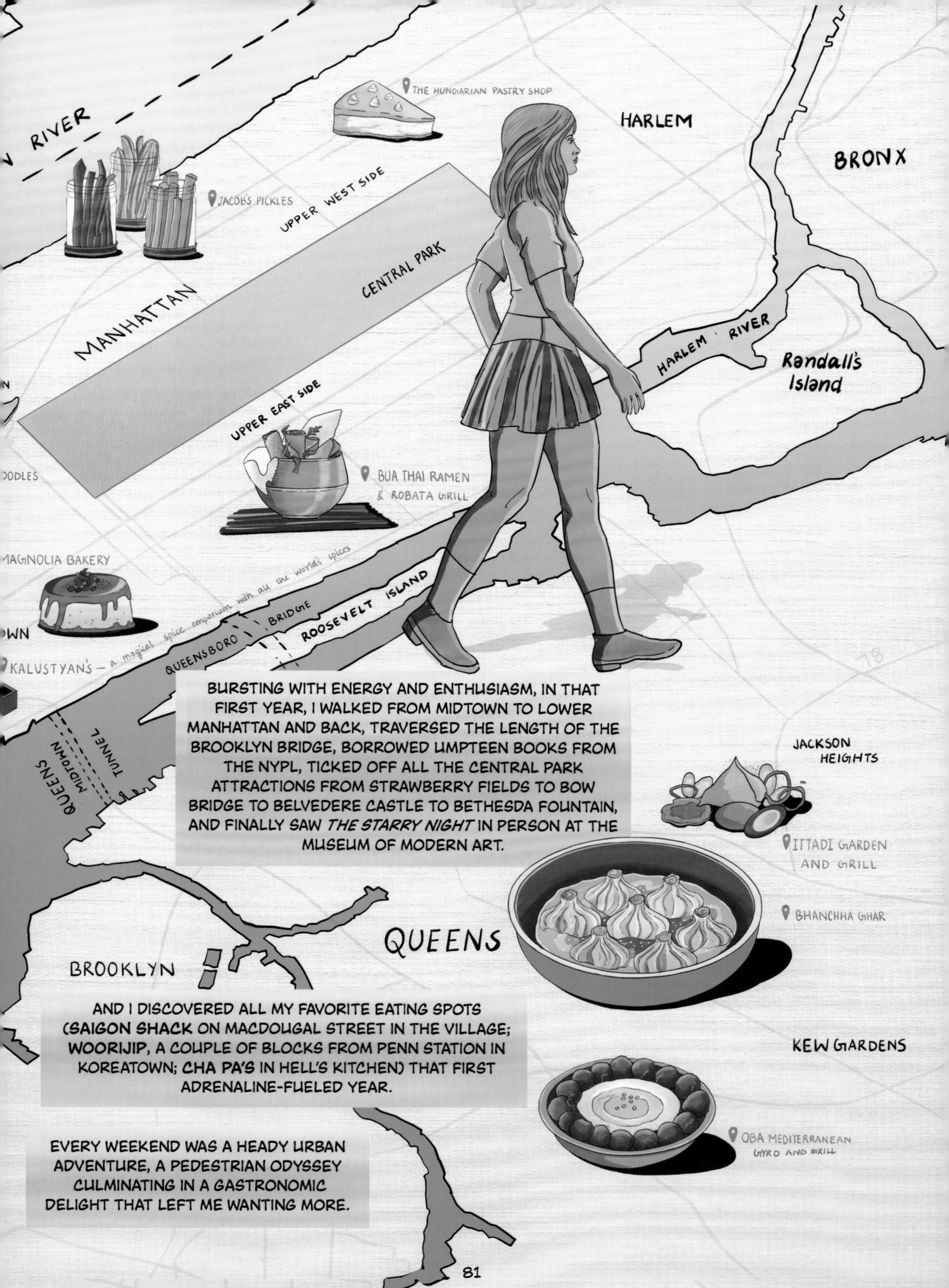
RIVER
THE HUNGARIAN PASTRY SHOP
HARLEM
BRONX
JACOB'S PICKLES
UPPER WEST SIDE
CENTRAL PARK
MANHATTAN
HARLEM RIVER
Randall's Island
UPPER EAST SIDE
BUA THAI RAMEN & ROBATA GRILL
MAGNOLIA BAKERY
KALUSTYAN'S — a magical spice emporium with all the world's spices
QUEENSBORO BRIDGE
ROOSEVELT ISLAND
QUEENS MIDTOWN TUNNEL
BURSTING WITH ENERGY AND ENTHUSIASM, IN THAT FIRST YEAR, I WALKED FROM MIDTOWN TO LOWER MANHATTAN AND BACK, TRAVERSED THE LENGTH OF THE BROOKLYN BRIDGE, BORROWED UMPTEEN BOOKS FROM THE NYPL, TICKED OFF ALL THE CENTRAL PARK ATTRACTIONS FROM STRAWBERRY FIELDS TO BOW BRIDGE TO BELVEDERE CASTLE TO BETHESDA FOUNTAIN, AND FINALLY SAW *THE STARRY NIGHT* IN PERSON AT THE MUSEUM OF MODERN ART.
JACKSON HEIGHTS
ITTADI GARDEN AND GRILL
BHANCHHA GHAR
QUEENS
BROOKLYN
AND I DISCOVERED ALL MY FAVORITE EATING SPOTS (**SAIGON SHACK** ON MACDOUGAL STREET IN THE VILLAGE; **WOORIJIP**, A COUPLE OF BLOCKS FROM PENN STATION IN KOREATOWN; **CHA PA'S** IN HELL'S KITCHEN) THAT FIRST ADRENALINE-FUELED YEAR.
KEW GARDENS
OBA MEDITERRANEAN GYRO AND GRILL
EVERY WEEKEND WAS A HEADY URBAN ADVENTURE, A PEDESTRIAN ODYSSEY CULMINATING IN A GASTRONOMIC DELIGHT THAT LEFT ME WANTING MORE.

SAVE FOR A COUPLE OF FRIENDS TURNED FAMILY, I HAVE NEVER BEEN ONE FOR SOCIALIZING A LOT OR EVEN A LITTLE. I DO NOT MAKE NEW FRIENDS; I GO THROUGH ACQUAINTANCES, AMICABLY ENOUGH, BUT ALWAYS ON A TEMPORARY BASIS. ANYTHING MORE IS EMOTIONALLY TAXING AND TAKES TOO MUCH OUT OF ME AND TAKES ENTIRELY TOO LONG TO REPLENISH.

YET FOR MOST OF TWENTY-FOUR YEARS, I CARRIED A SENSE OF EMBARRASSING LONELINESS THAT WAS UNBECOMING FOR AN INCORRIGIBLE INTROVERT OF MY NATURE.

THAT WAS, UNTIL THE MOMENT I ARRIVED IN NEW YORK, AND STEPPED OUT OF PENN STATION ON TO 34TH STREET.

SUDDENLY, I WAS SURROUNDED BY THE LOW HUM OF THE BUSIEST CITY IN THE WORLD. SOME SAY THAT NEW YORK IS TOO LOUD, OTHERS SAY IT'S A FUN ENOUGH PLACE TO VISIT BUT THEY COULD NEVER LIVE HERE.

BUT I HEAR ONLY THE MOST COMFORTING WHITE NOISE IN THE WORLD. I KNEW ABSOLUTELY NOBODY AND FELT COMPLETELY UNBOTHERED BY IT.

IT WAS A BRIGHT, TURQUOISE-SKIED, SLIGHTLY-TOO-WARM SUMMER DAY, AND, IN A WAY THAT IS MILDLY INDICATIVE OF THE RAMPANT CONSUMERISM OF OUR TIMES...

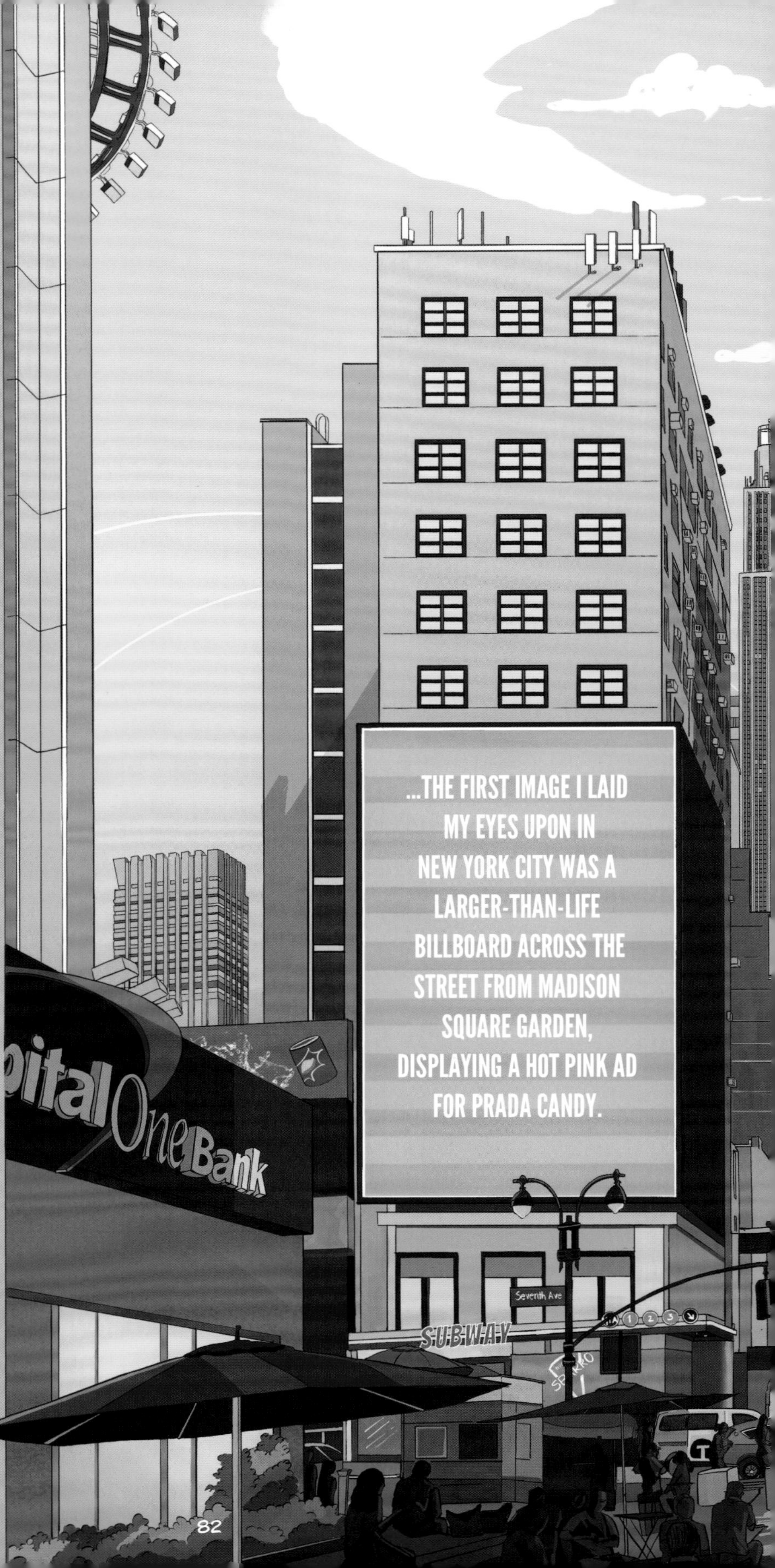
...THE FIRST IMAGE I LAID MY EYES UPON IN NEW YORK CITY WAS A LARGER-THAN-LIFE BILLBOARD ACROSS THE STREET FROM MADISON SQUARE GARDEN, DISPLAYING A HOT PINK AD FOR PRADA CANDY.
pital One Bank
Seventh Ave
SUBWAY

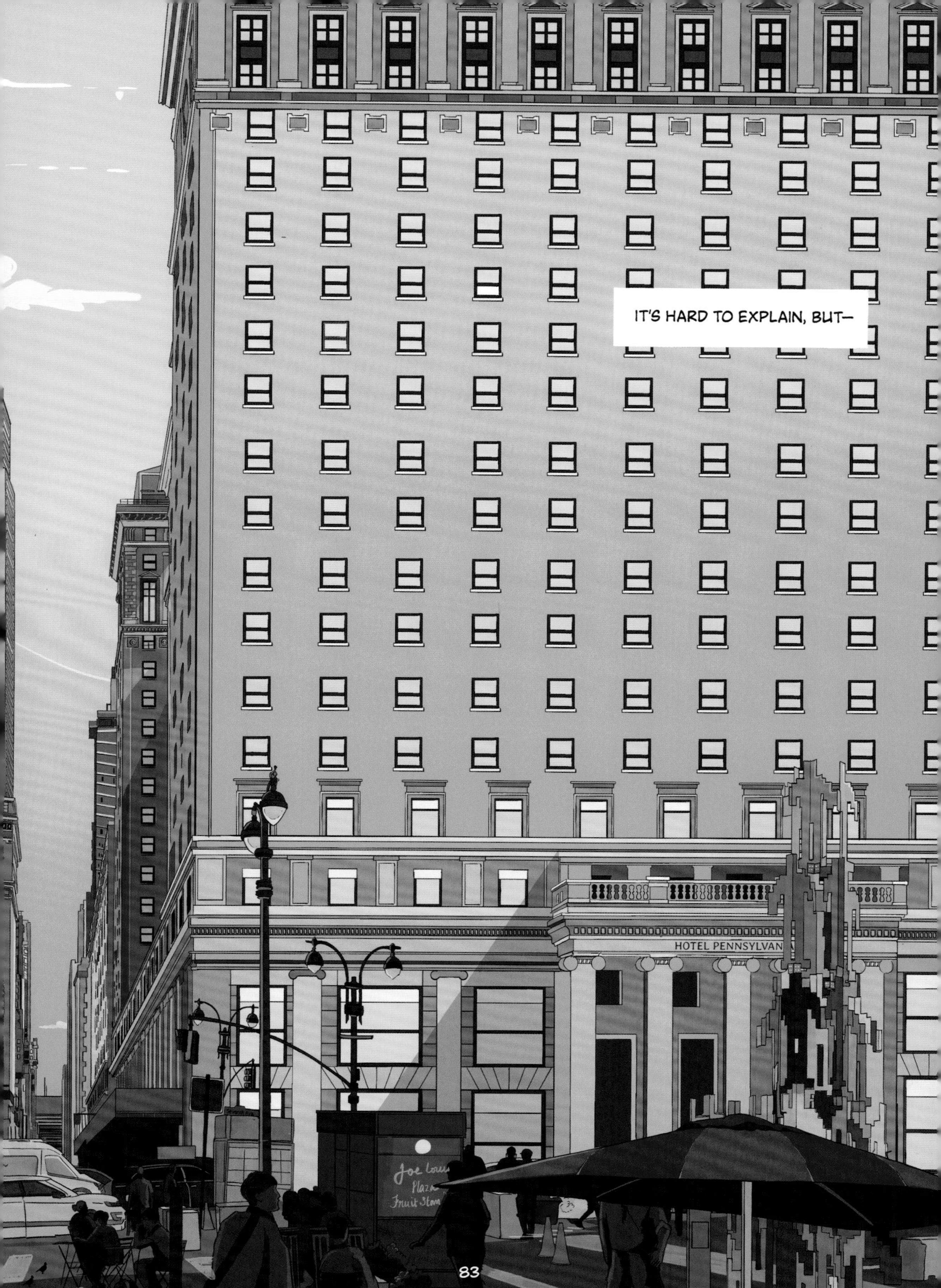
IT'S HARD TO EXPLAIN, BUT—
HOTEL PENNSYLVAN

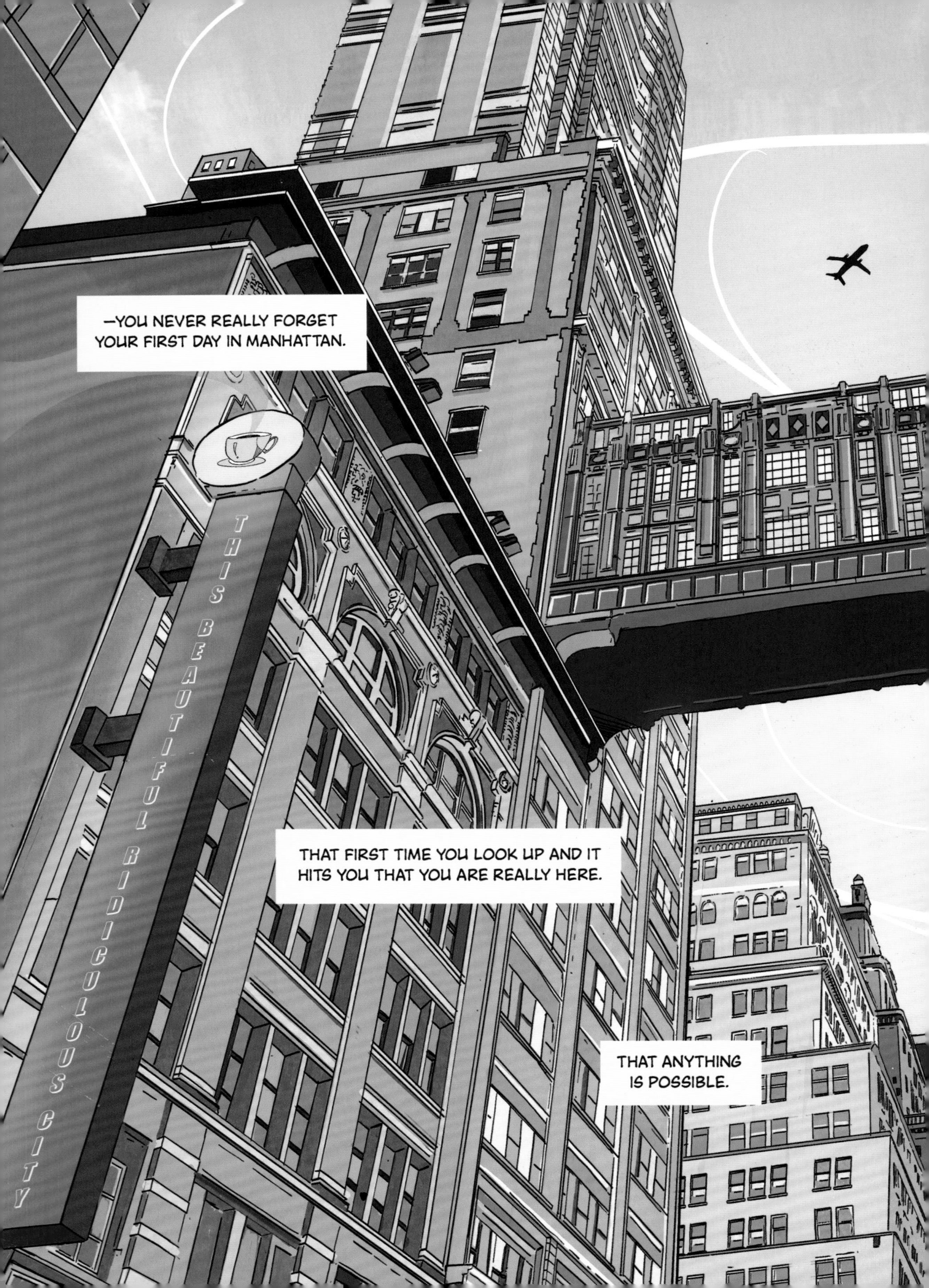
—YOU NEVER REALLY FORGET YOUR FIRST DAY IN MANHATTAN.
THIS BEAUTIFUL RIDICULOUS CITY
THAT FIRST TIME YOU LOOK UP AND IT HITS YOU THAT YOU ARE REALLY HERE.
THAT ANYTHING IS POSSIBLE.

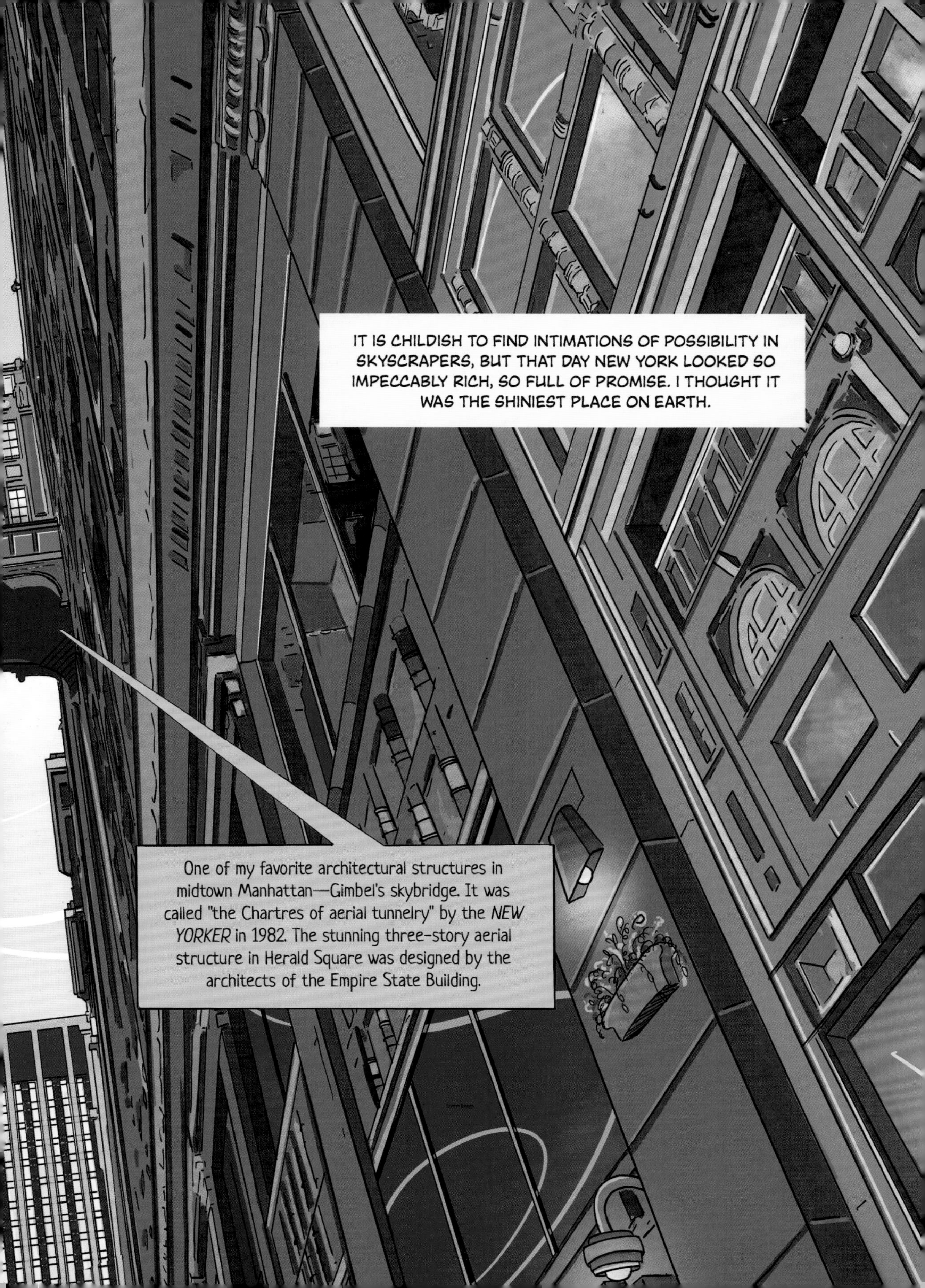
IT IS CHILDISH TO FIND INTIMATIONS OF POSSIBILITY IN SKYSCRAPERS, BUT THAT DAY NEW YORK LOOKED SO IMPECCABLY RICH, SO FULL OF PROMISE. I THOUGHT IT WAS THE SHINIEST PLACE ON EARTH.
One of my favorite architectural structures in midtown Manhattan—Gimbel's skybridge. It was called "the Chartres of aerial tunnelry" by the *NEW YORKER* in 1982. The stunning three-story aerial structure in Herald Square was designed by the architects of the Empire State Building.

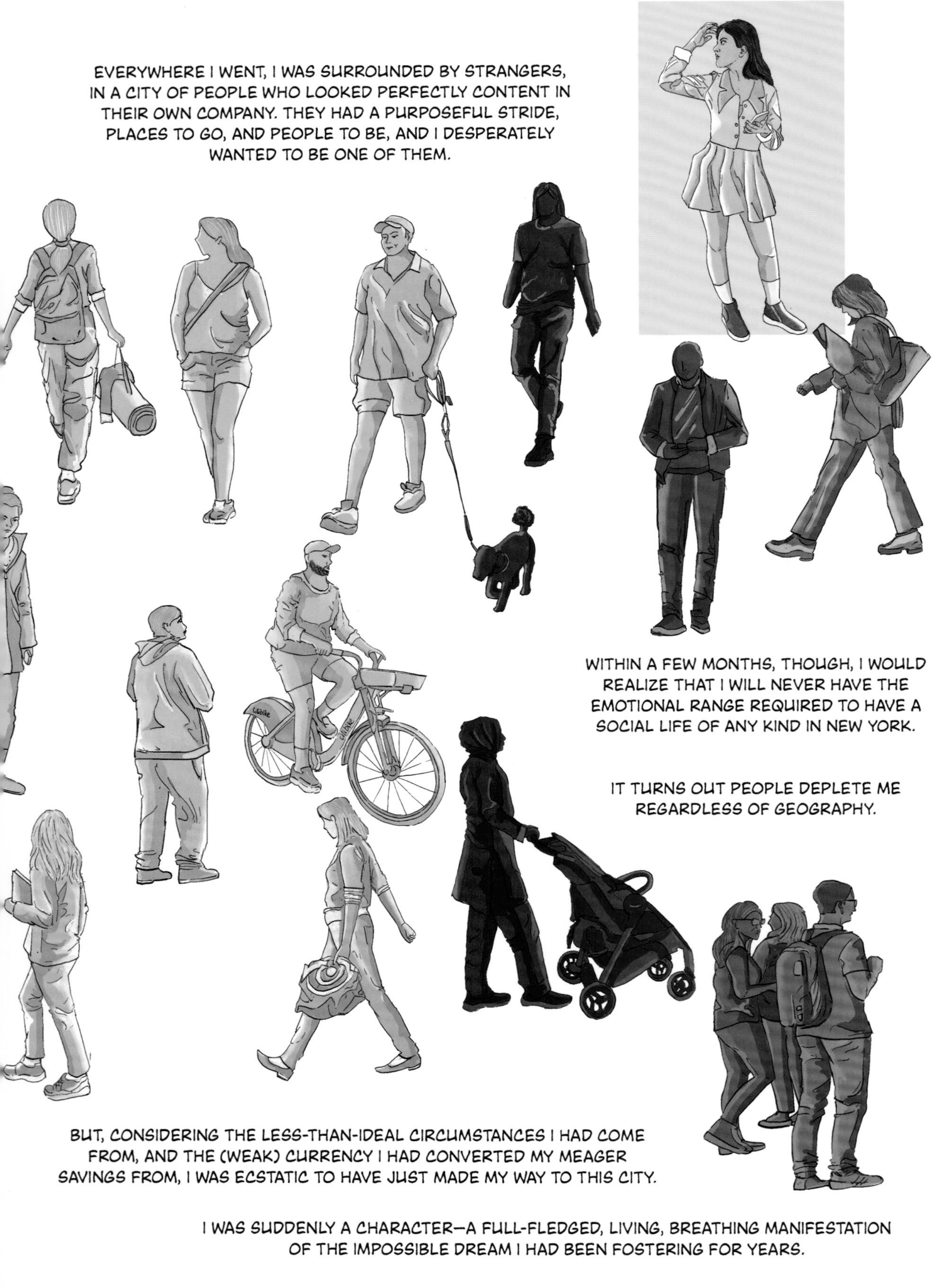
EVERYWHERE I WENT, I WAS SURROUNDED BY STRANGERS, IN A CITY OF PEOPLE WHO LOOKED PERFECTLY CONTENT IN THEIR OWN COMPANY. THEY HAD A PURPOSEFUL STRIDE, PLACES TO GO, AND PEOPLE TO BE, AND I DESPERATELY WANTED TO BE ONE OF THEM.
WITHIN A FEW MONTHS, THOUGH, I WOULD REALIZE THAT I WILL NEVER HAVE THE EMOTIONAL RANGE REQUIRED TO HAVE A SOCIAL LIFE OF ANY KIND IN NEW YORK.
IT TURNS OUT PEOPLE DEPLETE ME REGARDLESS OF GEOGRAPHY.
BUT, CONSIDERING THE LESS-THAN-IDEAL CIRCUMSTANCES I HAD COME FROM, AND THE (WEAK) CURRENCY I HAD CONVERTED MY MEAGER SAVINGS FROM, I WAS ECSTATIC TO HAVE JUST MADE MY WAY TO THIS CITY.
I WAS SUDDENLY A CHARACTER—A FULL-FLEDGED, LIVING, BREATHING MANIFESTATION OF THE IMPOSSIBLE DREAM I HAD BEEN FOSTERING FOR YEARS.

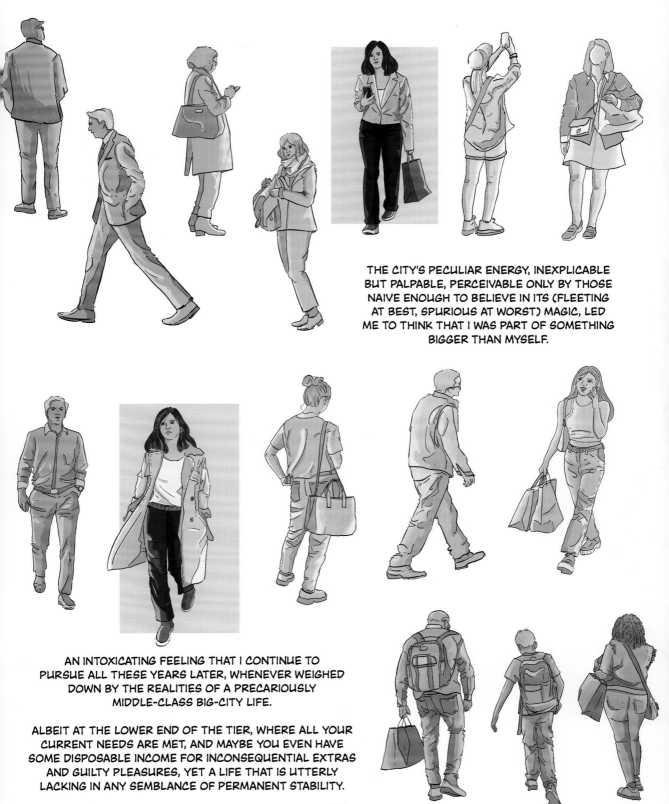

E. B. WHITE'S *HERE IS NEW YORK* BEGINS WITH THE LINE, "ON ANY PERSON WHO DESIRES SUCH QUEER PRIZES, NEW YORK WILL BESTOW THE GIFT OF LONELINESS AND THE GIFT OF PRIVACY."

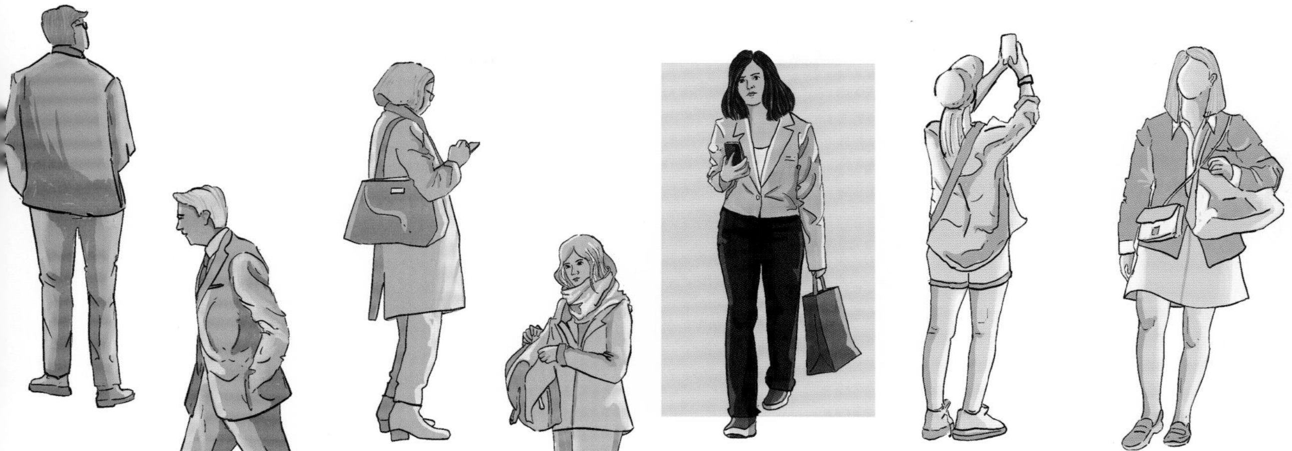

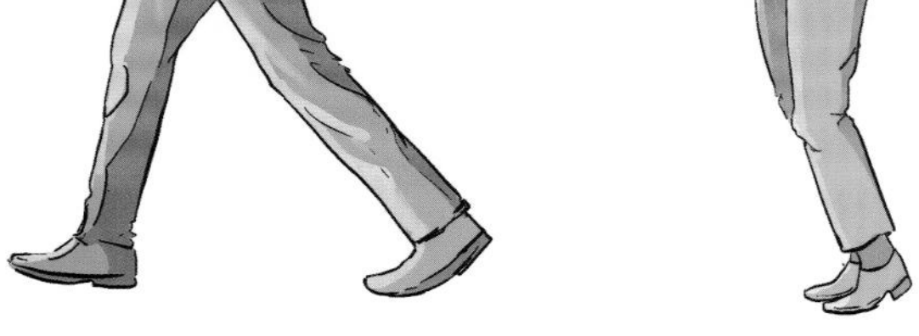

THE CITY'S PECULIAR ENERGY, INEXPLICABLE BUT PALPABLE, PERCEIVABLE ONLY BY THOSE NAIVE ENOUGH TO BELIEVE IN ITS (FLEETING AT BEST, SPURIOUS AT WORST) MAGIC, LED ME TO THINK THAT I WAS PART OF SOMETHING BIGGER THAN MYSELF.

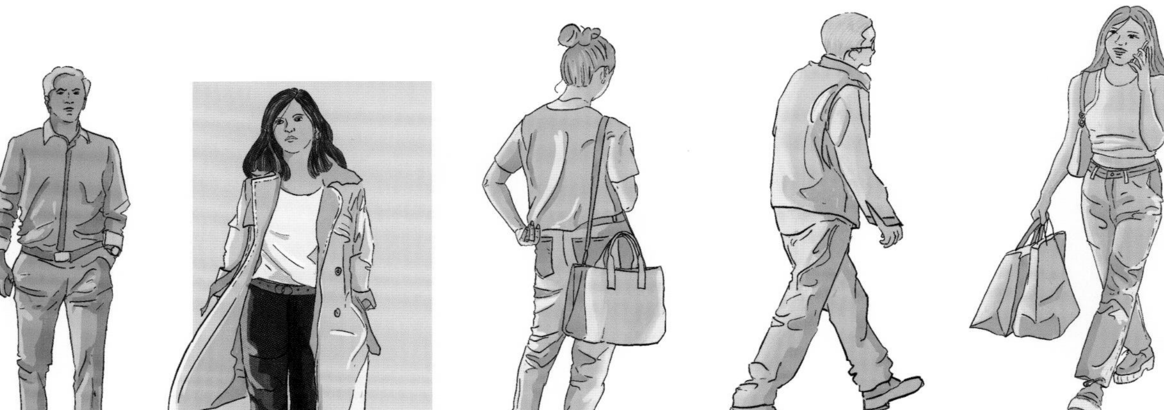

AN INTOXICATING FEELING THAT I CONTINUE TO PURSUE ALL THESE YEARS LATER, WHENEVER WEIGHED DOWN BY THE REALITIES OF A PRECARIOUSLY MIDDLE-CLASS BIG-CITY LIFE.

ALBEIT AT THE LOWER END OF THE TIER, WHERE ALL YOUR CURRENT NEEDS ARE MET, AND MAYBE YOU EVEN HAVE SOME DISPOSABLE INCOME FOR INCONSEQUENTIAL EXTRAS AND GUILTY PLEASURES, YET A LIFE THAT IS UTTERLY LACKING IN ANY SEMBLANCE OF PERMANENT STABILITY.

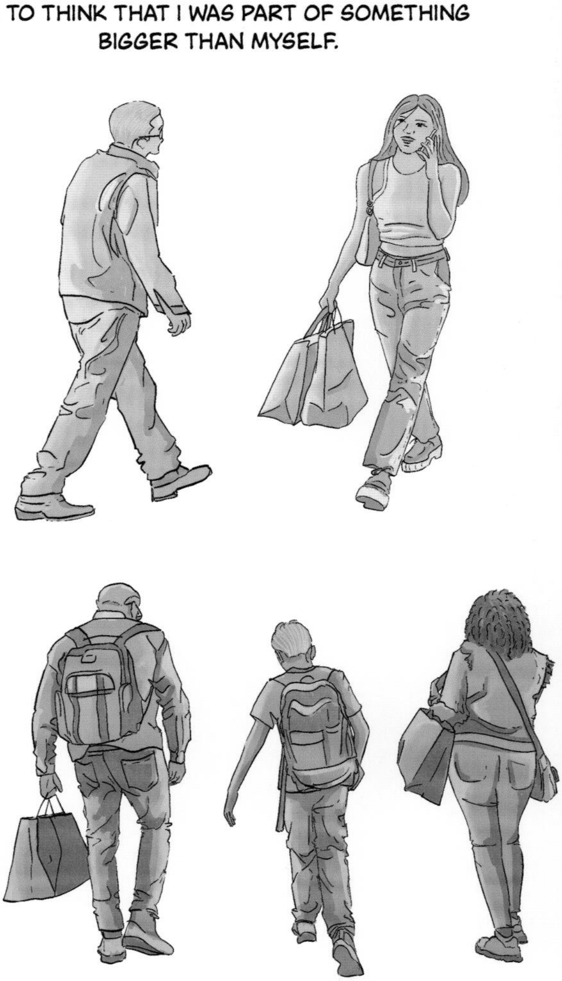

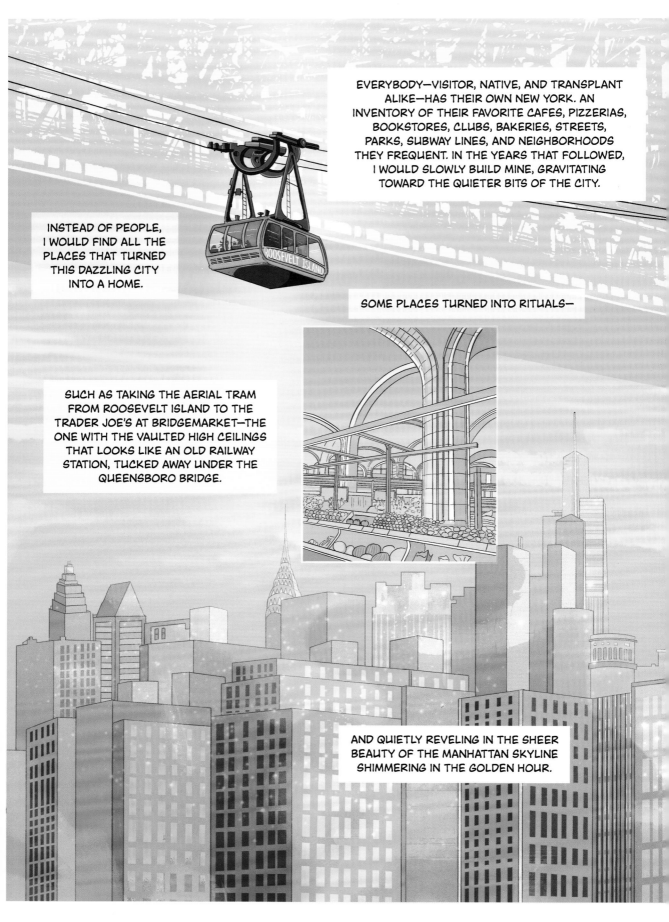

EVERYBODY—VISITOR, NATIVE, AND TRANSPLANT ALIKE—HAS THEIR OWN NEW YORK. AN INVENTORY OF THEIR FAVORITE CAFES, PIZZERIAS, BOOKSTORES, CLUBS, BAKERIES, STREETS, PARKS, SUBWAY LINES, AND NEIGHBORHOODS THEY FREQUENT. IN THE YEARS THAT FOLLOWED, I WOULD SLOWLY BUILD MINE, GRAVITATING TOWARD THE QUIETER BITS OF THE CITY.

INSTEAD OF PEOPLE, I WOULD FIND ALL THE PLACES THAT TURNED THIS DAZZLING CITY INTO A HOME.

SOME PLACES TURNED INTO RITUALS—

SUCH AS TAKING THE AERIAL TRAM FROM ROOSEVELT ISLAND TO THE TRADER JOE'S AT BRIDGEMARKET—THE ONE WITH THE VAULTED HIGH CEILINGS THAT LOOKS LIKE AN OLD RAILWAY STATION, TUCKED AWAY UNDER THE QUEENSBORO BRIDGE.

AND QUIETLY REVELING IN THE SHEER BEAUTY OF THE MANHATTAN SKYLINE SHIMMERING IN THE GOLDEN HOUR.

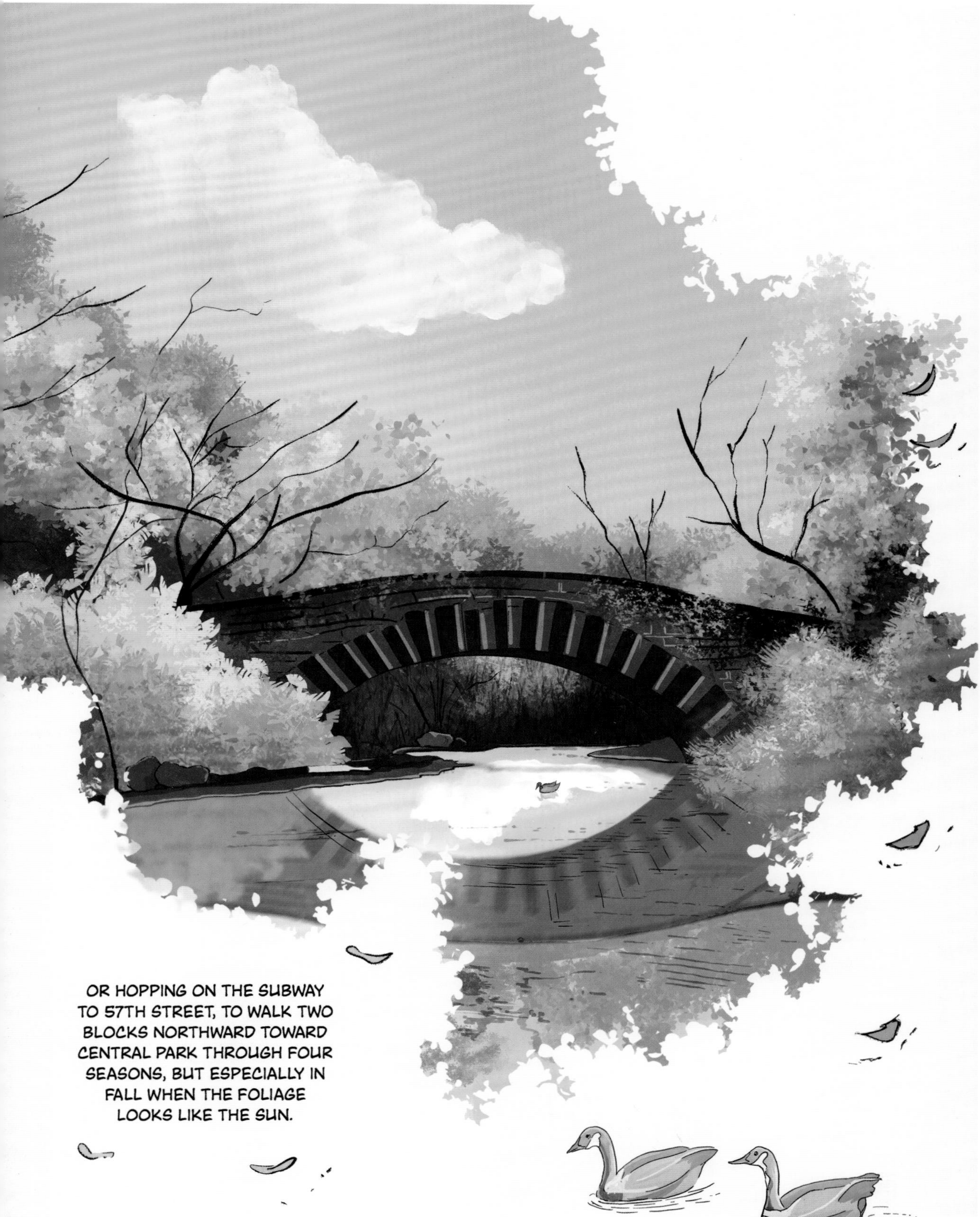
OR HOPPING ON THE SUBWAY TO 57TH STREET, TO WALK TWO BLOCKS NORTHWARD TOWARD CENTRAL PARK THROUGH FOUR SEASONS, BUT ESPECIALLY IN FALL WHEN THE FOLIAGE LOOKS LIKE THE SUN.

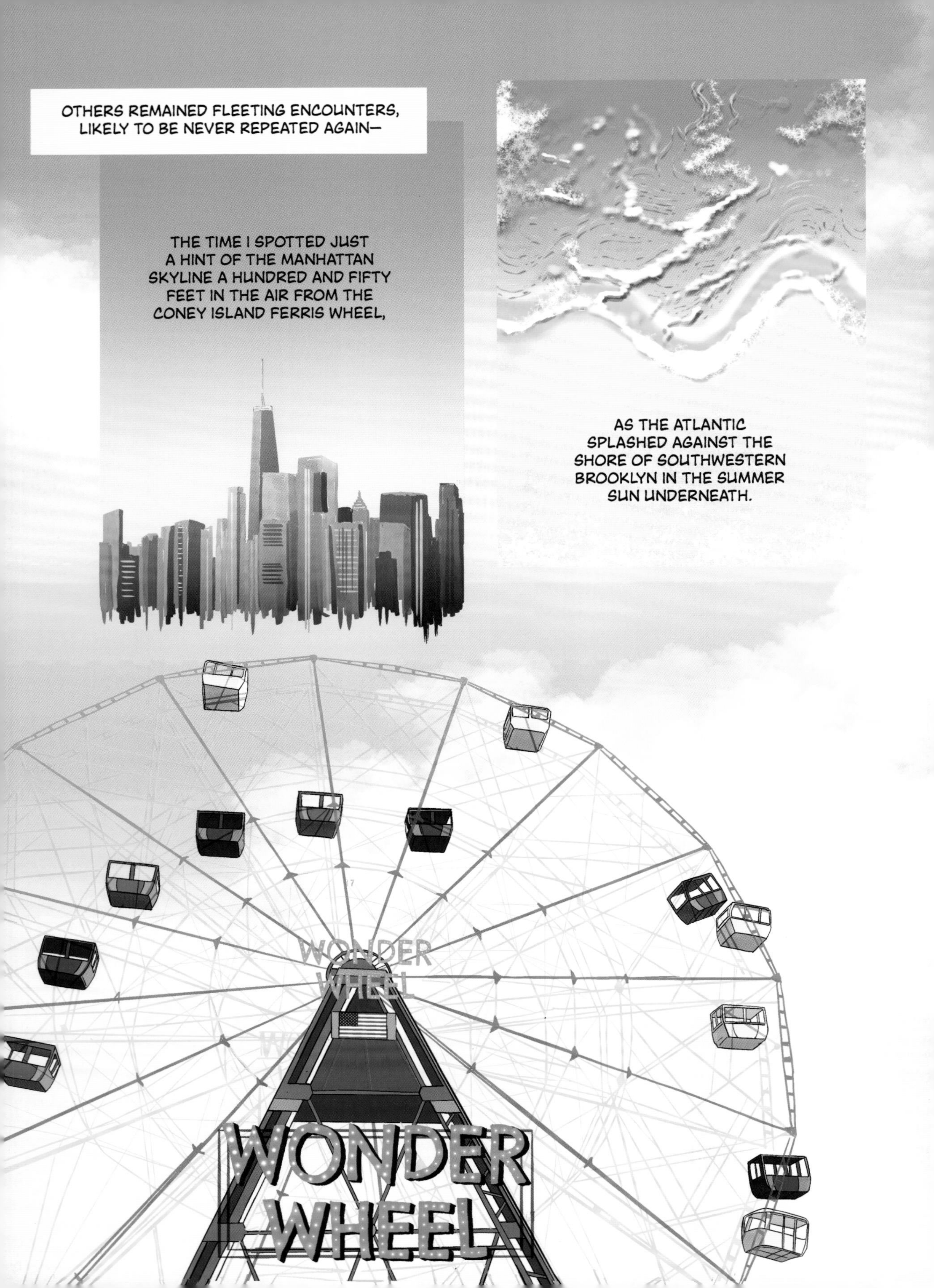
OTHERS REMAINED FLEETING ENCOUNTERS, LIKELY TO BE NEVER REPEATED AGAIN—
THE TIME I SPOTTED JUST A HINT OF THE MANHATTAN SKYLINE A HUNDRED AND FIFTY FEET IN THE AIR FROM THE CONEY ISLAND FERRIS WHEEL,
AS THE ATLANTIC SPLASHED AGAINST THE SHORE OF SOUTHWESTERN BROOKLYN IN THE SUMMER SUN UNDERNEATH.
WONDER WHEEL

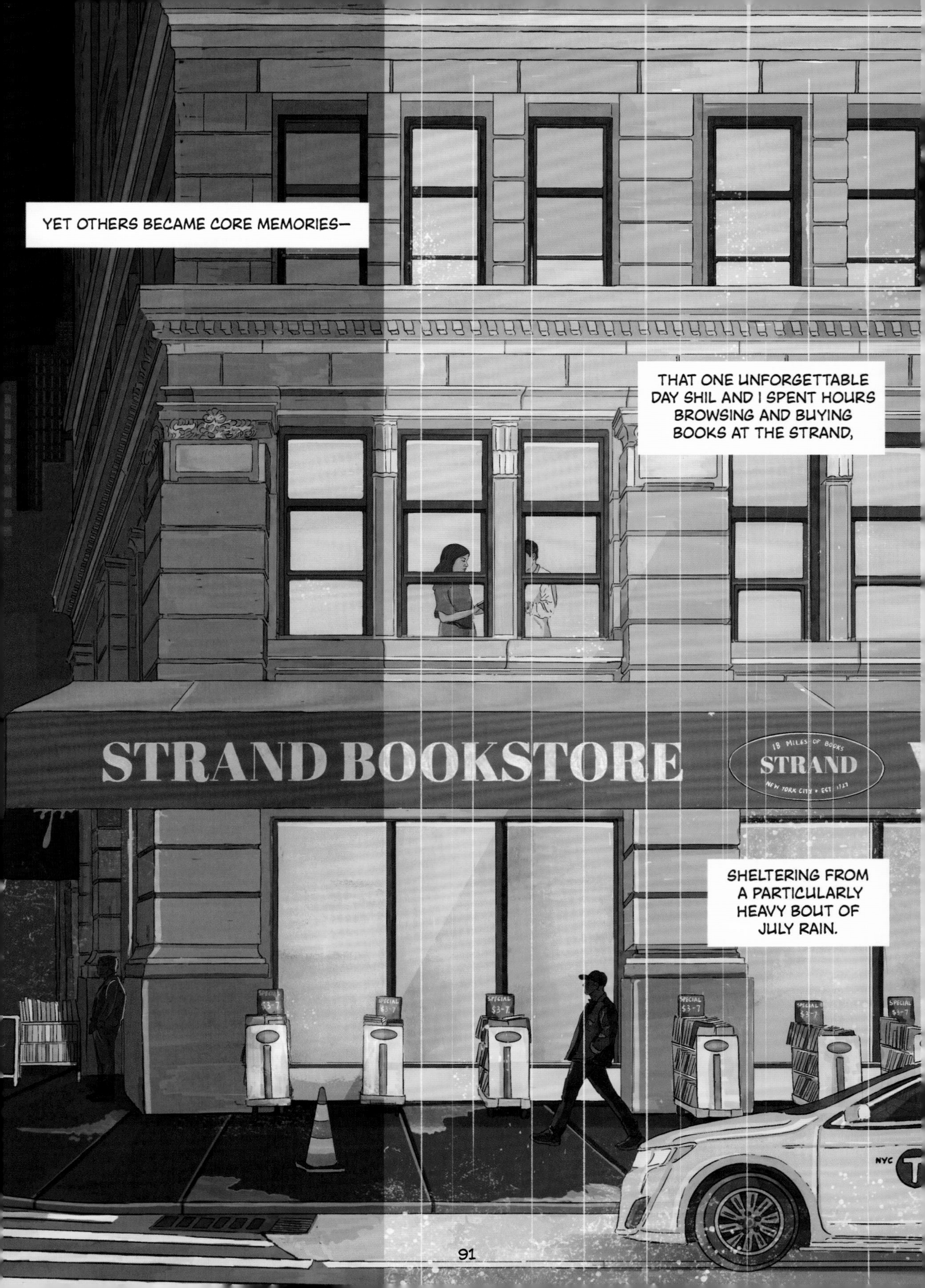
YET OTHERS BECAME CORE MEMORIES—
THAT ONE UNFORGETTABLE DAY SHIL AND I SPENT HOURS BROWSING AND BUYING BOOKS AT THE STRAND,
STRAND BOOKSTORE
18 MILES OF BOOKS
STRAND
NEW YORK CITY
SHELTERING FROM A PARTICULARLY HEAVY BOUT OF JULY RAIN.
NYC

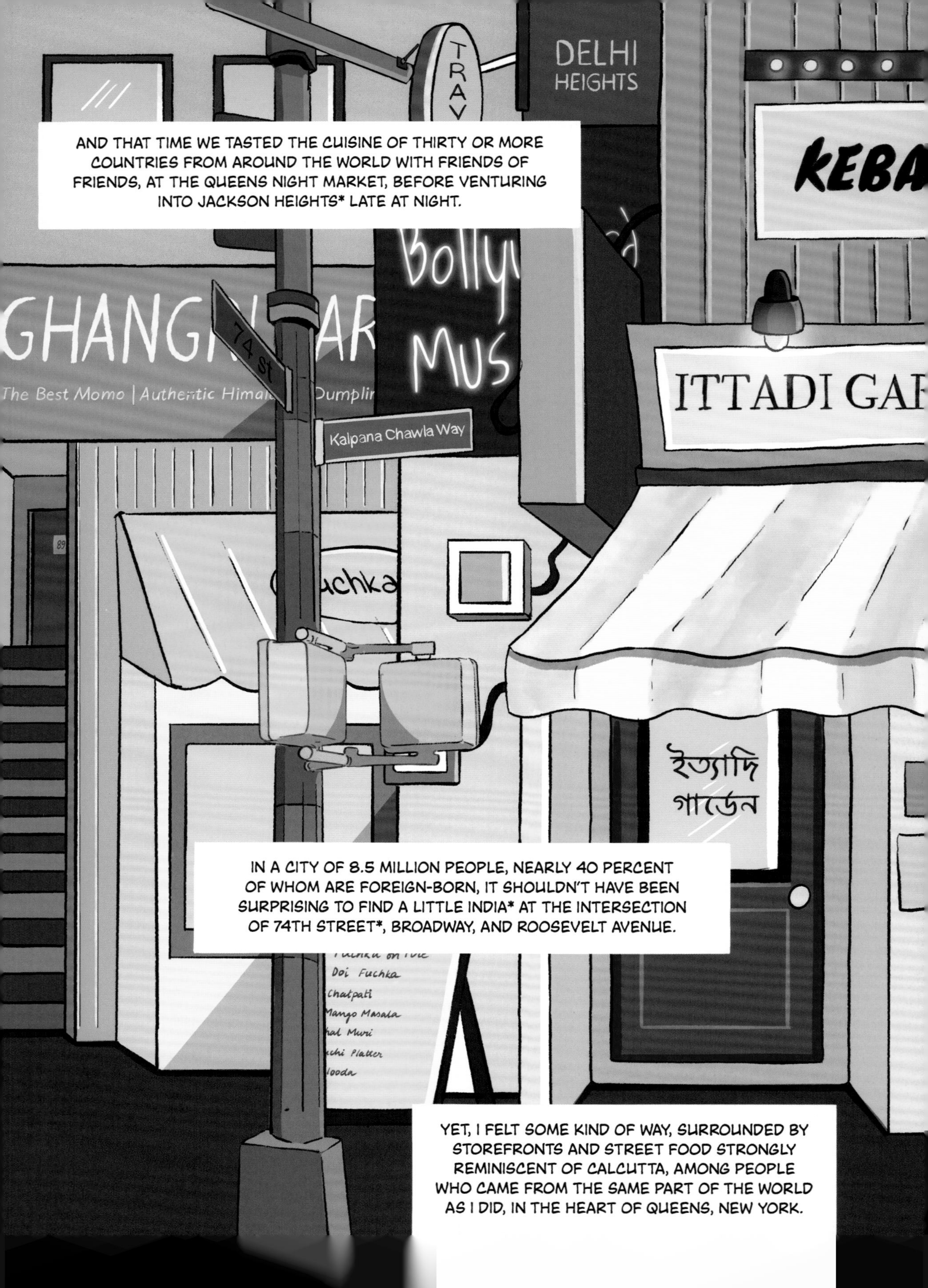
AND THAT TIME WE TASTED THE CUISINE OF THIRTY OR MORE COUNTRIES FROM AROUND THE WORLD WITH FRIENDS OF FRIENDS, AT THE QUEENS NIGHT MARKET, BEFORE VENTURING INTO JACKSON HEIGHTS* LATE AT NIGHT.
DELHI HEIGHTS
74 st
Kalpana Chawla Way
ইত্যাদি গার্ডেন
IN A CITY OF 8.5 MILLION PEOPLE, NEARLY 40 PERCENT OF WHOM ARE FOREIGN-BORN, IT SHOULDN'T HAVE BEEN SURPRISING TO FIND A LITTLE INDIA* AT THE INTERSECTION OF 74TH STREET*, BROADWAY, AND ROOSEVELT AVENUE.
Doi Fuchka
Chatpati
Mango Masala
YET, I FELT SOME KIND OF WAY, SURROUNDED BY STOREFRONTS AND STREET FOOD STRONGLY REMINISCENT OF CALCUTTA, AMONG PEOPLE WHO CAME FROM THE SAME PART OF THE WORLD AS I DID, IN THE HEART OF QUEENS, NEW YORK.

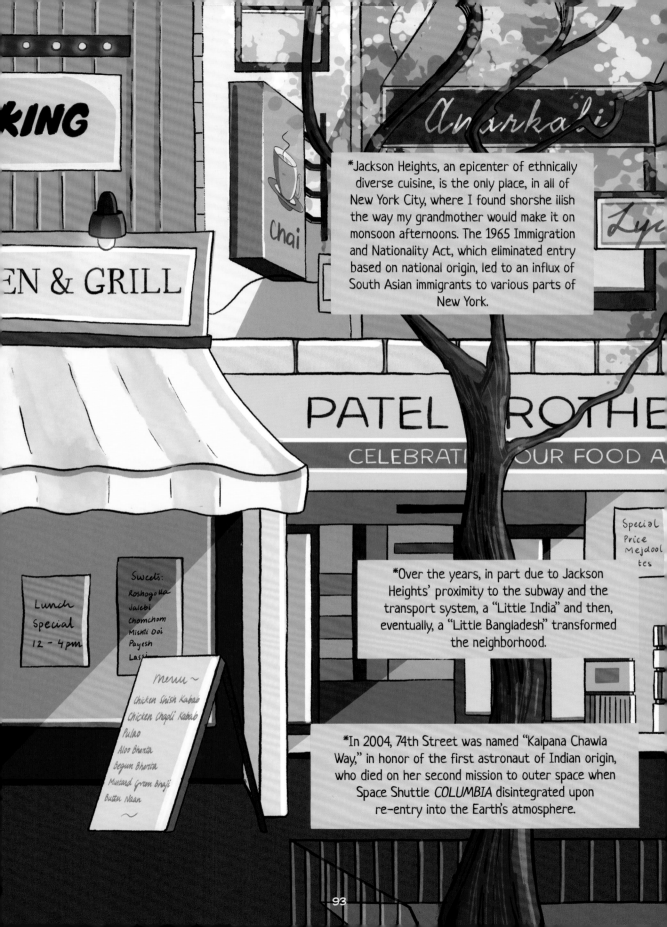

*Jackson Heights, an epicenter of ethnically diverse cuisine, is the only place, in all of New York City, where I found shorshe ilish the way my grandmother would make it on monsoon afternoons. The 1965 Immigration and Nationality Act, which eliminated entry based on national origin, led to an influx of South Asian immigrants to various parts of New York.

*Over the years, in part due to Jackson Heights' proximity to the subway and the transport system, a "Little India" and then, eventually, a "Little Bangladesh" transformed the neighborhood.

*In 2004, 74th Street was named "Kalpana Chawla Way," in honor of the first astronaut of Indian origin, who died on her second mission to outer space when Space Shuttle *COLUMBIA* disintegrated upon re-entry into the Earth's atmosphere.

KING

EN & GRILL

Chai

Anarkali

Ly

PATEL ROTHE

CELEBRATI OUR FOOD A

Special Price Mejdool tes

Lunch Special 12 - 4 pm

Sweets:
Roshogolla
Jalebi
Chomchom
Mishti Doi
Payesh
Lassi

Menu ~
Chicken Shish Kabab
Chicken Chapli Kabab
Pulao
Aloo Bharta
Begun Bharta
Mustard Green Braji
Butta Naan
~

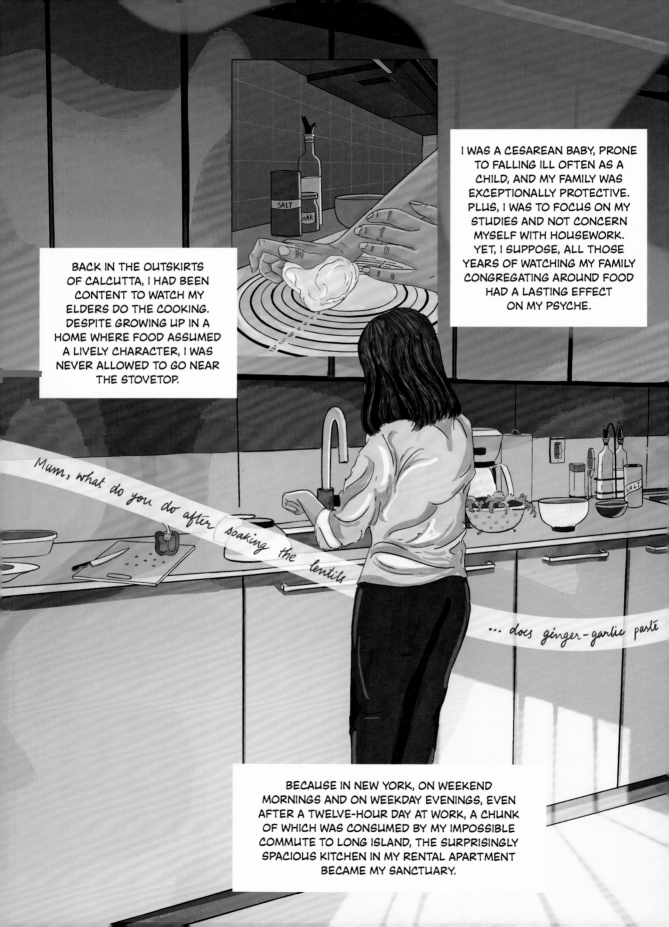

I WAS A CESAREAN BABY, PRONE TO FALLING ILL OFTEN AS A CHILD, AND MY FAMILY WAS EXCEPTIONALLY PROTECTIVE. PLUS, I WAS TO FOCUS ON MY STUDIES AND NOT CONCERN MYSELF WITH HOUSEWORK. YET, I SUPPOSE, ALL THOSE YEARS OF WATCHING MY FAMILY CONGREGATING AROUND FOOD HAD A LASTING EFFECT ON MY PSYCHE.

BACK IN THE OUTSKIRTS OF CALCUTTA, I HAD BEEN CONTENT TO WATCH MY ELDERS DO THE COOKING. DESPITE GROWING UP IN A HOME WHERE FOOD ASSUMED A LIVELY CHARACTER, I WAS NEVER ALLOWED TO GO NEAR THE STOVETOP.

Mum, what do you do after soaking the lentils

... does ginger-garlic paste

BECAUSE IN NEW YORK, ON WEEKEND MORNINGS AND ON WEEKDAY EVENINGS, EVEN AFTER A TWELVE-HOUR DAY AT WORK, A CHUNK OF WHICH WAS CONSUMED BY MY IMPOSSIBLE COMMUTE TO LONG ISLAND, THE SURPRISINGLY SPACIOUS KITCHEN IN MY RENTAL APARTMENT BECAME MY SANCTUARY.

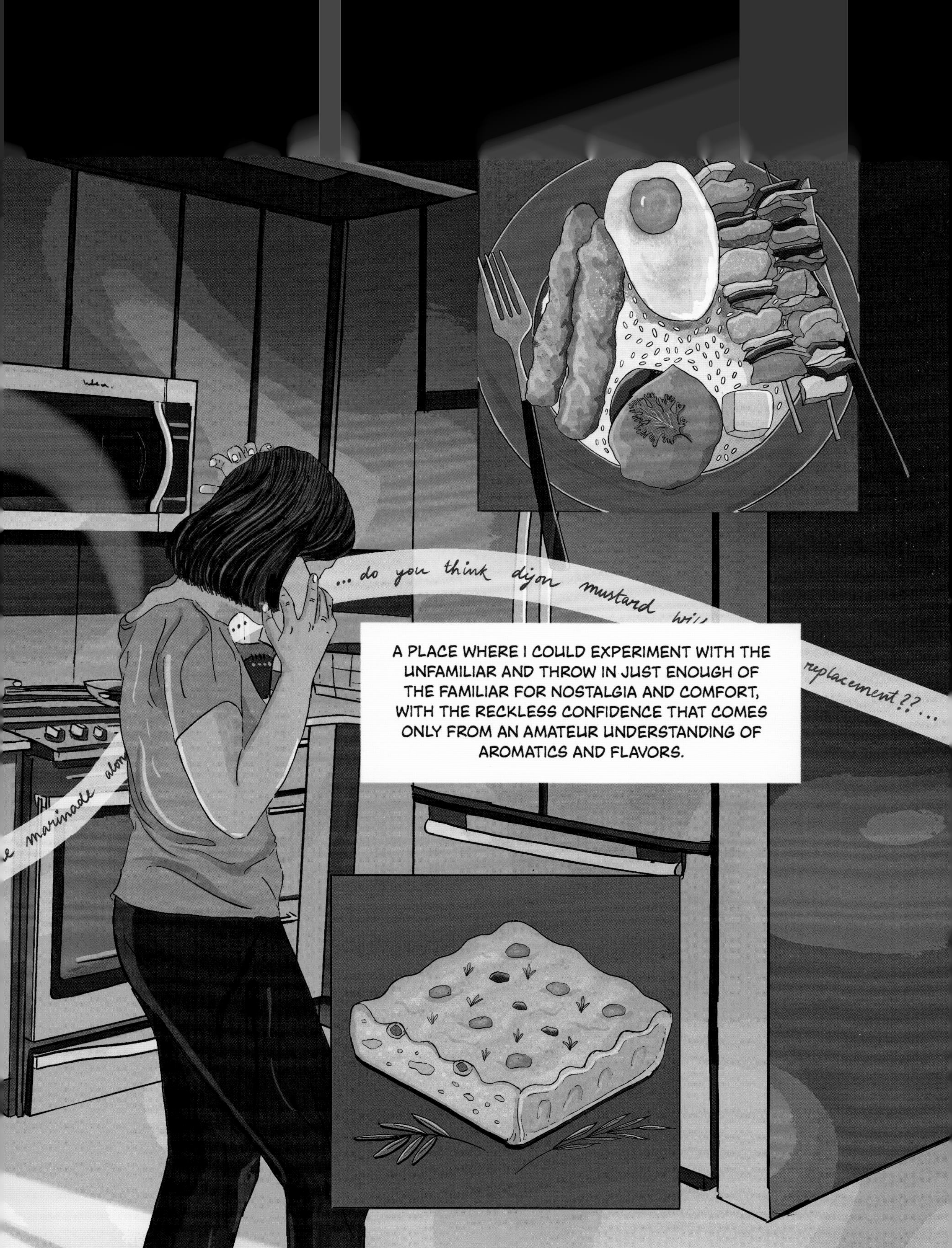
... do you think dijon mustard
replacement ??...
marinade
A PLACE WHERE I COULD EXPERIMENT WITH THE UNFAMILIAR AND THROW IN JUST ENOUGH OF THE FAMILIAR FOR NOSTALGIA AND COMFORT, WITH THE RECKLESS CONFIDENCE THAT COMES ONLY FROM AN AMATEUR UNDERSTANDING OF AROMATICS AND FLAVORS.

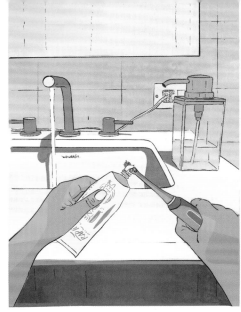

But
first
coffee

WHENEVER I FOUND MYSELF
BEING HELPLESSLY DRAWN
BACK TO THE DARKNESS I
HAD MOVED ACROSS THE
WORLD TO ESCAPE...

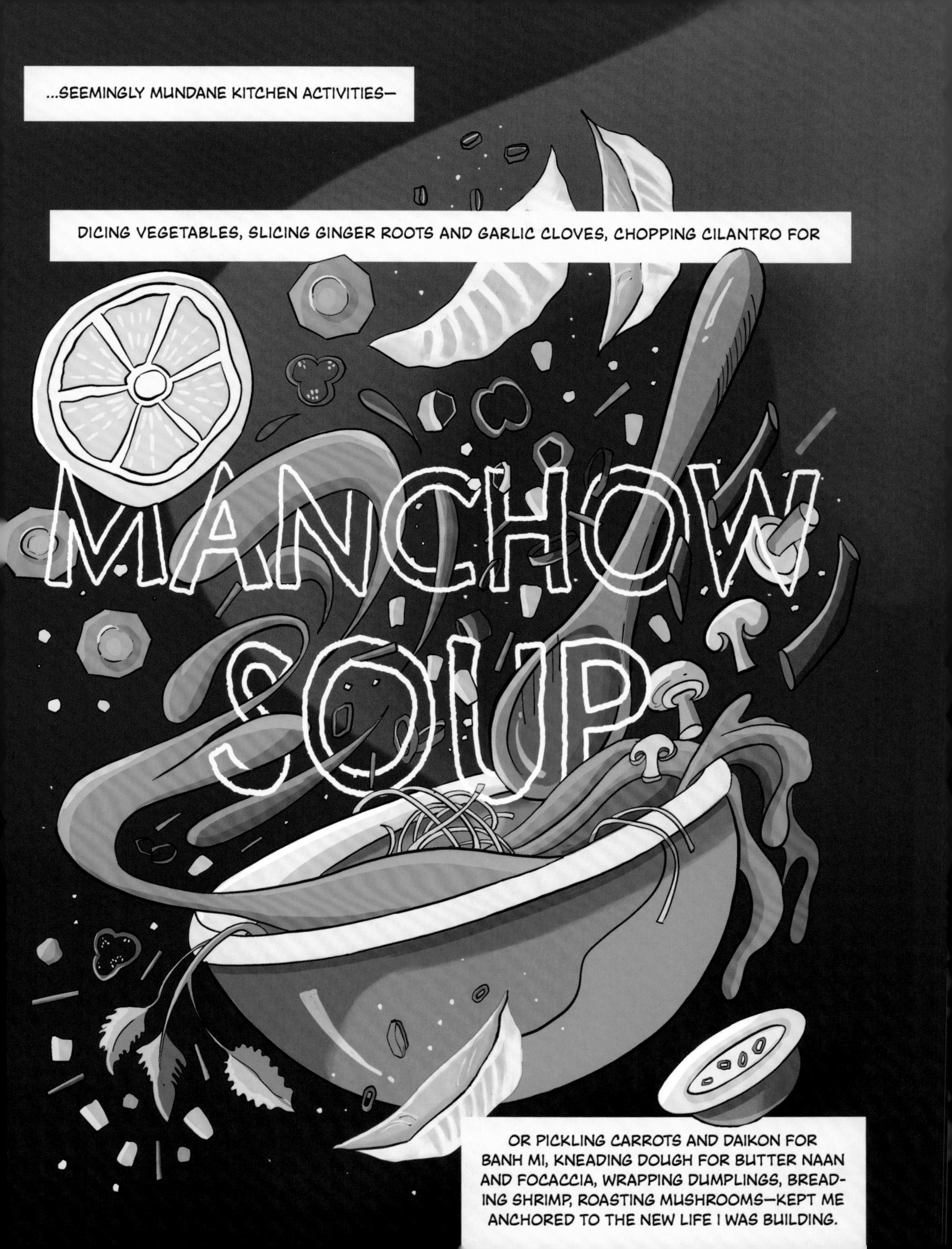
...SEEMINGLY MUNDANE KITCHEN ACTIVITIES—
DICING VEGETABLES, SLICING GINGER ROOTS AND GARLIC CLOVES, CHOPPING CILANTRO FOR
MANCHOW SOUP
OR PICKLING CARROTS AND DAIKON FOR BANH MI, KNEADING DOUGH FOR BUTTER NAAN AND FOCACCIA, WRAPPING DUMPLINGS, BREADING SHRIMP, ROASTING MUSHROOMS—KEPT ME ANCHORED TO THE NEW LIFE I WAS BUILDING.

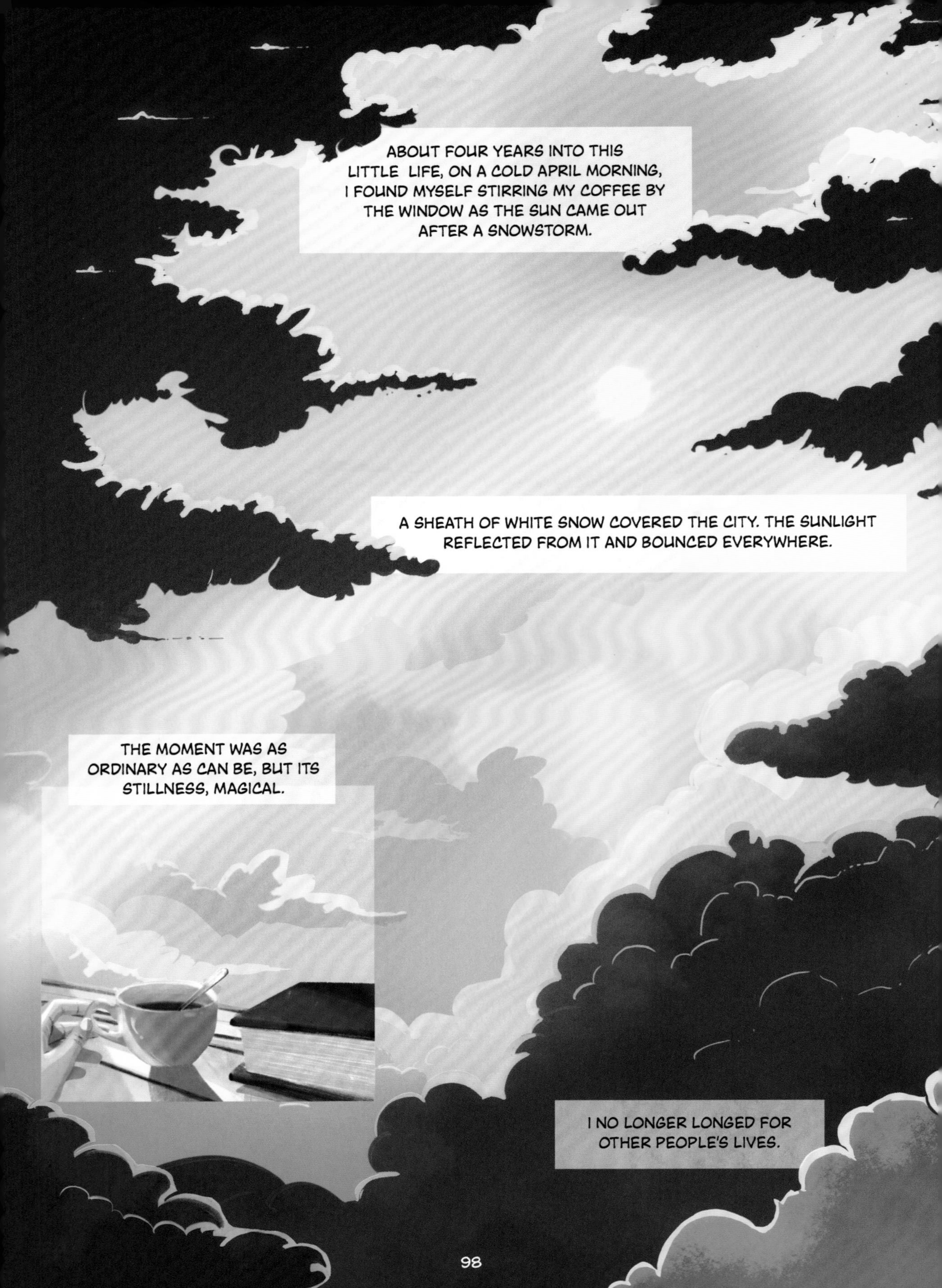
ABOUT FOUR YEARS INTO THIS LITTLE LIFE, ON A COLD APRIL MORNING, I FOUND MYSELF STIRRING MY COFFEE BY THE WINDOW AS THE SUN CAME OUT AFTER A SNOWSTORM.
A SHEATH OF WHITE SNOW COVERED THE CITY. THE SUNLIGHT REFLECTED FROM IT AND BOUNCED EVERYWHERE.
THE MOMENT WAS AS ORDINARY AS CAN BE, BUT ITS STILLNESS, MAGICAL.
I NO LONGER LONGED FOR OTHER PEOPLE'S LIVES.

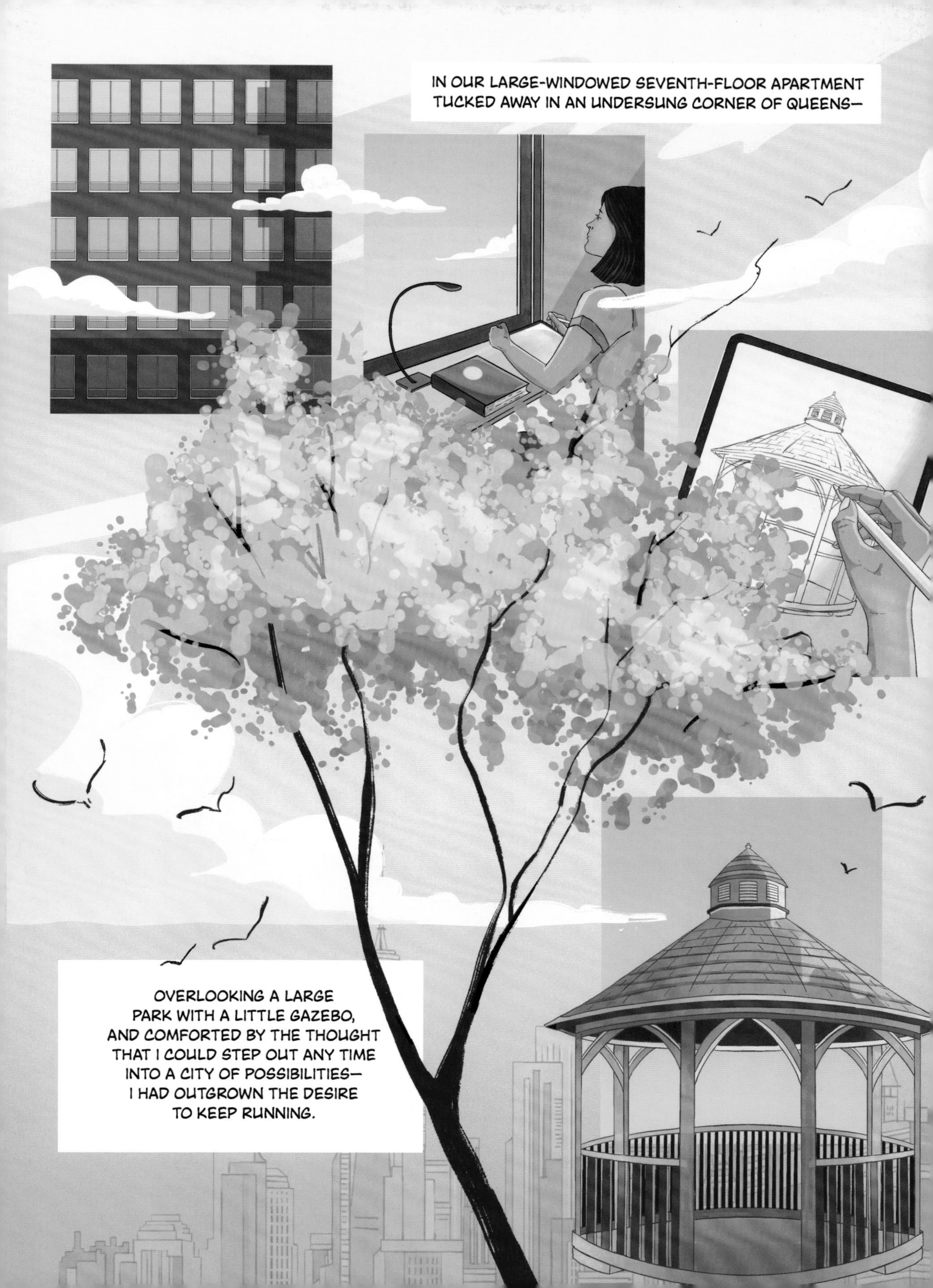
IN OUR LARGE-WINDOWED SEVENTH-FLOOR APARTMENT TUCKED AWAY IN AN UNDERSUNG CORNER OF QUEENS—
OVERLOOKING A LARGE PARK WITH A LITTLE GAZEBO, AND COMFORTED BY THE THOUGHT THAT I COULD STEP OUT ANY TIME INTO A CITY OF POSSIBILITIES— I HAD OUTGROWN THE DESIRE TO KEEP RUNNING.

A ROOM OF ONE'S OWN

in THIS BEAUTIFUL, RIDICULOUS CITY

"This is the city's centripetal force: its power to attract to itself the hungry who hope to make their own stories here and its sometimes-as-fierce will to cast them off."

Joshua Jelly-Schapiro, *Names of New York*

I THINK A LOT ABOUT HOME, BELONGING, AND ITS CONTINGENCIES

IN A FIGURATIVE SENSE, AS AN IMMIGRANT, AND IN A LITERAL SENSE, BECAUSE I HAVE NEVER REALLY HAD A HOME THAT I COULD FULLY CALL MY OWN.

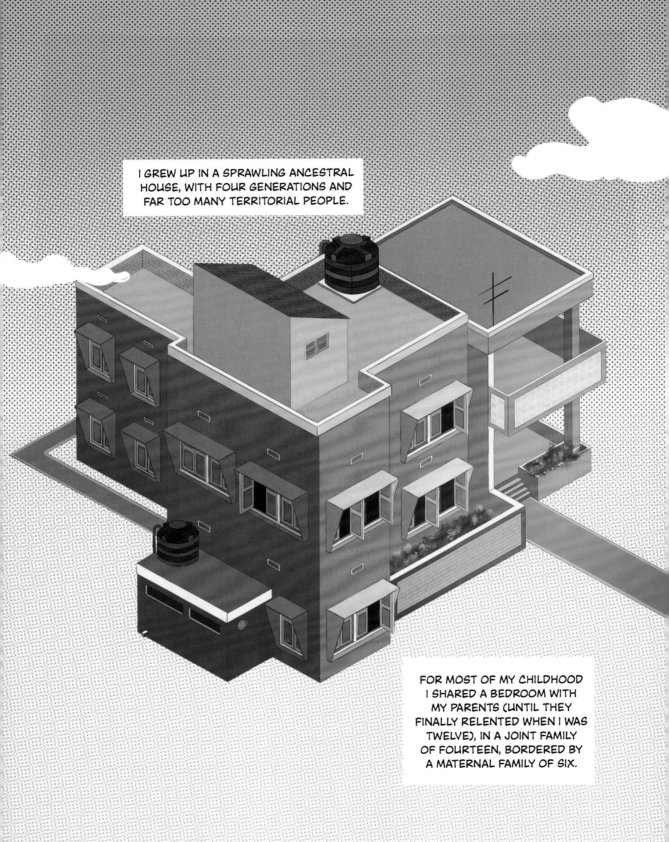

I GREW UP IN A SPRAWLING ANCESTRAL HOUSE, WITH FOUR GENERATIONS AND FAR TOO MANY TERRITORIAL PEOPLE.

FOR MOST OF MY CHILDHOOD I SHARED A BEDROOM WITH MY PARENTS (UNTIL THEY FINALLY RELENTED WHEN I WAS TWELVE), IN A JOINT FAMILY OF FOURTEEN, BORDERED BY A MATERNAL FAMILY OF SIX.

EVEN IN SMALL-TOWN INDIA, IT WAS AN UNUSUAL ARRANGEMENT. THE NINETIES AND NEW-WORLD SENSIBILITIES HAD MADE THE NUCLEAR FAMILY POPULAR. THE JOINT, EXTENDED FAMILY HAD ALREADY BECOME OUTMODED. YET MY FRIENDS, OUR NEIGHBORS, AND OUR RELATIVES FROM OTHER PARTS NEVER MISSED AN OPPORTUNITY TO TELL US HOW LUCKY WE WERE TO HAVE EACH OTHER, OR HOW LUCKY OUR PARENTS WERE TO HAVE CONSIDERABLE HELP IN RAISING CHILDREN.

PERHAPS SO. BUT THERE WAS SO MUCH MORE TO A JOINT FAMILY OF FOURTEEN (PLUS SIX*) THAN WHAT APPEARED ON THE SURFACE. THEY SAY IT TAKES A VILLAGE. WHAT THEY DO NOT SAY IS HOW THE VILLAGE IS RUN ON THE BACKS OF WOMEN WHO GIVE UP THEIR DREAMS TO MAKE SPACE FOR THOSE OF THEIR HUSBANDS, TO RAISE CHILDREN, AND TO CEASELESSLY CATER TO THE NEEDS OF OTHERS.

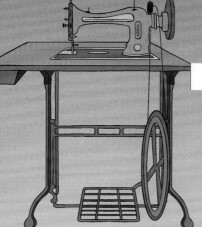

*We lived next door to my mother's maternal home.

MY GRANDMOTHER GAVE UP DRESSMAKING;

MY MOTHER GAVE UP SINGING;

AND MY PATERNAL GRANDMOTHER, ONCE AN OUTDOORSY YOUNG GIRL WHO TAUGHT HERSELF HOW TO SWIM BY CLINGING ON TO AN ABANDONED PITCHER, BECAME COMPLETELY HOMEBOUND AFTER MARRIAGE IN THE SERVICE OF HER IN-LAWS.

I COME FROM A FAMILY OF CREATIVE WOMEN WHO PUT THEIR OWN ARTISTIC PURSUITS AND DREAMS ON PERPETUAL HOLD TO MAKE ROOM FOR THEIR CHILDREN.

But, you may say, we asked you to speak about women and fiction—what has that got to do with a room of her own? I will try to explain. When you asked me to speak about women and fiction I sat down on the banks of a river and began to wonder what the words meant. They might mean simply a few remarks about Fanny Burney; a few more about Jane Austen; a tribute to the Brontës and a sketch of Haworth Parsonage under snow; some witticisms if possible about Miss Mitford; a respectful allusion to George Eliot; a reference to Mrs Gaskell and one would have done. But at second sight the words seemed not so simple. The title women and fiction might mean, and you may have meant it to mean, women and what they are like; or it might mean women and the fiction that they write; or it might mean women and the fiction that is written about them; or it might mean that somehow all three are inextricably mixed together and you want me to consider them in that light. But when I began to consider the subject in this last way, which seemed the most interesting, I soon saw that it had one fatal drawback. I should never be able to come to a conclusion. I should never be able to fulfil what is, I understand, the first duty of a lecturer— to hand you after an hour's discourse a nugget of pure truth to wrap up between the pages of your notebooks and keep on the mantel-piece for ever. All I could do was to offer you an opinion upon one minor point— **a woman must have money and a room of her own if she is to write fiction;** and that, as you will see, leaves the great problem of the true nature of woman and the true nature of fiction unsolved. I have shirked the duty of coming to a conclusion upon these two questions—women and fiction remain, so far as I am concerned, unsolved problems. But in order to make some amends I am going to do what I can to show you how I arrived at this opinion about the room and the money. I am going to develop in your presence as fully and freely as I can the train of thought which led me to think this. Perhaps if I lay bare the ideas, the prejudices, the idiosyncrasies which lie behind this statement you will find that they have some bearing upon women and some upon fiction. At any rate, when a subject is highly controversial—and any question about sex is that—one cannot hope to tell the truth. One can only show how one came to hold whatever opinion one does hold. One can only give one's audience the chance of drawing their own conclusions as they observe the limitations, the prejudices, the idiosyncrasies of the speaker. Fiction here is likely to contain more truth than fact.

IN 1929, THE INIMITABLE VIRGINIA WOOLF WROTE:

AS I GET TO PURSUE MY DREAMS OF BECOMING A WRITER, ALBEIT PRECARIOUSLY, FROM MY 550-SQUARE-FOOT RENTAL IN QUEENS, I THINK ABOUT THE THREE GENERATIONS OF WOMEN STUCK IN SPACES NEVER ENTIRELY THEIR OWN, IN A COUNTRY THAT IS CONTINGENT ON THE INVISIBLE LABOR OF MILLIONS OF WOMEN, MANY WITHOUT A ROOF OVER THEIR HEADS, MUCH LESS **A ROOM OF THEIR OWN.**

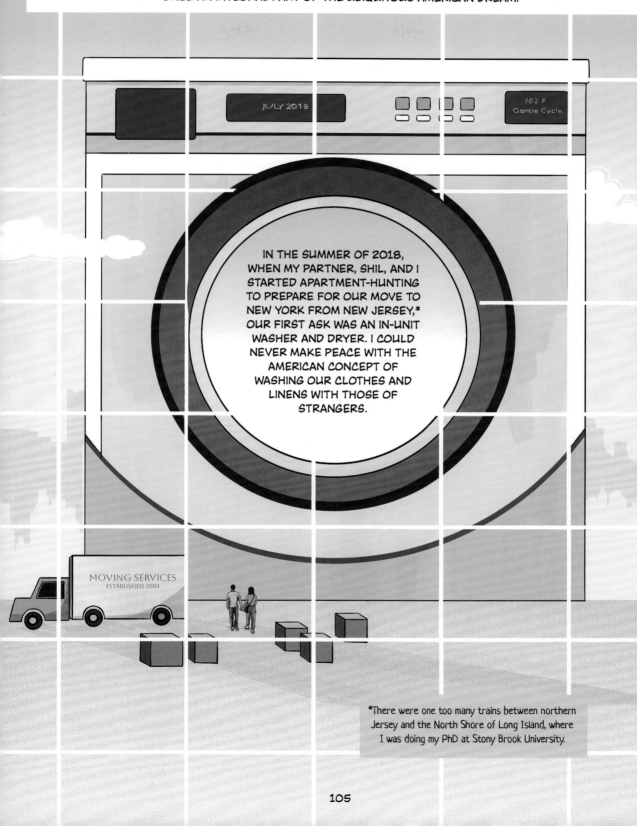

TODAY, IN NEW YORK, EVEN AS THE NUMBER OF SINGLE WOMEN WHO ARE HOMEOWNERS RISES IN THE UNITED STATES, MANY, ESPECIALLY THOSE WHO ARE LOWER-INCOME, QUEER, IMMIGRANT, OR DISABLED, GET LEFT BEHIND BY THE CITY'S UNEQUAL POLICIES AND PRICED OUT OF HOUSING, A BASIC RIGHT AND ONCE AN INTEGRAL PART OF THE UBIQUITOUS AMERICAN DREAM.

JULY 2018

102 F
Gentle Cycle

IN THE SUMMER OF 2018, WHEN MY PARTNER, SHIL, AND I STARTED APARTMENT-HUNTING TO PREPARE FOR OUR MOVE TO NEW YORK FROM NEW JERSEY,* OUR FIRST ASK WAS AN IN-UNIT WASHER AND DRYER. I COULD NEVER MAKE PEACE WITH THE AMERICAN CONCEPT OF WASHING OUR CLOTHES AND LINENS WITH THOSE OF STRANGERS.

MOVING SERVICES
ESTABLISHED 2003

*There were one too many trains between northern Jersey and the North Shore of Long Island, where I was doing my PhD at Stony Brook University.

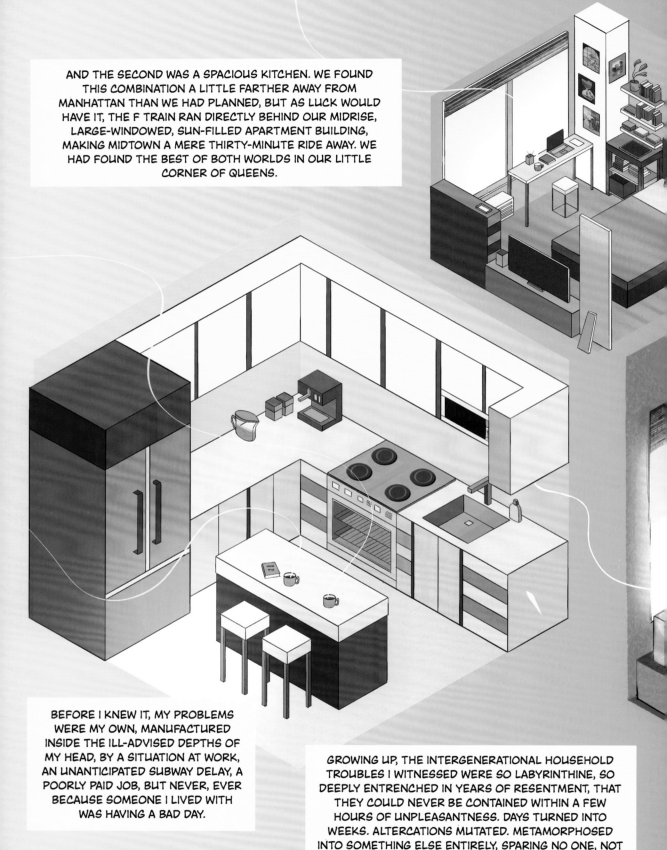

AND THE SECOND WAS A SPACIOUS KITCHEN. WE FOUND THIS COMBINATION A LITTLE FARTHER AWAY FROM MANHATTAN THAN WE HAD PLANNED, BUT AS LUCK WOULD HAVE IT, THE F TRAIN RAN DIRECTLY BEHIND OUR MIDRISE, LARGE-WINDOWED, SUN-FILLED APARTMENT BUILDING, MAKING MIDTOWN A MERE THIRTY-MINUTE RIDE AWAY. WE HAD FOUND THE BEST OF BOTH WORLDS IN OUR LITTLE CORNER OF QUEENS.

BEFORE I KNEW IT, MY PROBLEMS WERE MY OWN, MANUFACTURED INSIDE THE ILL-ADVISED DEPTHS OF MY HEAD, BY A SITUATION AT WORK, AN UNANTICIPATED SUBWAY DELAY, A POORLY PAID JOB, BUT NEVER, EVER BECAUSE SOMEONE I LIVED WITH WAS HAVING A BAD DAY.

GROWING UP, THE INTERGENERATIONAL HOUSEHOLD TROUBLES I WITNESSED WERE SO LABYRINTHINE, SO DEEPLY ENTRENCHED IN YEARS OF RESENTMENT, THAT THEY COULD NEVER BE CONTAINED WITHIN A FEW HOURS OF UNPLEASANTNESS. DAYS TURNED INTO WEEKS. ALTERCATIONS MUTATED. METAMORPHOSED INTO SOMETHING ELSE ENTIRELY, SPARING NO ONE, NOT EVEN MERE SPECTATORS.

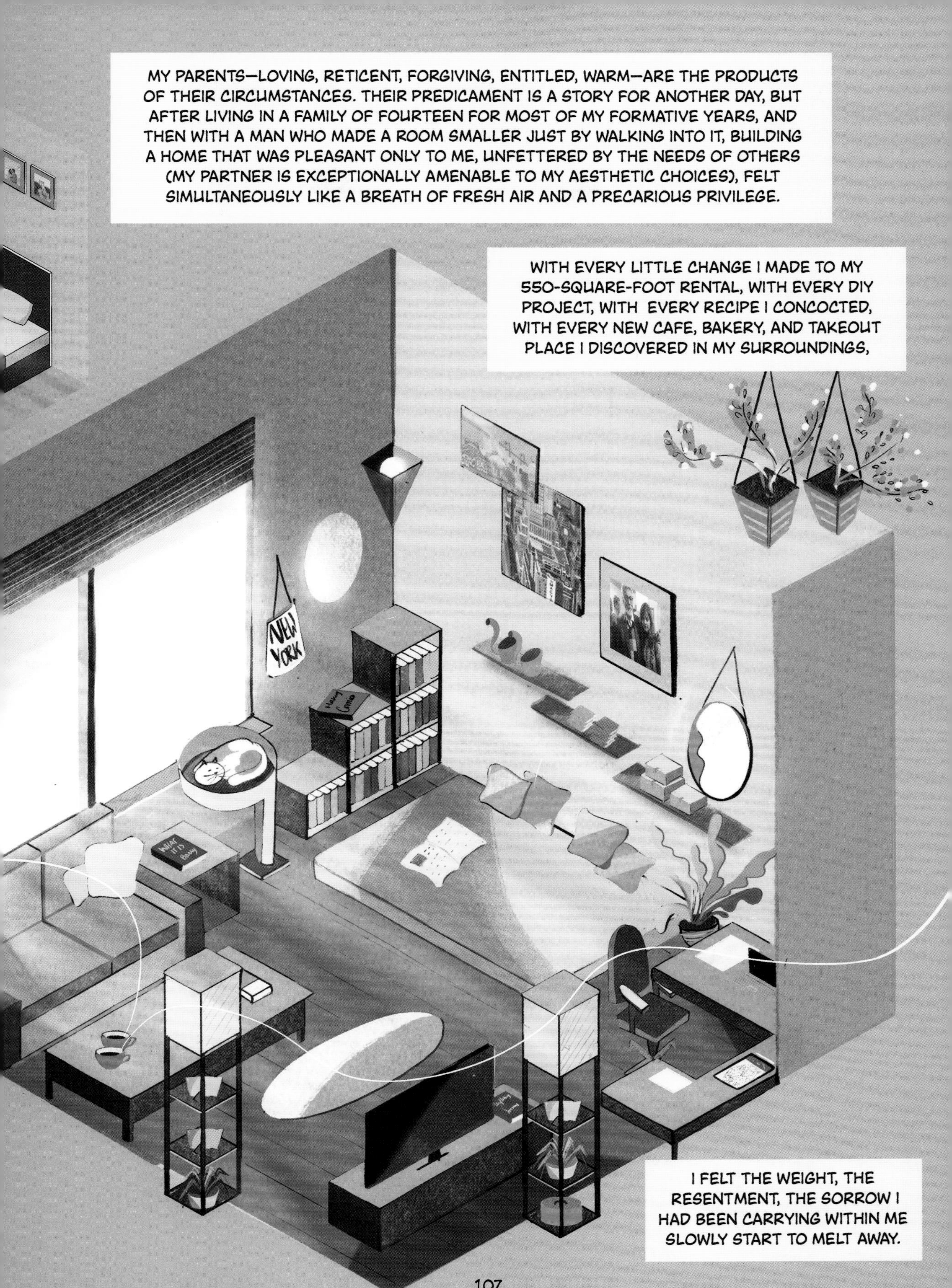
MY PARENTS—LOVING, RETICENT, FORGIVING, ENTITLED, WARM—ARE THE PRODUCTS OF THEIR CIRCUMSTANCES. THEIR PREDICAMENT IS A STORY FOR ANOTHER DAY, BUT AFTER LIVING IN A FAMILY OF FOURTEEN FOR MOST OF MY FORMATIVE YEARS, AND THEN WITH A MAN WHO MADE A ROOM SMALLER JUST BY WALKING INTO IT, BUILDING A HOME THAT WAS PLEASANT ONLY TO ME, UNFETTERED BY THE NEEDS OF OTHERS (MY PARTNER IS EXCEPTIONALLY AMENABLE TO MY AESTHETIC CHOICES), FELT SIMULTANEOUSLY LIKE A BREATH OF FRESH AIR AND A PRECARIOUS PRIVILEGE.
WITH EVERY LITTLE CHANGE I MADE TO MY 550-SQUARE-FOOT RENTAL, WITH EVERY DIY PROJECT, WITH EVERY RECIPE I CONCOCTED, WITH EVERY NEW CAFE, BAKERY, AND TAKEOUT PLACE I DISCOVERED IN MY SURROUNDINGS,
NEW YORK
I FELT THE WEIGHT, THE RESENTMENT, THE SORROW I HAD BEEN CARRYING WITHIN ME SLOWLY START TO MELT AWAY.

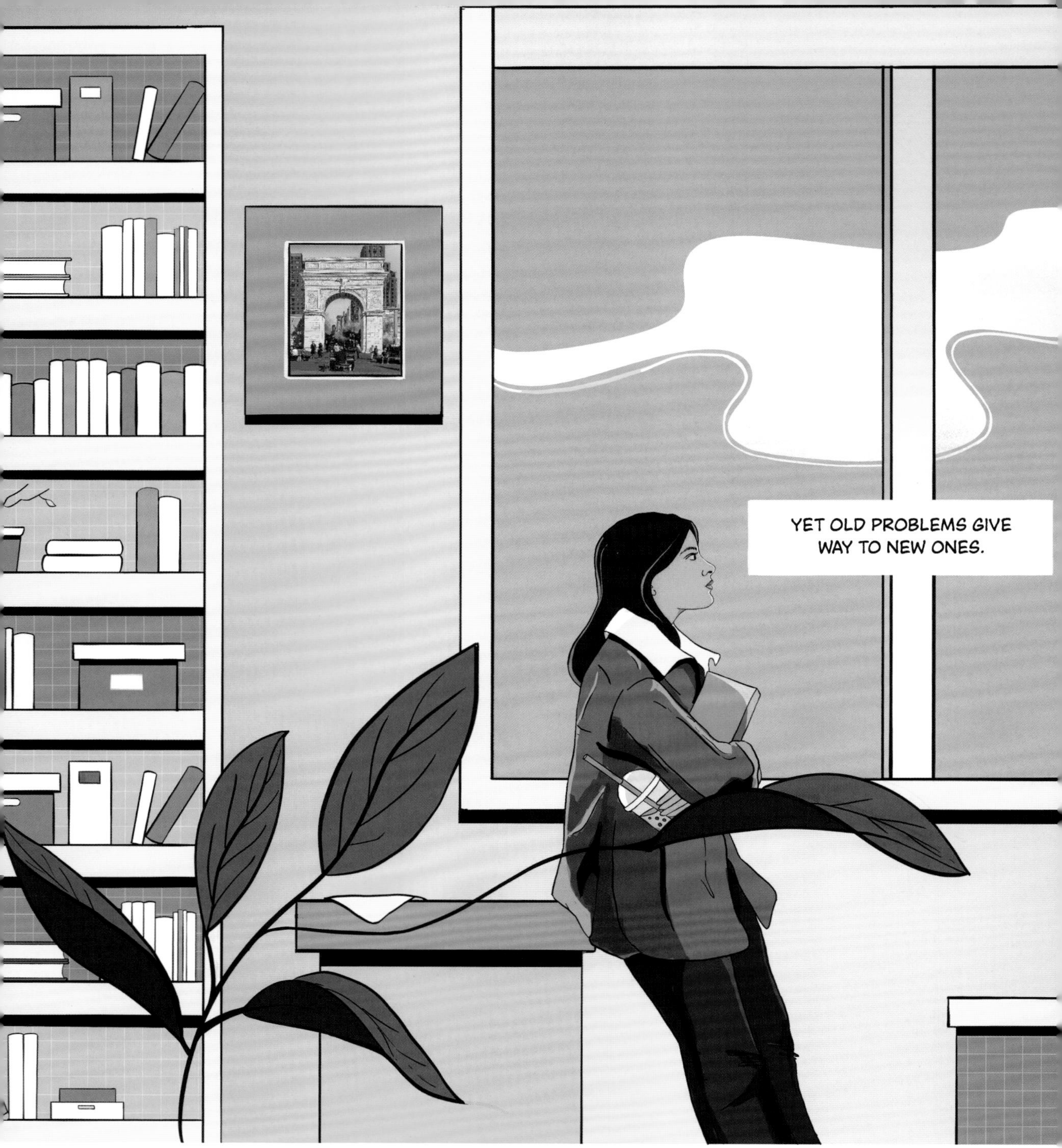
YET OLD PROBLEMS GIVE WAY TO NEW ONES.

IN MY SIX YEARS IN THIS NEIGHBORHOOD IN QUEENS, I HAVE WATCHED IT GENTRIFY, LUXURY CONDOS SHOOT UP SKYWARD, BOBA TEA CAFES (WHICH I ADMITTEDLY LOVE VERY MUCH) POP UP ON EVERY BLOCK, AND THE SKYLINE CHANGE. I HAVE SEEN, FROM MY WINDOW, MULTIPLE SINGLE-FAMILY HOMES GET DEMOLISHED TO MAKE ROOM FOR A LUXURY BUILDING WITH 220 APARTMENTS, ALL RENTAL, NONE FOR OWNERSHIP.

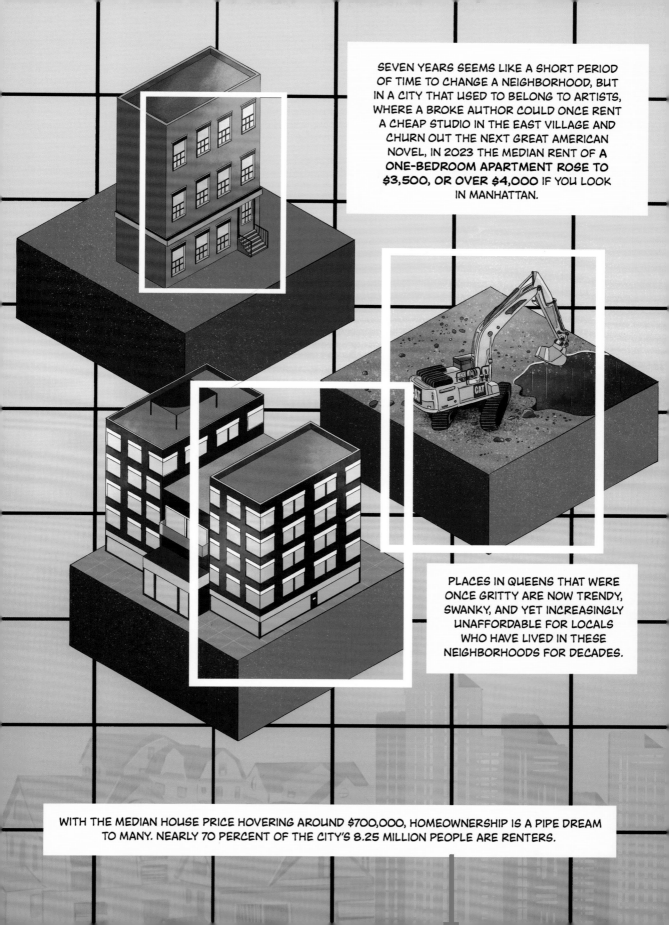

SEVEN YEARS SEEMS LIKE A SHORT PERIOD OF TIME TO CHANGE A NEIGHBORHOOD, BUT IN A CITY THAT USED TO BELONG TO ARTISTS, WHERE A BROKE AUTHOR COULD ONCE RENT A CHEAP STUDIO IN THE EAST VILLAGE AND CHURN OUT THE NEXT GREAT AMERICAN NOVEL, IN 2023 THE MEDIAN RENT OF A ONE-BEDROOM APARTMENT ROSE TO $3,500, OR OVER $4,000 IF YOU LOOK IN MANHATTAN.

PLACES IN QUEENS THAT WERE ONCE GRITTY ARE NOW TRENDY, SWANKY, AND YET INCREASINGLY UNAFFORDABLE FOR LOCALS WHO HAVE LIVED IN THESE NEIGHBORHOODS FOR DECADES.

WITH THE MEDIAN HOUSE PRICE HOVERING AROUND $700,000, HOMEOWNERSHIP IS A PIPE DREAM TO MANY. NEARLY 70 PERCENT OF THE CITY'S 8.25 MILLION PEOPLE ARE RENTERS.

A 2023 REPORT BY THE ATTORNEY GENERAL OF NEW YORK, LETITIA JAMES, REVEALED THAT NOT ONLY DO PEOPLE OF COLOR HAVE LOWER RATES OF HOMEOWNERSHIP ACROSS THE STATE, THEY ALSO ARE MORE LIKELY TO BE DENIED LOANS AND MORTGAGES, IRRESPECTIVE OF CREDIT SCORE AND INCOME.

REZONINGS DISPROPORTIONATELY DISPLACE BLACK AND BROWN RESIDENTS. AMONG WOMEN, LACK OF ACCESS TO STABLE HOUSING INCREASES THEIR RISK OF DOMESTIC AND INTIMATE PARTNER VIOLENCE. YET THOUSANDS OF RENT-STABILIZED APARTMENTS REMAIN VACANT DUE TO BARRIERS PERTAINING TO REPAIRS AND POLICY FAILURES.

Percentage of statewide owner-occupied units
70
60
50
40
30
20
10
0
ASIAN
BLACK
LATINO
OTHER
WHITE
POC

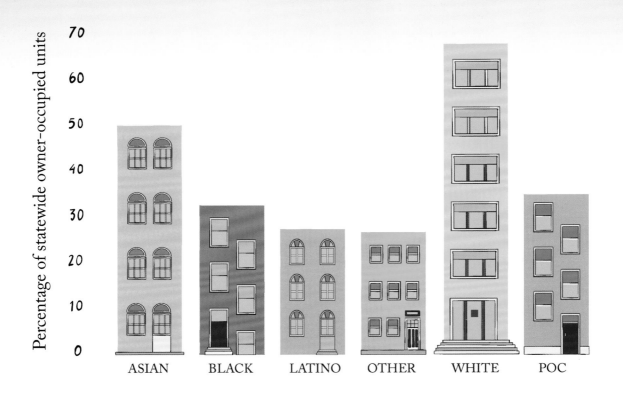

AS RECENTLY AS 2023, FOUR THOUSAND PEOPLE SLEEP ON THE STREETS EVERY NIGHT, AND OVER A HUNDRED THOUSAND EXPERIENCE HOMELESSNESS IN A GIVEN YEAR.

THE HOUSING SITUATION IN NEW YORK, ALWAYS TEETERING ON THE BRINK OF AN EMERGENCY, HAS ESCALATED TO A FULL-BLOWN CRISIS OF LATE IN THE WAKE OF HIGH RENTS, RISING INTEREST RATES, AND CLIMATE-CHANGE-RELATED WEATHER EVENTS THAT DISPROPORTIONATELY AFFECT LOWER-INCOME NEIGHBORHOODS.

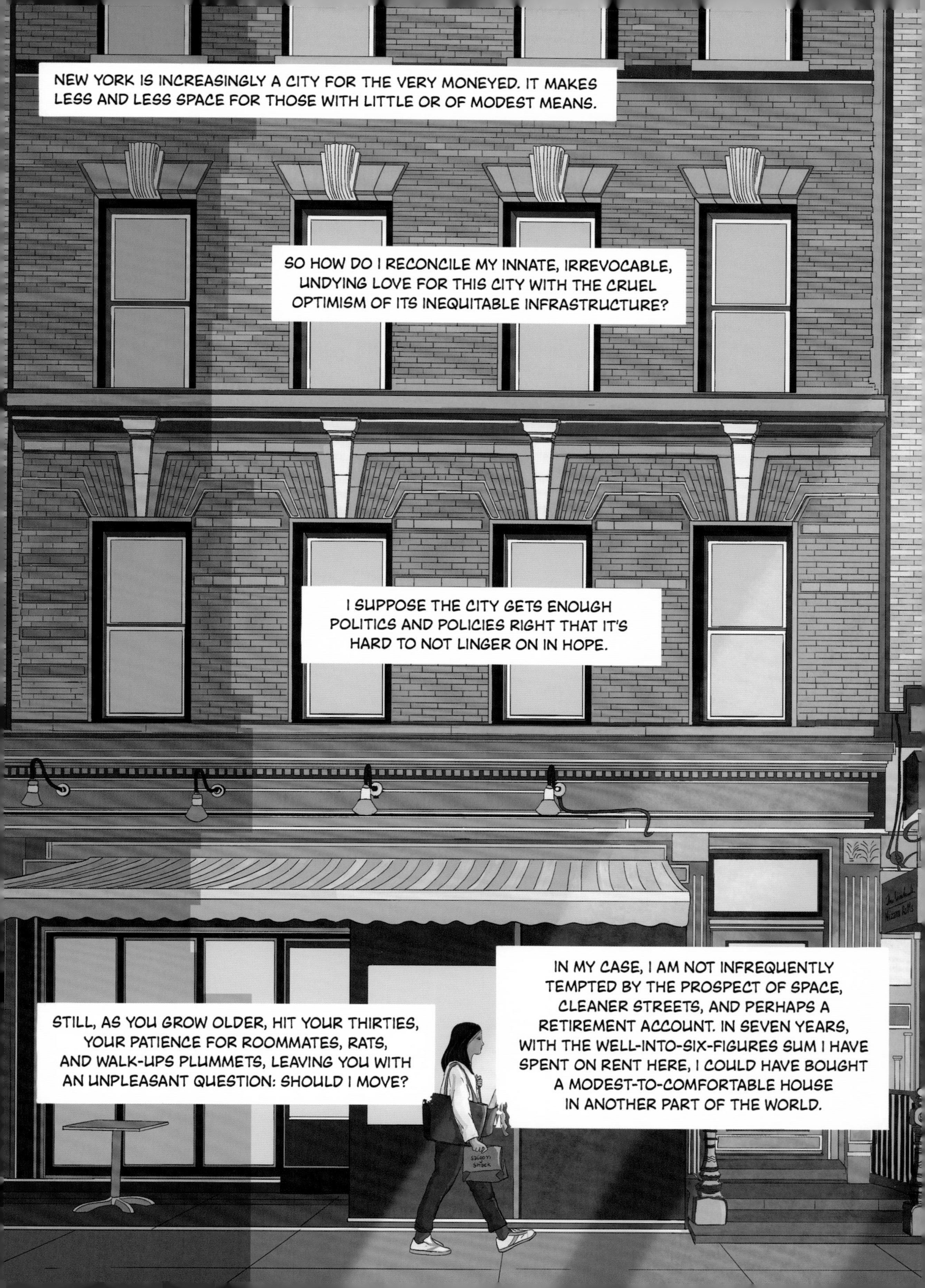
NEW YORK IS INCREASINGLY A CITY FOR THE VERY MONEYED. IT MAKES LESS AND LESS SPACE FOR THOSE WITH LITTLE OR OF MODEST MEANS.
SO HOW DO I RECONCILE MY INNATE, IRREVOCABLE, UNDYING LOVE FOR THIS CITY WITH THE CRUEL OPTIMISM OF ITS INEQUITABLE INFRASTRUCTURE?
I SUPPOSE THE CITY GETS ENOUGH POLITICS AND POLICIES RIGHT THAT IT'S HARD TO NOT LINGER ON IN HOPE.
STILL, AS YOU GROW OLDER, HIT YOUR THIRTIES, YOUR PATIENCE FOR ROOMMATES, RATS, AND WALK-UPS PLUMMETS, LEAVING YOU WITH AN UNPLEASANT QUESTION: SHOULD I MOVE?
IN MY CASE, I AM NOT INFREQUENTLY TEMPTED BY THE PROSPECT OF SPACE, CLEANER STREETS, AND PERHAPS A RETIREMENT ACCOUNT. IN SEVEN YEARS, WITH THE WELL-INTO-SIX-FIGURES SUM I HAVE SPENT ON RENT HERE, I COULD HAVE BOUGHT A MODEST-TO-COMFORTABLE HOUSE IN ANOTHER PART OF THE WORLD.
saigon shack

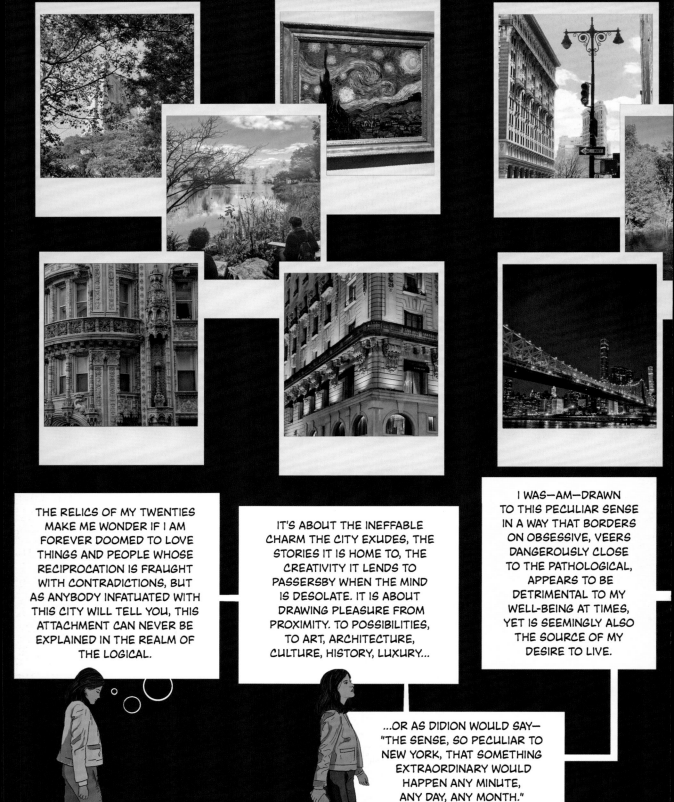

THE RELICS OF MY TWENTIES MAKE ME WONDER IF I AM FOREVER DOOMED TO LOVE THINGS AND PEOPLE WHOSE RECIPROCATION IS FRAUGHT WITH CONTRADICTIONS, BUT AS ANYBODY INFATUATED WITH THIS CITY WILL TELL YOU, THIS ATTACHMENT CAN NEVER BE EXPLAINED IN THE REALM OF THE LOGICAL.

IT'S ABOUT THE INEFFABLE CHARM THE CITY EXUDES, THE STORIES IT IS HOME TO, THE CREATIVITY IT LENDS TO PASSERSBY WHEN THE MIND IS DESOLATE. IT IS ABOUT DRAWING PLEASURE FROM PROXIMITY. TO POSSIBILITIES, TO ART, ARCHITECTURE, CULTURE, HISTORY, LUXURY...

I WAS—AM—DRAWN TO THIS PECULIAR SENSE IN A WAY THAT BORDERS ON OBSESSIVE, VEERS DANGEROUSLY CLOSE TO THE PATHOLOGICAL, APPEARS TO BE DETRIMENTAL TO MY WELL-BEING AT TIMES, YET IS SEEMINGLY ALSO THE SOURCE OF MY DESIRE TO LIVE.

...OR AS DIDION WOULD SAY— "THE SENSE, SO PECULIAR TO NEW YORK, THAT SOMETHING EXTRAORDINARY WOULD HAPPEN ANY MINUTE, ANY DAY, ANY MONTH."

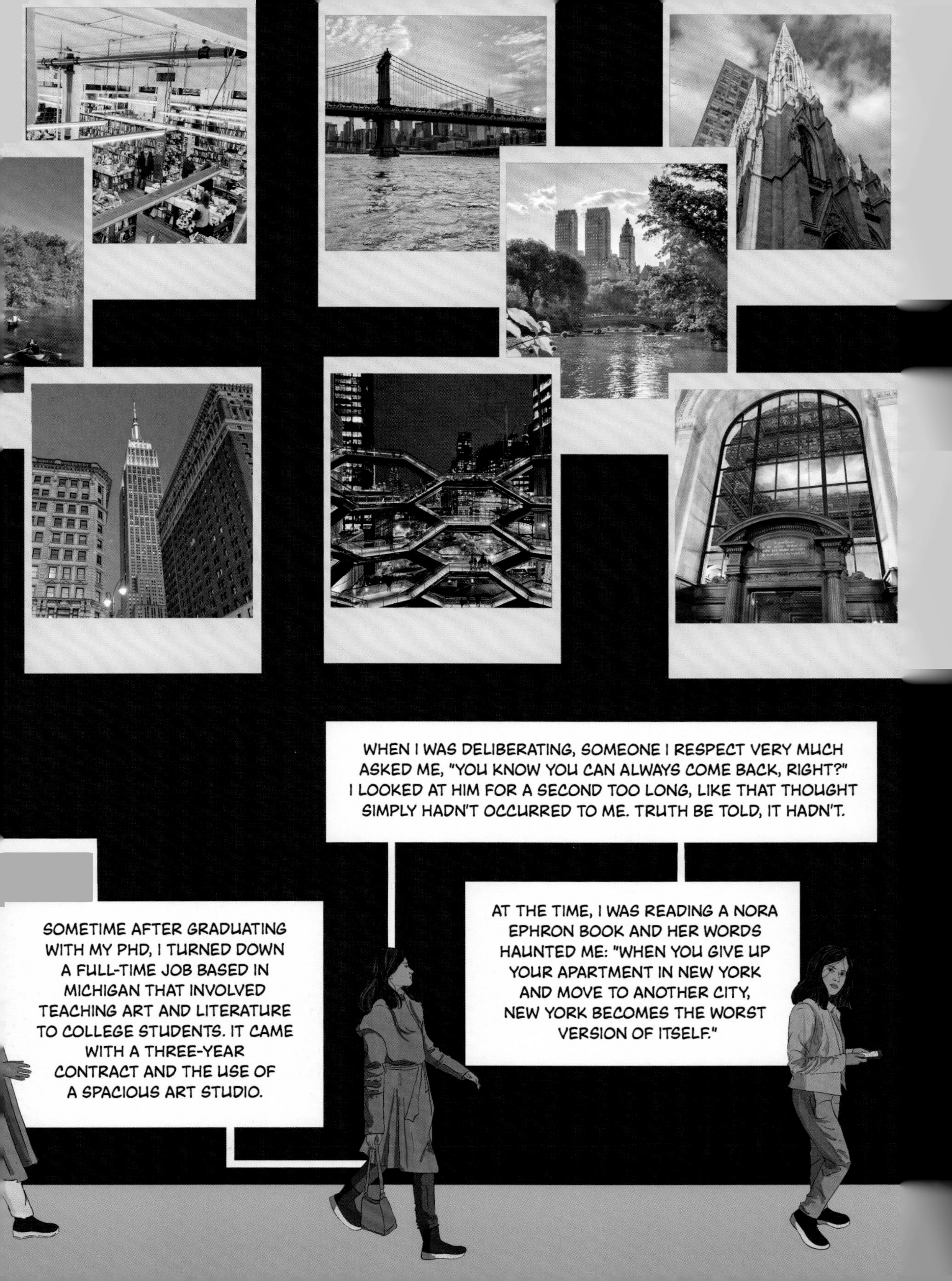

WHEN I WAS DELIBERATING, SOMEONE I RESPECT VERY MUCH ASKED ME, "YOU KNOW YOU CAN ALWAYS COME BACK, RIGHT?" I LOOKED AT HIM FOR A SECOND TOO LONG, LIKE THAT THOUGHT SIMPLY HADN'T OCCURRED TO ME. TRUTH BE TOLD, IT HADN'T.
SOMETIME AFTER GRADUATING WITH MY PHD, I TURNED DOWN A FULL-TIME JOB BASED IN MICHIGAN THAT INVOLVED TEACHING ART AND LITERATURE TO COLLEGE STUDENTS. IT CAME WITH A THREE-YEAR CONTRACT AND THE USE OF A SPACIOUS ART STUDIO.
AT THE TIME, I WAS READING A NORA EPHRON BOOK AND HER WORDS HAUNTED ME: "WHEN YOU GIVE UP YOUR APARTMENT IN NEW YORK AND MOVE TO ANOTHER CITY, NEW YORK BECOMES THE WORST VERSION OF ITSELF."

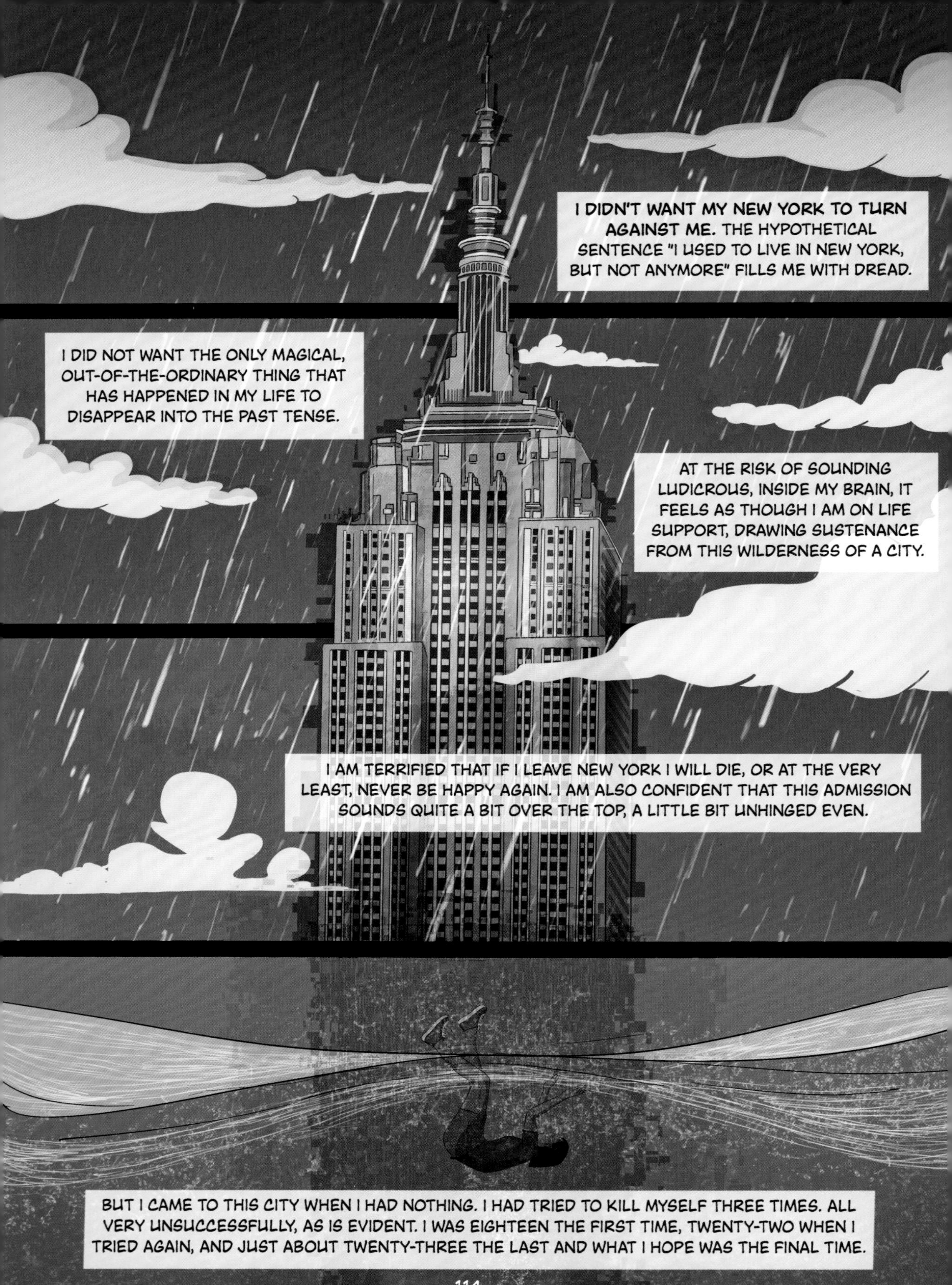
I DIDN'T WANT MY NEW YORK TO TURN AGAINST ME. THE HYPOTHETICAL SENTENCE "I USED TO LIVE IN NEW YORK, BUT NOT ANYMORE" FILLS ME WITH DREAD.
I DID NOT WANT THE ONLY MAGICAL, OUT-OF-THE-ORDINARY THING THAT HAS HAPPENED IN MY LIFE TO DISAPPEAR INTO THE PAST TENSE.
AT THE RISK OF SOUNDING LUDICROUS, INSIDE MY BRAIN, IT FEELS AS THOUGH I AM ON LIFE SUPPORT, DRAWING SUSTENANCE FROM THIS WILDERNESS OF A CITY.
I AM TERRIFIED THAT IF I LEAVE NEW YORK I WILL DIE, OR AT THE VERY LEAST, NEVER BE HAPPY AGAIN. I AM ALSO CONFIDENT THAT THIS ADMISSION SOUNDS QUITE A BIT OVER THE TOP, A LITTLE BIT UNHINGED EVEN.
BUT I CAME TO THIS CITY WHEN I HAD NOTHING. I HAD TRIED TO KILL MYSELF THREE TIMES. ALL VERY UNSUCCESSFULLY, AS IS EVIDENT. I WAS EIGHTEEN THE FIRST TIME, TWENTY-TWO WHEN I TRIED AGAIN, AND JUST ABOUT TWENTY-THREE THE LAST AND WHAT I HOPE WAS THE FINAL TIME.

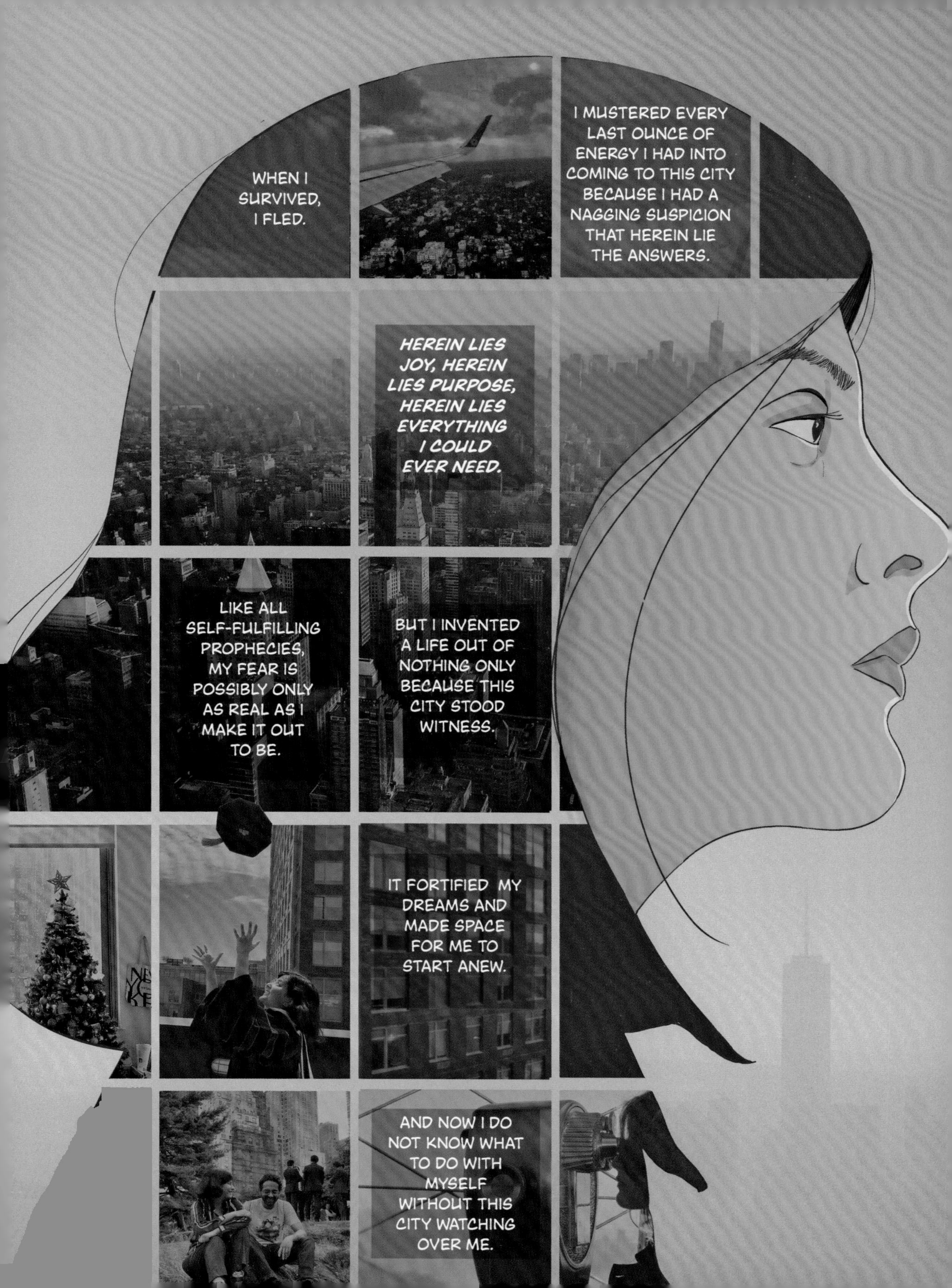
WHEN I SURVIVED, I FLED.
I MUSTERED EVERY LAST OUNCE OF ENERGY I HAD INTO COMING TO THIS CITY BECAUSE I HAD A NAGGING SUSPICION THAT HEREIN LIE THE ANSWERS.
HEREIN LIES JOY, HEREIN LIES PURPOSE, HEREIN LIES EVERYTHING I COULD EVER NEED.
LIKE ALL SELF-FULFILLING PROPHECIES, MY FEAR IS POSSIBLY ONLY AS REAL AS I MAKE IT OUT TO BE.
BUT I INVENTED A LIFE OUT OF NOTHING ONLY BECAUSE THIS CITY STOOD WITNESS.
IT FORTIFIED MY DREAMS AND MADE SPACE FOR ME TO START ANEW.
AND NOW I DO NOT KNOW WHAT TO DO WITH MYSELF WITHOUT THIS CITY WATCHING OVER ME.

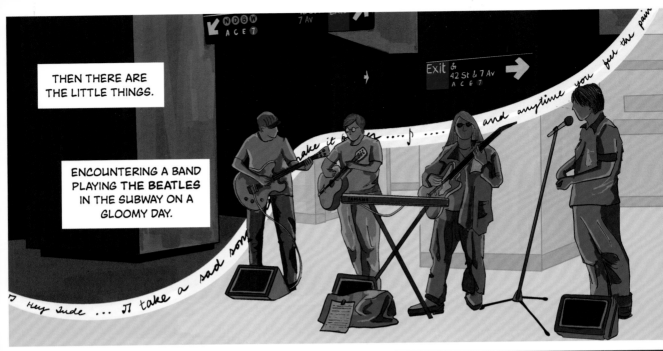

THEN THERE ARE THE LITTLE THINGS.
ENCOUNTERING A BAND PLAYING THE BEATLES IN THE SUBWAY ON A GLOOMY DAY.
N Q R W
A C E 7
7 Av
Exit 42 St & 7 Av A C E 7
Hey Jude ... take a sad son
ake it b
.... and anytime you feel the pain
YAMAHA
THIS MIDTOWN SIGN ON THE WALL OF
THE COMMUNITY CHURCH OF NEW YORK
KNOWING NOT SECT CLASS NATION OR RACE WELCOMES EACH TO THE SERVICE OF ALL
THAT ONE TILE ON THE SIDEWALK
IT'S JUST LOVE
NEAR THE TRADER JOE'S AT CHELSEA.
THE FACT THAT PEOPLE WAIT IN LINES FOR VAN LEEUWEN ACROSS THE STREET FROM ADEL'S HALAL CART.
ADEL'S FAMOUS
NEW YORK CITY'S BEST HALAL FOOD
ONE WAY
VanLeeuwen
VanLeeuwen

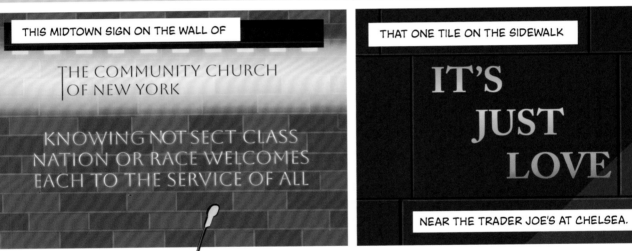

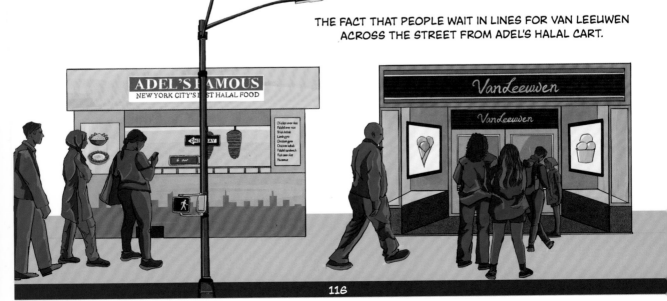

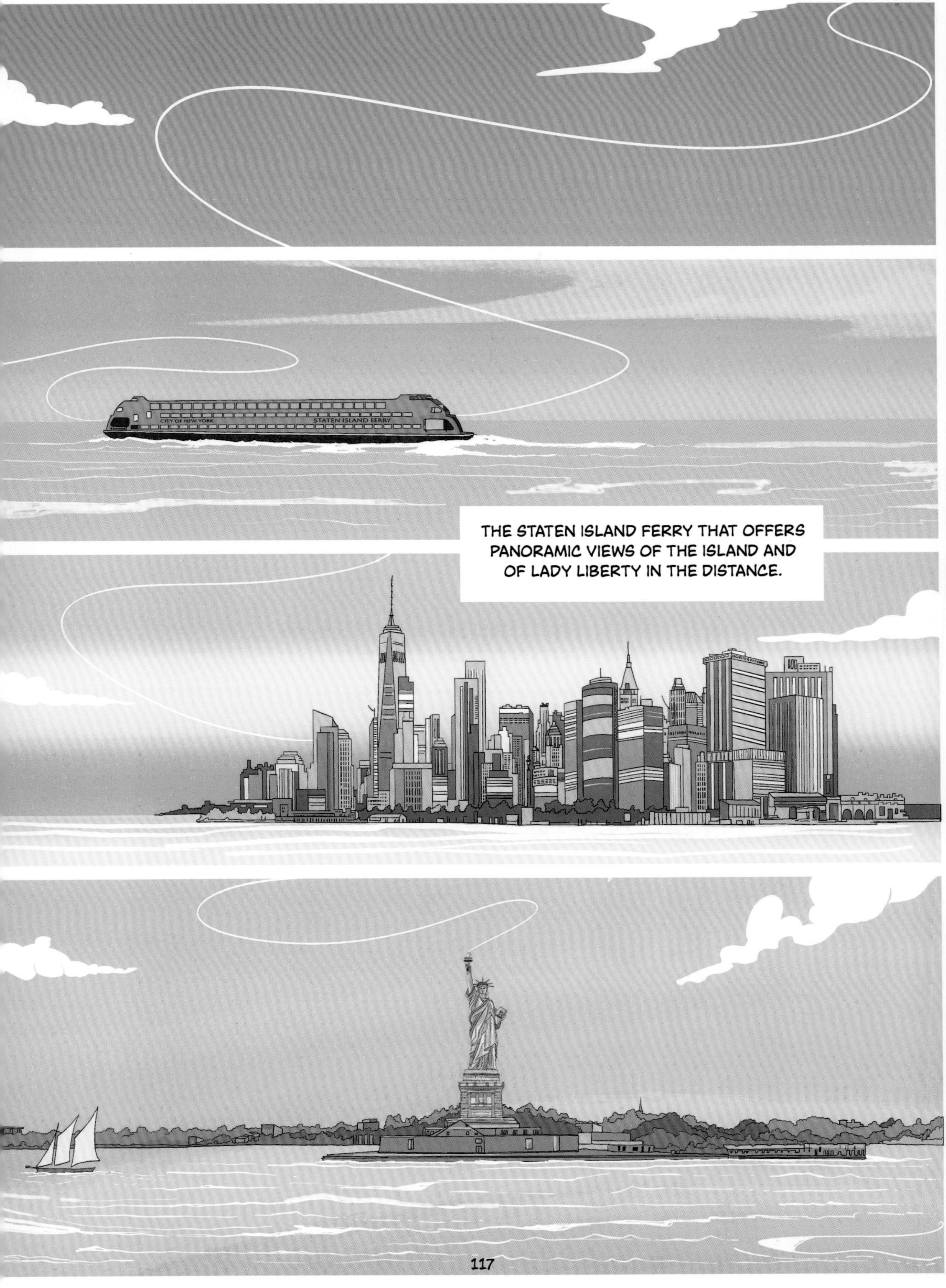
CITY OF NEW YORK
STATEN ISLAND FERRY
THE STATEN ISLAND FERRY THAT OFFERS PANORAMIC VIEWS OF THE ISLAND AND OF LADY LIBERTY IN THE DISTANCE.

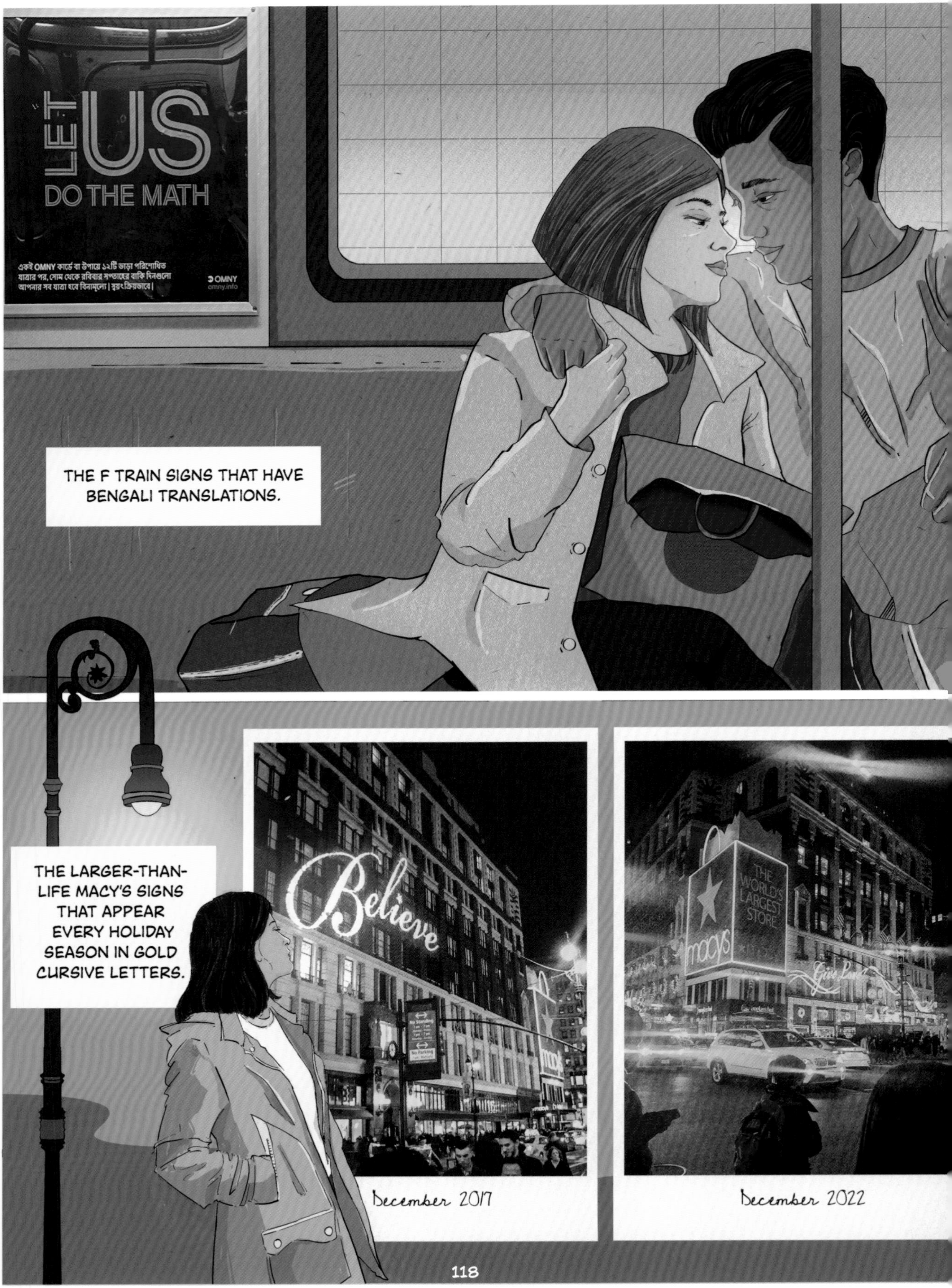
LET US
DO THE MATH
একই OMNY কার্ডে বা উপায়ে ১২টি ভাড়া পরিশোধিত যাত্রার পর, সোম থেকে রবিবার সপ্তাহের বাকি দিনগুলো আপনার সব যাত্রা হবে বিনামূল্যে। স্বয়ংক্রিয়ভাবে।
OMNY
omny.info
THE F TRAIN SIGNS THAT HAVE BENGALI TRANSLATIONS.
THE LARGER-THAN-LIFE MACY'S SIGNS THAT APPEAR EVERY HOLIDAY SEASON IN GOLD CURSIVE LETTERS.
Believe
December 2017
THE WORLD'S LARGEST STORE
macys
December 2022

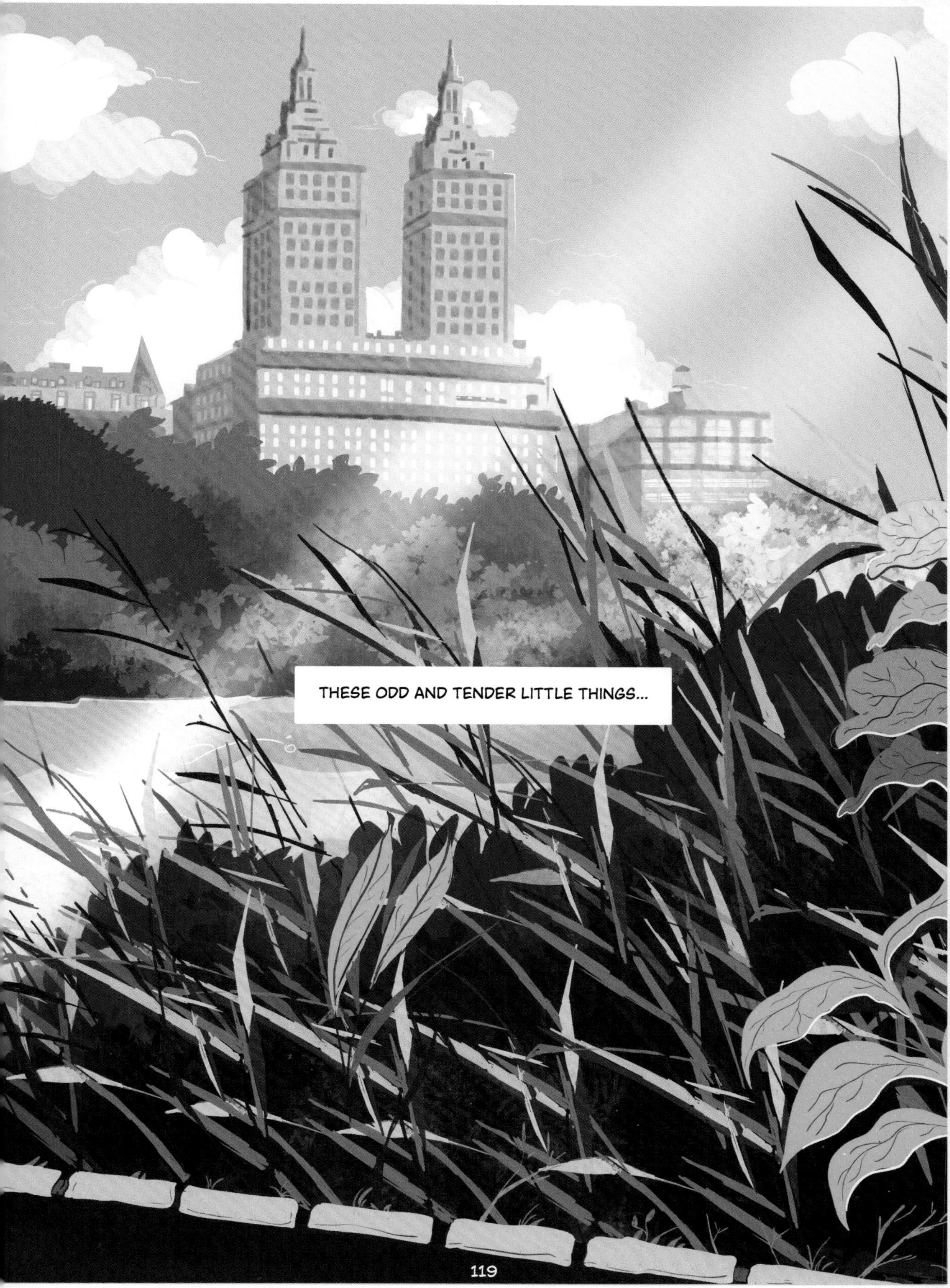
THESE ODD AND TENDER LITTLE THINGS...

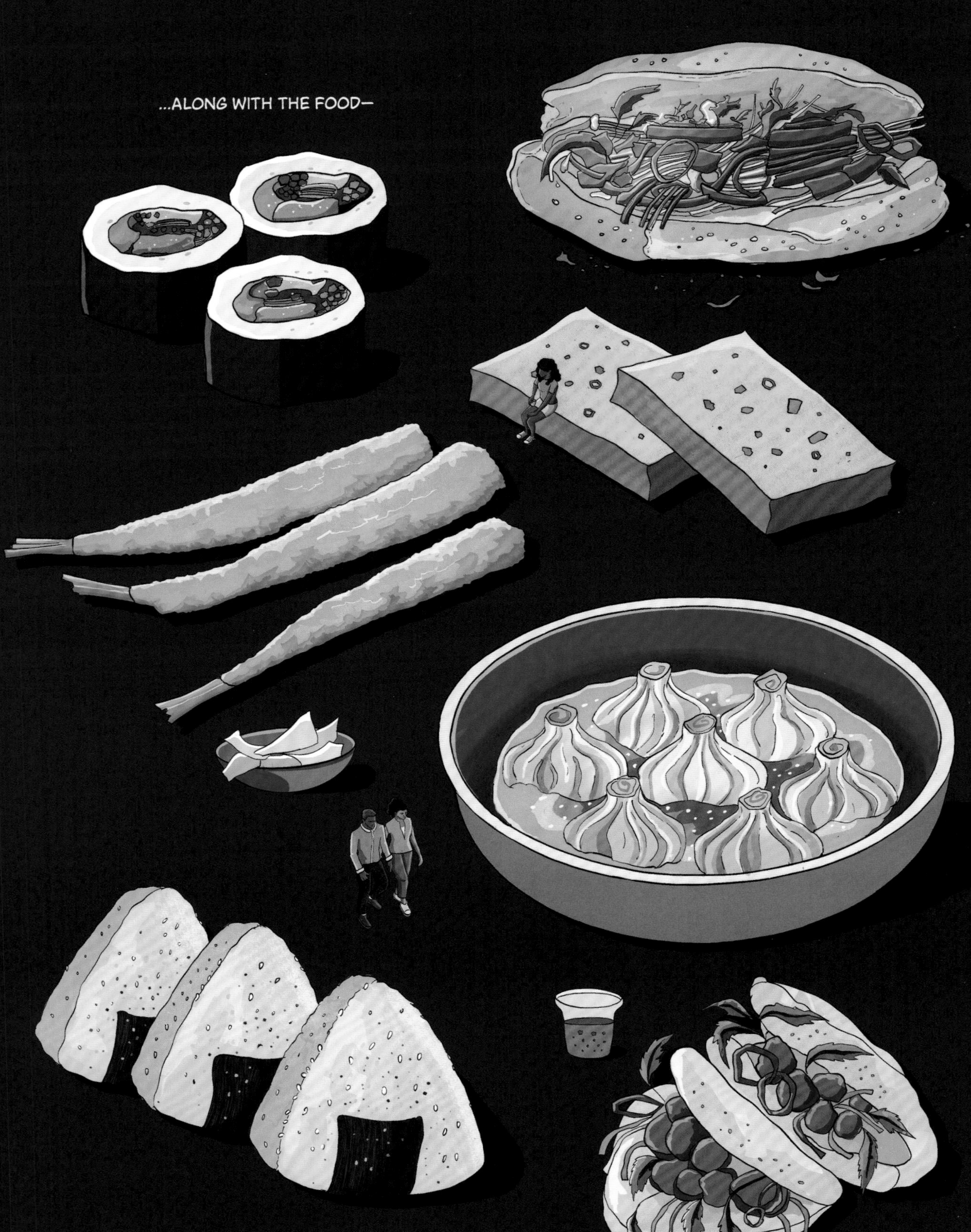
...ALONG WITH THE FOOD—

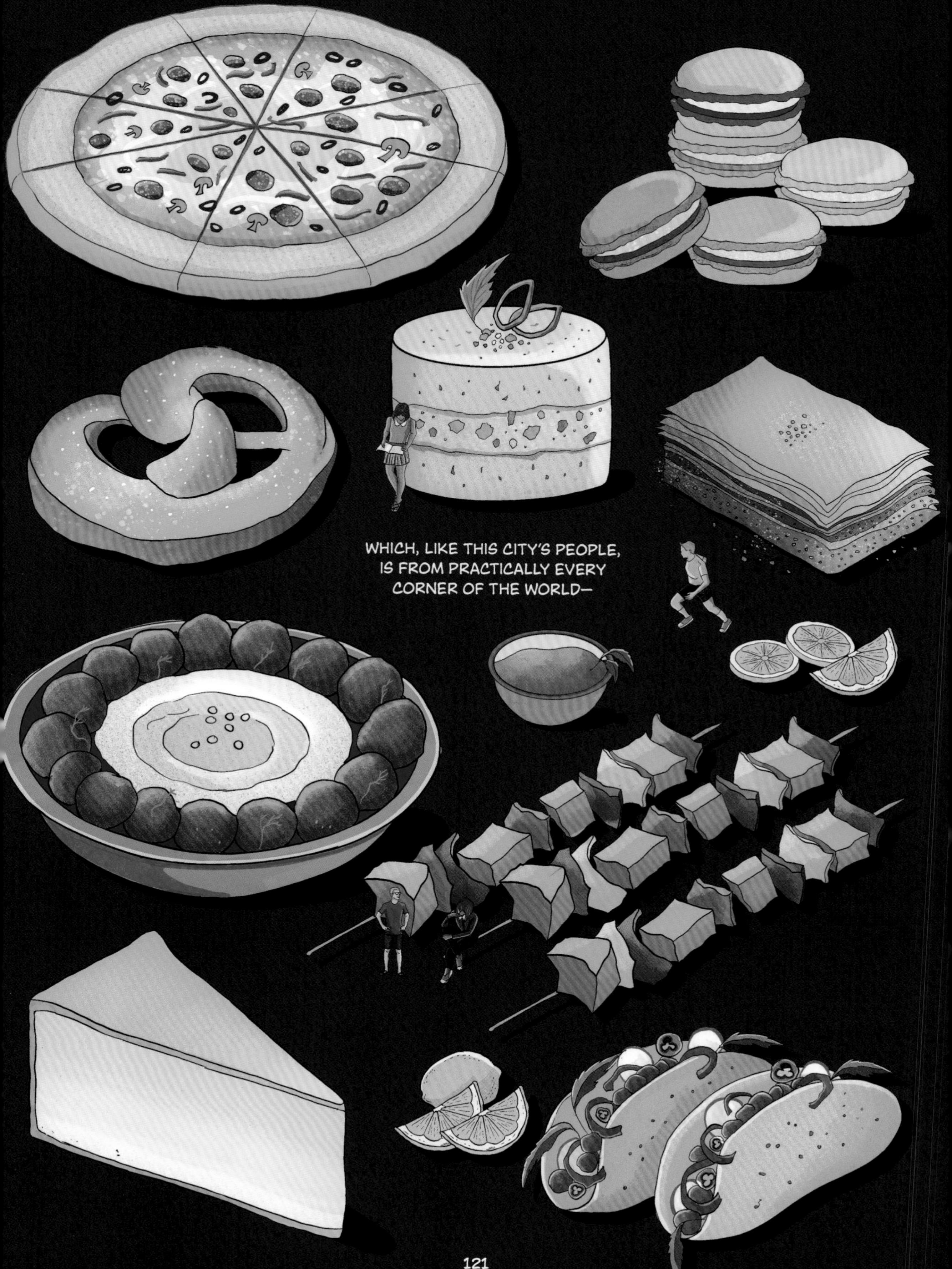
WHICH, LIKE THIS CITY'S PEOPLE, IS FROM PRACTICALLY EVERY CORNER OF THE WORLD—

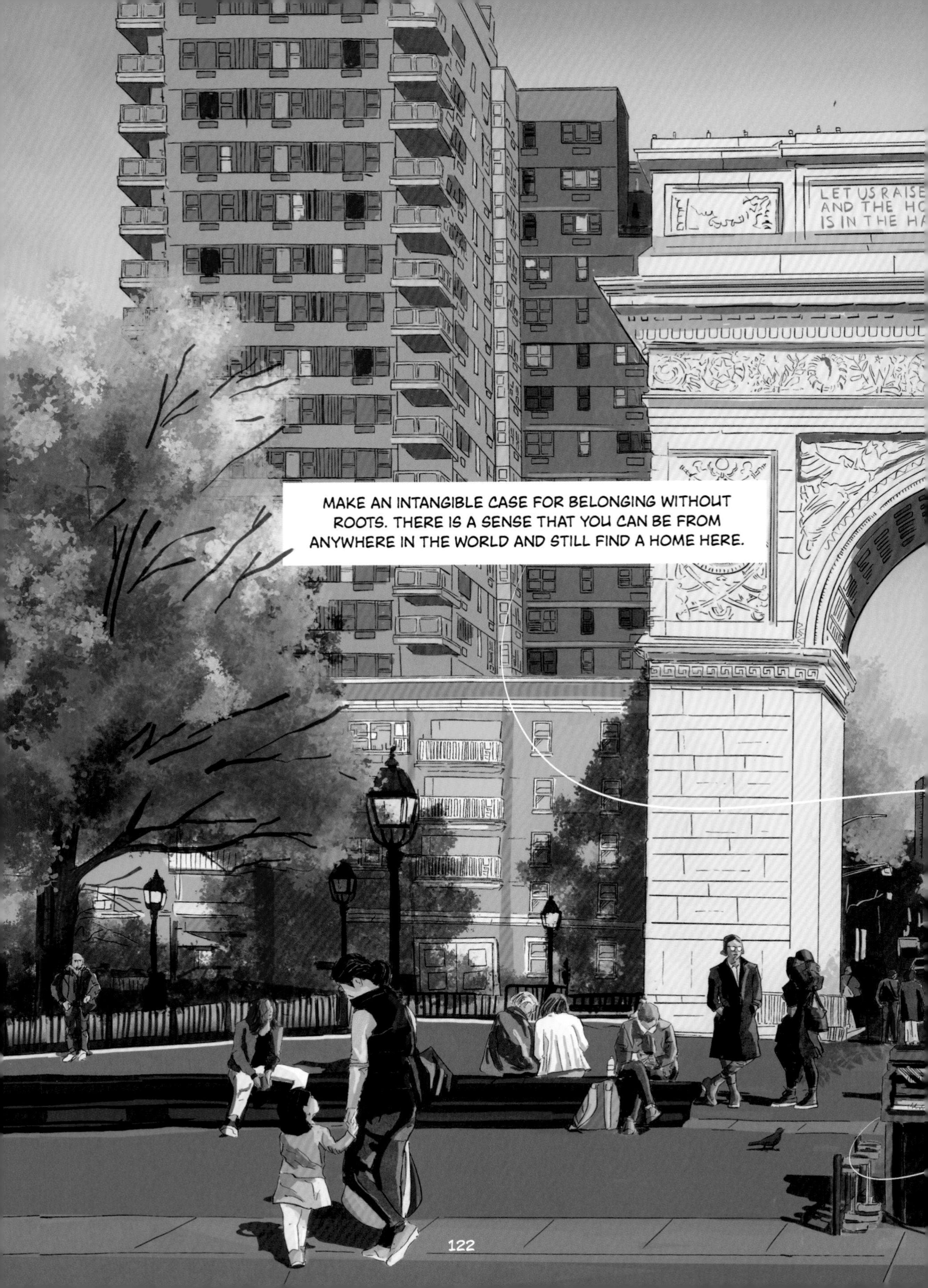
MAKE AN INTANGIBLE CASE FOR BELONGING WITHOUT ROOTS. THERE IS A SENSE THAT YOU CAN BE FROM ANYWHERE IN THE WORLD AND STILL FIND A HOME HERE.

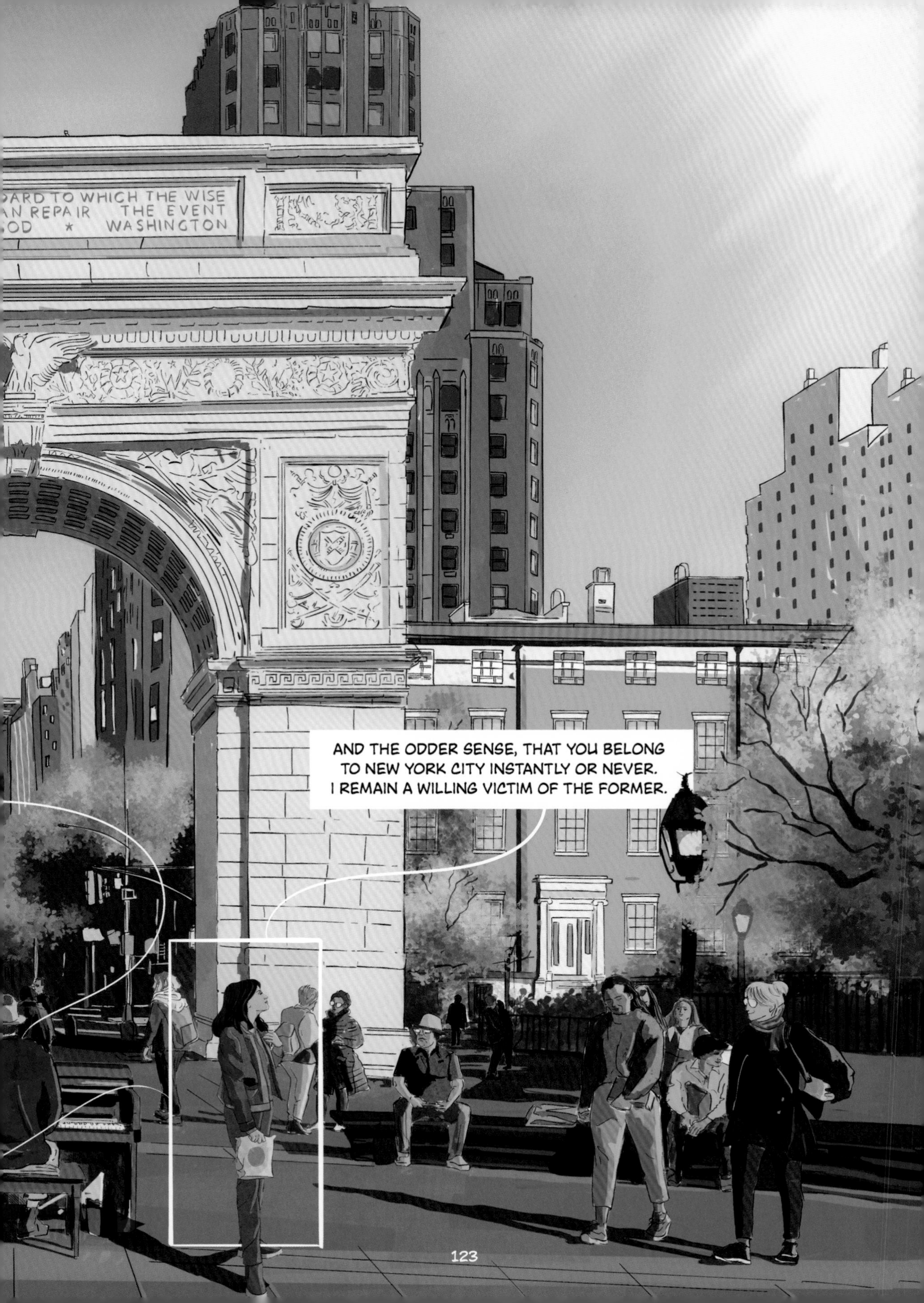
DARD TO WHICH THE WISE
AN REPAIR THE EVENT
OD ★ WASHINGTON
AND THE ODDER SENSE, THAT YOU BELONG TO NEW YORK CITY INSTANTLY OR NEVER. I REMAIN A WILLING VICTIM OF THE FORMER.

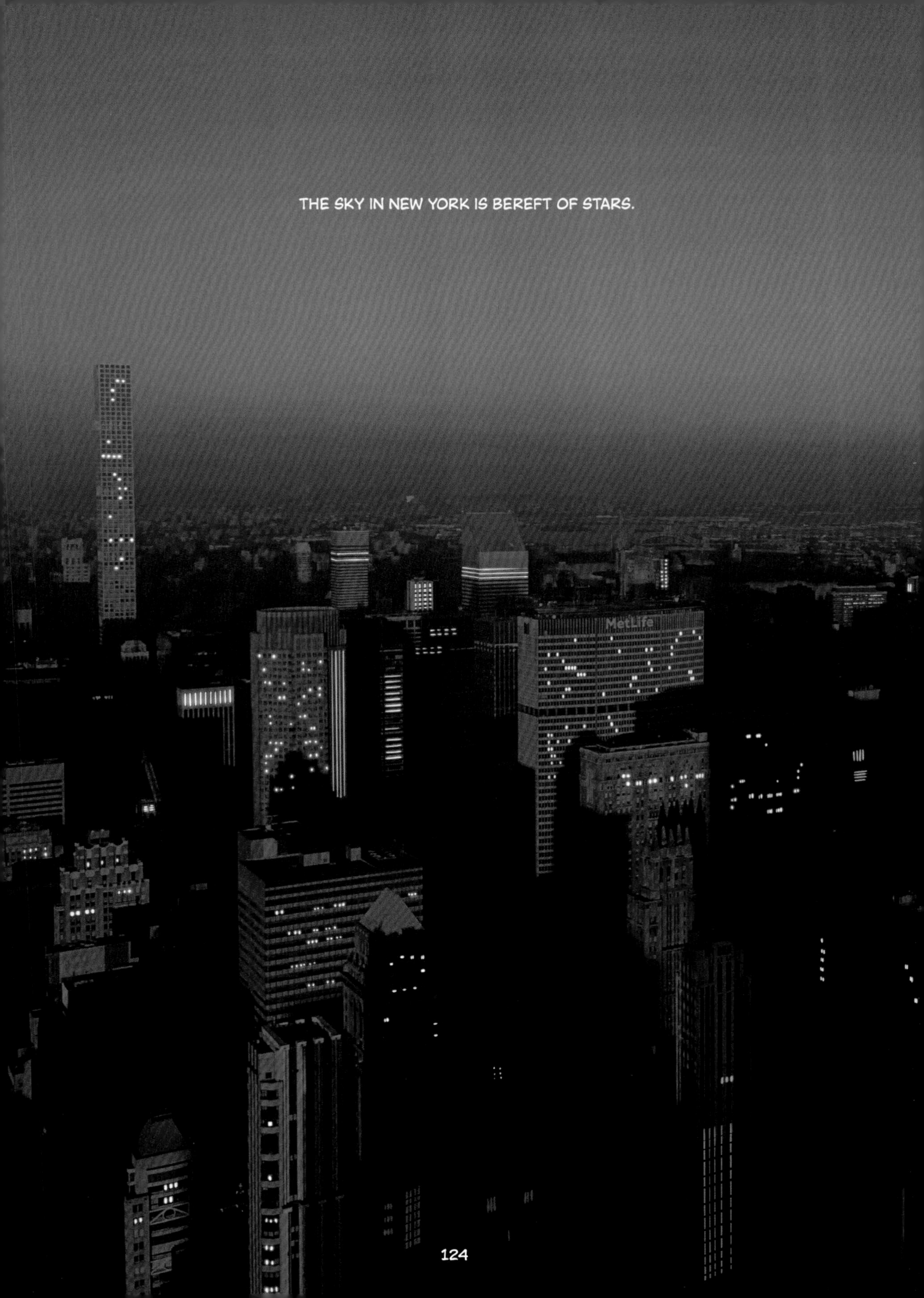
THE SKY IN NEW YORK IS BEREFT OF STARS.
MetLife

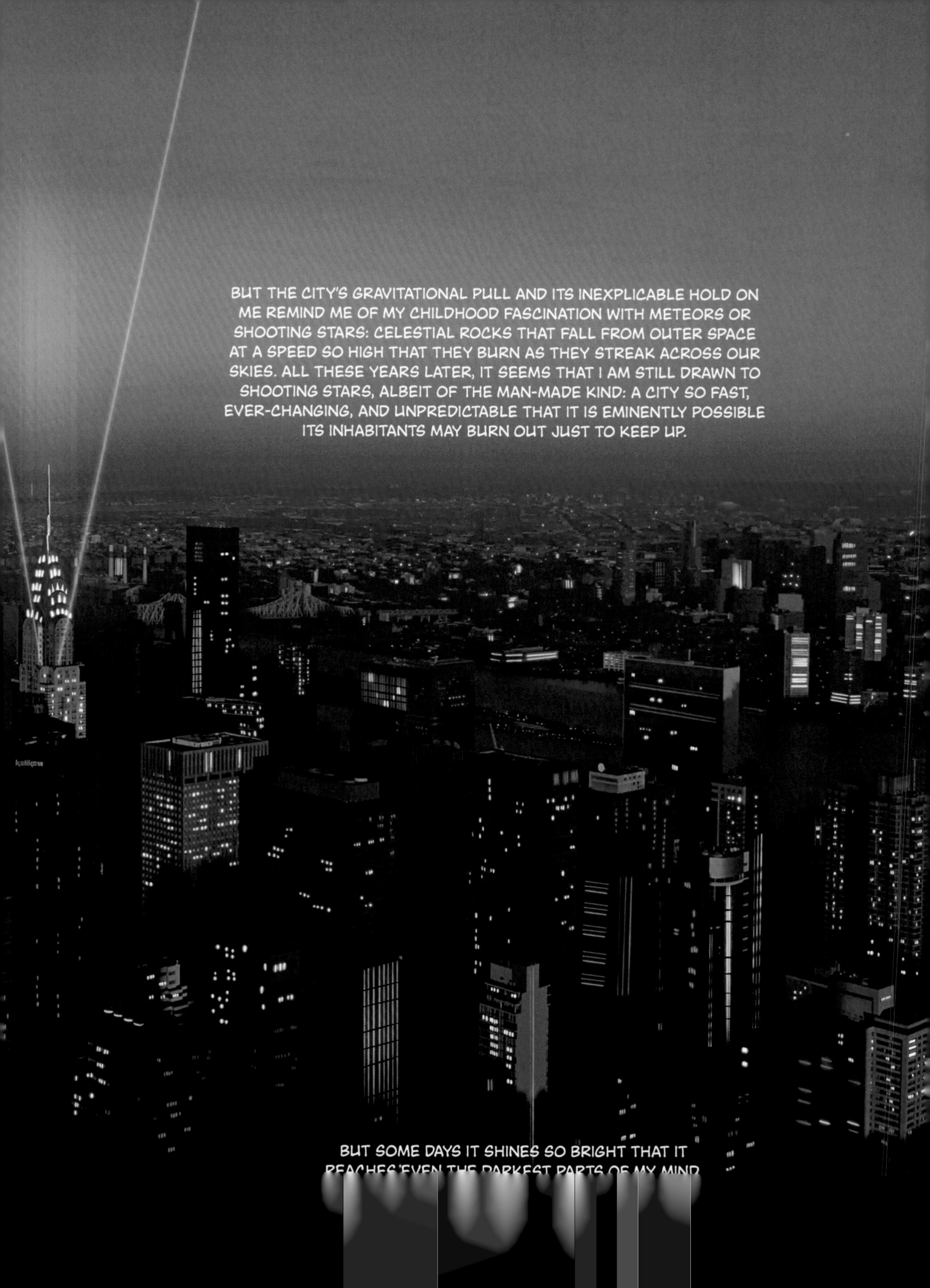
BUT THE CITY'S GRAVITATIONAL PULL AND ITS INEXPLICABLE HOLD ON ME REMIND ME OF MY CHILDHOOD FASCINATION WITH METEORS OR SHOOTING STARS: CELESTIAL ROCKS THAT FALL FROM OUTER SPACE AT A SPEED SO HIGH THAT THEY BURN AS THEY STREAK ACROSS OUR SKIES. ALL THESE YEARS LATER, IT SEEMS THAT I AM STILL DRAWN TO SHOOTING STARS, ALBEIT OF THE MAN-MADE KIND: A CITY SO FAST, EVER-CHANGING, AND UNPREDICTABLE THAT IT IS EMINENTLY POSSIBLE ITS INHABITANTS MAY BURN OUT JUST TO KEEP UP.
BUT SOME DAYS IT SHINES SO BRIGHT THAT IT REACHES EVEN THE DARKEST PARTS OF MY MIND

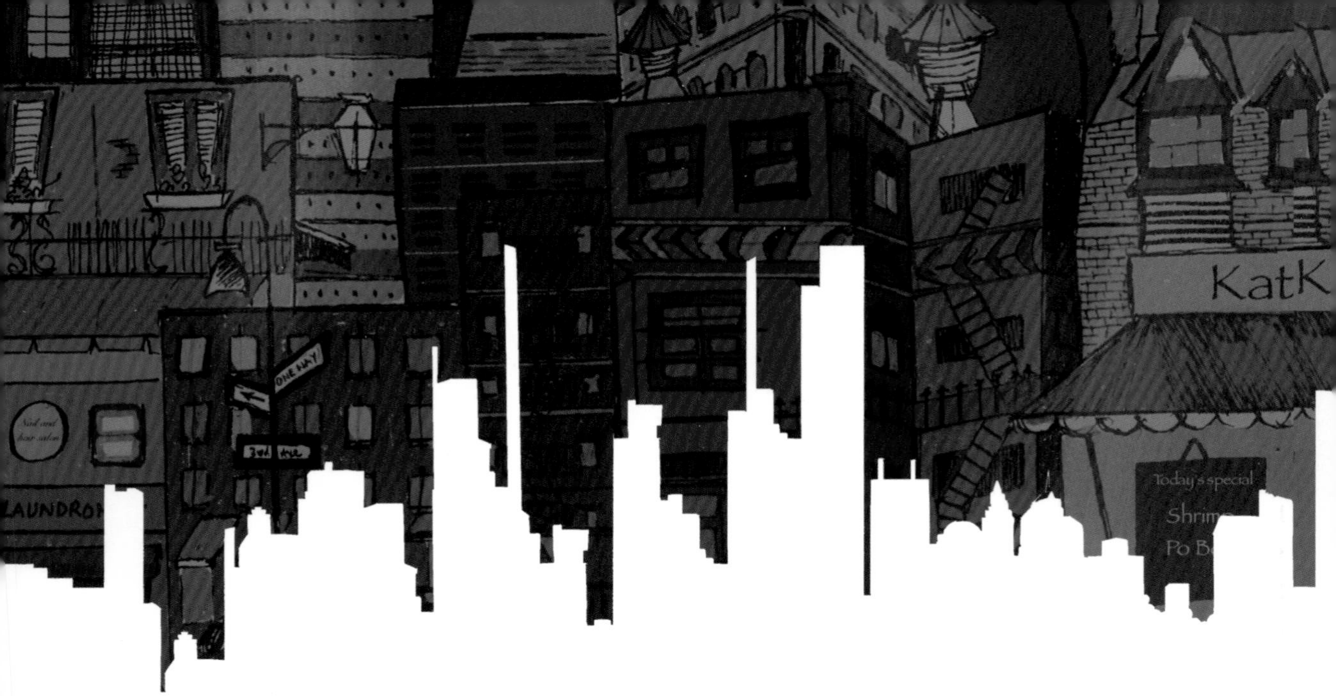
KatK
ONE WAY
3rd Ave
LAUNDRO
Today's special
Shrim
Po B

EPILOGUE

I do not know what I expected New York to do for me when I bought a one-way ticket from Calcutta to JFK (on a student visa and with barely enough money to last two months), after years of poring over Didion, Bechdel, Fitzgerald, Kerouac, and others as though their lives were at all relatable to mine. I surely was not hoping for a literary life considering I had not written a single thing outside of college assignments since graduating high school, or if I was, I certainly did not have the optimism to acknowledge it even to myself.

By the time this book is out in the world, it will be my eighth year, only two short of a decade in this beautiful, ridiculous city. In my time here, I have earned a doctorate, have learned how to make comics, and have—much to my surprise and gratitude—made or taught art for a living on most days. I do not know what lies ahead. These things, as I keep saying, are precarious, and I love this city enough to feel let down by it not infrequently, for myself, but also for others in circumstances worse than mine. Yet here I am, writing this confession of a story about a city that did save me. Maybe not in the steadfast way that I had hoped it would, but in the chaotic and inconclusive way you'd expect if you have ever lived here.

CREDITS

I have visually referred to several book covers, comics, iconic scenes from movies, photographs, and film posters in this book. A full list of references can be found below:

Page 15: *Are You My Mother?* (Alison Bechdel, Jonathan Cape)
Page 30: *When Harry Met Sally* (Nora Ephron, Rob Reiner, Castle Rock Entertainment, Nelson Entertainment), *Friends* (Bright/Kauffman/Crane Productions, Warner Bros. Television), *The Great Gatsby* (F. Scott Fitzgerald, Pocket Books), *You've Got Mail* (Nora Ephron, Lauren Shuler Donner Productions), *Passing* (Nella Larsen, Alfred A. Knopf), *Breakfast at Tiffany's* (Truman Capote, Vintage), *Open City* (Teju Cole, Random House), *Desolation Angels* (Jack Kerouac, Penguin Books), *How I Met Your Mother* (Pamela Fryman, Rob Greenberg, Michael Shea, Neil Patrick Harris, Bays & Thomas Productions, 20th Century Fox Television), *Catcher in the Rye* (J. D. Salinger; Little, Brown and Company), *Kal Ho Naa Ho* (Karan Johar, Nikhil Advani, Dharma Productions)
Page 35: *New Kings of the World: Dispatches from Bollywood, Dizi, and K-Pop* (Fatima Bhutto, Columbia Global Reports)
Page 38-39: *Dilwale Dulhania Le Jayenge* (Aditya Chopra, Yash Raj Films)
Page 40: *Kal Ho Naa Ho* (Karan Johar, Nikhil Advani, Dharma Productions)
Page 41: A version of this page first appeared on page 9 of *Dencity: Stories of Crowds and Cities*, a comics anthology edited by Jordan Collver and Colin McFarlane
Page 104: Virginia Woolf's side-facing portrait, photographed by George Charles Beresford

ACKNOWLEDGMENTS

To my editor, Dan Franklin. For finding me and finding my work good enough for Cape.

To Vedika Khanna, Anjali Nathani, Konrad Kirkham, Jane Link, Rhiannon Roy, and the rest of the incredible teams at Ten Speed Graphic and Jonathan Cape, thank you for this opportunity and for taking care of my book.

To my mentors: Lisa Diedrich, Jeffrey Santa Ana, Nick Sousanis. I was supposed to write a dissertation and you let me draw a comic instead. Thank you for being so generous with your time and expertise, and for believing in my ideas before they were fully formed.

To my friend and writer extraordinaire Ravynn K. Stringfield. Thank you for Leah and for the camaraderie. And to Leah Pierre, my agent, thank you for helping me navigate this world.

To the comics community, and everyone else who cheered me on over the last couple of years: thank you for humoring my little drawings.

To all the cartoonists whose work inspired me to make comics: Alison Bechdel, Emil Ferris, Marjane Satrapi, Thi Bui, Joe Sacco, Art Spiegelman, Scott McCloud, Lynda Barry, Malik Sajad, Kristen Radtke, Mira Jacob, Ebony Flowers, and too many extraordinary others to fit into this page. Thank you for your stories and for this beautiful medium.

To my best friend in the whole world, Poorvi Ghosh, who wanted to read this book even before I'd written it—thank you, babe. You are my rock.

To my parents, for loving me enough to let me go. Your faith in me and my eccentric career choices melts my heart, and this is the only time I will say this in words so cherish it while you can.

And to my beloved husband, Shil Sen. For deseeding dozens and dozens of pomegranates for me to snack on, for reading all my drafts, and for seeing me through the days when nothing made sense. What would I have done without you?

Penguin Random House values and supports copyright. Copyright fuels creativity, encourages diverse voices, promotes free speech, and creates a vibrant culture. Thank you for buying an authorized copy of this book and for complying with copyright laws by not reproducing, scanning, or distributing any part of it in any form without permission. You are supoorting writers and allowing Penguin Random House to continue to publish books for every reader. Please note that no part of this book may be used or reproduced in any manner for the purpose of training artificial intelligence technologies or systems.

Published in the United States by Ten Speed Graphic, an imprint of the Crown Publishing Group, a division of Penguin Random House LLC., New York.
TenSpeed.com

TEN SPEED GRAPHIC and colophon are trademarks of Penguin Random House LLC

First published in the United Kingdom in 2025 by Jonathan Cape, an imprint of Vintage. Vintage is part of the Penguin Random House group of companies.

Typefaces: Dominik Jáger's Aboreto; Adobe's Caslon, Minion, and Myriad; Vernor Adams's Bangers and Oswald; Comicraft's Face Front; Kimberley Geswein's Cedarville; Tart Workshop's Chelsea Market and Fredericka the Great; Jovanny Lemonad's Neucha; and Astigmatic's Special Elite.

Library of Congress Cataloging-in-Publication Data is on file with the publisher.
Library of Congress Control Number: 2024943723

Hardcover ISBN: 978-0-593-83615-6
eBook ISBN: 978-0-593-83616-3

Printed in China

Acquiring editor: Vedika Khanna | Production editor: Sohayla Farman | Editorial assistant: Gabby Urena
Designer: Meggie Ramm | Art director: Chloe Rawlins | Production designer: Hannah Hunt
Colorist: Kay Sohini | Letterer: Kay Sohini
Production manager: Dan Myers
Compositor: Hannah Hunt
Proofreaders: Mikayla Butchart and Bridget Sweet
Publicist: Maya Bradford | Marketer: Paola Crespo

10 9 8 7 6 5 4 3 2 1

First US Edition

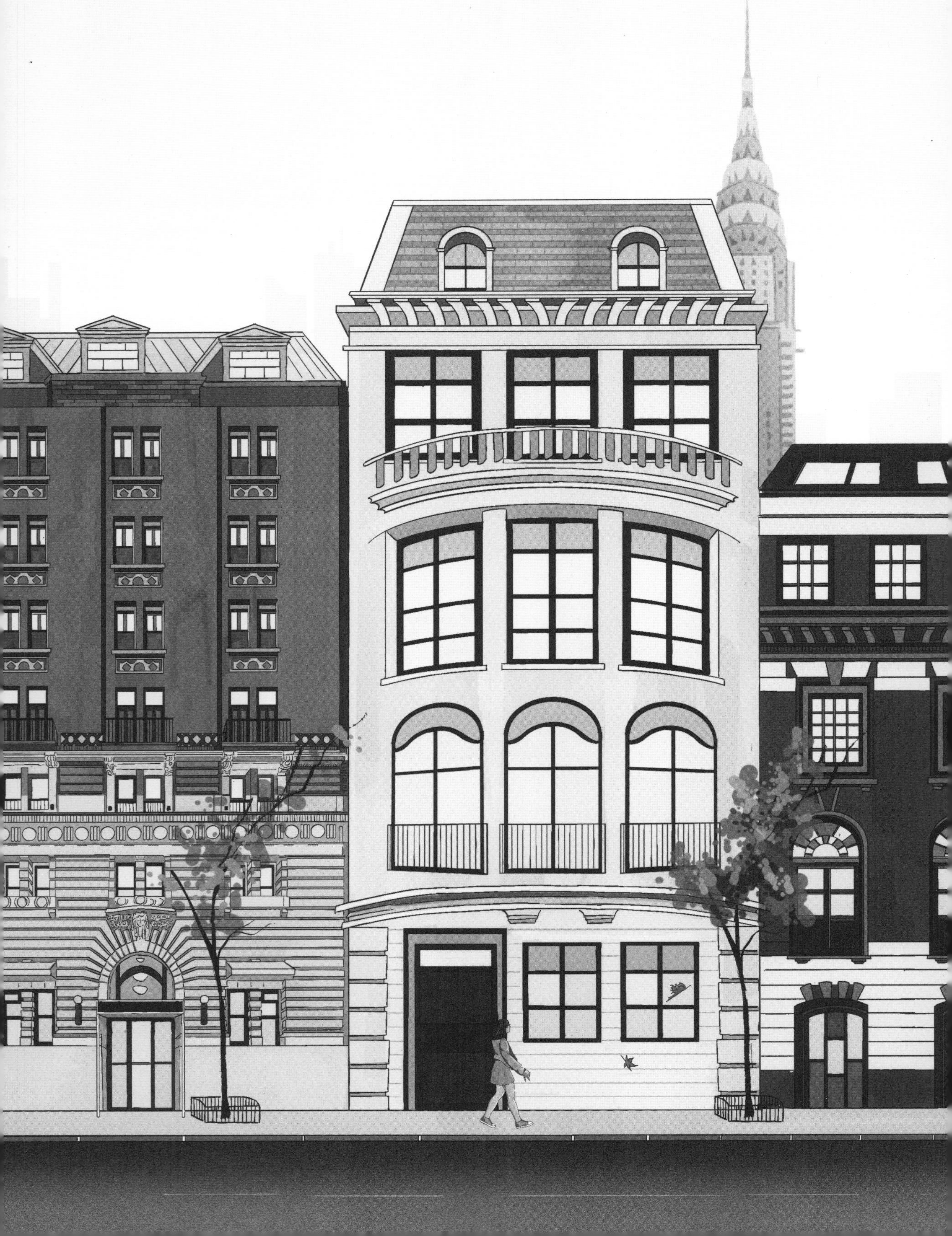